AF228058

MINDLESS

How the Education System is Indoctrinating Children and Destroying Our Civilisation

Bella d'Abrera

Mindless: How the Education System is Indoctrinating Children and Destroying Our Civilisation
Copyright © 2026 Bella d'Abrera

Cover design by Julia Kuris designerbility.com.au

Contents

Introduction

We have arrived at a stage in Western Civilisation in which sending our children to school is no longer a guarantee that they will emerge literate, numerate, or with enough knowledge of the world to successfully navigate life. The foundations of education have been deliberately removed from the curriculum and replaced with indoctrination. By the time they finish school in the public education system[1], your children will not be able to fill out a tax return or recite lines from Shakespeare, but they will certainly be able to lecture you on the patriarchy, systemic racism, the dangers of farting cows, and how to be a transgender ally.

Schools across the West have been transformed from centres of instruction into purveyors of dogma. Teachers are preying on the natural iconoclasm of children to instil in them a range of deranged theories about sex, gender, race, and history. These ideas have been *de rigueur* among university academics for decades and are now the unquestionable orthodoxy on campuses in the West. Our universities are no longer in the business of imparting knowledge. Rather, as Allan Bloom foresaw in America in the 1980s, they are now closing young minds across the Western world.

This is where the rot begins. Almost all future schoolteachers attend university faculties that have comprehensively embraced the new ideology with religious fervour. Critical Race Theory, queer theory, gender theory, postcolonial theory, critical disability theory, intersectionality, identity politics, decolonisation, and ecocentrism now form the basis of the global education system which has been rolled out across the Anglosphere. If you had to design an educational system to wreak maximum damage on generations of people, this would be it, because it is founded on the toxic idea that all of life is defined by an oppressor/oppressed binary.

The new educational establishment has naturally deemed any criticism of this as a 'far-right' conspiracy designed to induce moral panic.[2] The numbers tell us otherwise. In England, 72 per cent of schools are teaching that people have a gender identity that may be different from their biological sex, 25 per cent are teaching that some people or children 'may be born in the wrong body' and 30 per cent are teaching pupils that 'a person who self identifies as a man or a woman should be treated as a man or woman in all circumstances, even if this does not match their biological sex.'[3] In the United States, surveys show large shares of students being taught or hearing that America is systemically racist and that whites have 'white privilege, with one survey showing 62 per cent.'[4] Meanwhile, the authors of the government-mandated kindergarten syllabus in Australia are breathless with excitement at the prospect of teaching 1.5 million children aged four and under about sex and gender.

But it's not just the raw numbers that reveal the endemic levels of indoctrination in Western schools, it is the type of individual who is emerging into society having had their brains re-wired with anti-scientific, anti-rational magical thinking. The system is producing the sort of individual who will hire an angle grinder, don a balaclava and venture out under the cover of darkness to saw through the ankles of Captain Cook's bronze likeness in a park in Australia, to punish him for being a 'racist coloniser.' It is producing the type of delusional person who believes that tossing the statue of a Bristol merchant who died 300 years ago into a harbour will put an end to 'systemic racism' in the United States.

It is creating legions of young people such as 20-year-old university student Anna Holland who threw a tin of Heinz soup at Vincent Van Gogh's 'Sunflowers' on the understanding that her actions would somehow stop a climate apocalypse. This system creates individuals such as University of Pennsylvania student William Thomas, who changed his name to Lia, grew his hair, donned a women's swimsuit, and shot from being a mid-500s ranked male swimmer, to one of the top-ranked 'female' swimmers in the United States.

It is a system which produces individuals such as the aptly named Saga, a 19-year-old self-described 'Black Supremacist' who stood up at her white father's funeral and accused him of being a 'racist, misogynistic, xenophobic, Trump-loving, cis, straight white man.'[5] It clearly did not occur to Saga that she is the living embodiment of a man who was so utterly devoid of bigotry that he fathered a child with a woman of colour.

This is not how most parents would like their children to turn out. They anticipate that their beloved offspring will eulogise about how big- hearted, rather than bigoted, they were. They dream that their son will not grow into a man who gets perverse pleasure from beating a woman by lengths in the pool or shattering a woman's jaw in a boxing ring. They do not envisage that their child will grow up to be ignorantly and proudly dismissive of history and all those who have lived before us.

Unfortunately, it is at this juncture that the general public and the education system part ways. Many still believe that the twelve years at school will produce charitable, happy, well- adjusted, literate and numerate human beings who can think for themselves and who love their country. But the system clearly has other ideas. Classrooms have been transformed from places of learning into fertile training grounds for future generations of political revolutionaries who are ready to rise up and tear down Western Civilisation to make way for the new, improved socialist utopia.

This politicisation is taking place at the hands of a particularly militant set of teachers who believe that their primary duty to society is as agents of change in a world that they understand to be a zero-sum political struggle revolving around identity markers such as race, sex, gender, disability, and cultural background. Here's a tip for parents: When you go to a parent-teacher night and you are told that little Johnny is progressing well in his literacy, she is not referring to his chance of winning the Year 3 Spelling Bee, but that he is literate enough to read *The Hips on the Drag Queen Go Swish, Swish, Swish* by Lil Miss Hot Mess.[6]

When exactly did the Western education system cease being about education? For centuries, the curriculum was classical liberal, which could be traced back to ancient Greece and Rome, and which established the foundation of grammar, rhetoric, and logic. In the Middle Ages, these ideas were coalesced into the seven liberal arts: the trivium (grammar, logic, rhetoric) and the quadrivium (arithmetic, geometry, music, astronomy). The later emergence of cathedral schools and early universities led to the creation and adoption of the structured curriculum which has defined Western education for centuries.

In this classical model, the teacher's role was to transmit knowledge and to form children as virtuous citizens, capable of sustaining and renewing society. In substance, an Australian schoolboy in 1960s Perth still encountered an education recognisably descended from that of a grammar-school boy in 19th-century England, with its grounding in literature, history, and intellectual discipline.

Yet by the 1960s and 70s, progressive educators increasingly saw this continuity as a problem. To them, reproducing the cultural inheritance of the West was not a virtue but an obstacle. Over the following decades, they dismantled the old curriculum piece by piece. Today, though schools may look architecturally unchanged, what goes on inside is profoundly different. Behind the familiar façades lies a system redesigned to serve ideology rather than knowledge.

The sooner that society wakes up to the fact that the system is no longer what it was, the better. Home schooling is an increasingly popular alternative, but it still represents only a tiny fraction of the system. The establishment is now aggressively promoting its destructive goals. Florida preschool teacher DeDe Duffy, for example, boasts that 'the only thing these kids r learning from me is (to) be gay.' Her advice to kids whose parents object to this is: 'fuck your mom.'[7] The system does not take kindly to public criticism and is highly protective of itself. In 2022, mothers and fathers who attempted to discuss the education of their children by speaking out against Critical Race Theory and radical gender theory at board meetings were labelled domestic terrorists by the Biden Administration.[8] Herein lies a question central to this book: To whom do children belong? The parent or the system? Naturally, most parents still think that the children they brought into the world are theirs. The system thinks not. As a 2021 *Washington Post* op ed bluntly argued, 'Parents claim they have the right to shape their kids' school curriculum. They don't.'[9]

We have established that there are many forces working to make children anxious in the classroom. In fact, if one were inclined to err on the side of conspiracy, it could almost seem as though the system were deliberately designed to destabilise and weaken. Certainly, there are no metrics suggesting an improvement in skills, a strengthening of mental health, or a firm grasp of enduring principles. Added to all this is the rising tide of mental distress caused by smartphones, which is a troubling development documented by Jonathan Haidt in his aptly titled *The Anxious Generation*. The data is alarming; the harm being done to young people is beyond imagining. It is not within the remit of this book to explore the full psychological consequences of smartphones and social media use, but in light of this evidence, it is astonishing that some schools still allow personal devices at all, let alone on top of the ideological confusion already overwhelming the classroom.

Education is central to the continuation of Western Civilisation because it transmits the collective wisdom, skills, and values that allow societies to flourish, innovate, and sustain themselves across generations. However, it may just be that after thousands of years, ours is the first civilisation which is brought down by what is being taught in schools and universities. A combination of the erosion of critical thinking, abandonment of the pursuit of knowledge, obsession with political activism, high rates of illiteracy and numeracy and the prioritisation of feelings over fact might well prove fatal for our institutions.

The irony is that the educationalists who have put us on this path claim that it is all in the name of progress. Instead, they are discarding all the technological progress made during the past three centuries, and all the intellectual progress we have made in the past two thousand years. For what? They haven't fully explained, although I will do so in devastating detail later in this book. The education system is driving our culture towards superstition, division, and failure. We cannot let this happen.

1

New Education

In November 2021, a group of academics at the University of Cambridge proudly unveiled a likeness of a Paulo Freire to sit in the Faculty of Education's library. Even though he has been dead since 1997, Paulo Freire continues to be one of the most influential figures in the field of education you have probably never heard. It is also likely that you have never heard of his 1968 work, *Pedagogy of the Oppressed*, which is the most sacred of texts among the education fraternity. The ideas and practices Freire expounded fifty years ago have not only been embedded into university education faculties but also into primary and secondary school classrooms across the West.

It does not seem unreasonable that the Faculty of Education's employees would want to honour one of their patron saints. But what does seem odd is that Paulo Freire was a Marxist revolutionary who was thrown out of Brazil on account of his 'subversive activities' and whose heroes included Friedrich Hegel, Vladimir Lenin, Mao Zedong, Fidel Castro, and Che Guevara. *Pedagogy of the Oppressed,* penned by Freire while in exile, is as revolutionary as the title suggests. Among other appeals, it exhorts students to 'denounce' the world as it is and strive ceaselessly, even violently, for 'transformation'. This work is about as close as possible to the *Little Red Book.*

Yet, the academic staff at the University of Cambridge decided that they not only needed a monument to a man who called for revolution but that the same man be lauded as 'one of the greatest thinkers in education' and celebrated with a two-week Festival of Freire. In a social media post announcing the bust's installation, a young Brazilian student activist excitedly shows off the head of a bespectacled, bearded and kindly-looking old man and asks his audience, 'What is a statue of Paulo Freire doing at the University of Cambridge?' We might ask the same thing.

Part of the answer to this question is that Paulo Freire's likeness is now sitting in the Faculty of Education's library because it was a gift from the Landless Workers' Movement, which is a militant organisation whose *modus operandi* is to invade farmers' lands and colonise them through force and is the most prominent and most polarising social movement in Latin America. Judging from this particular gift, the Landless Workers' Movement also has invaded and colonised a bronze cast-making workshop somewhere in Brazil.

The other part of the answer to this question lies with faculty head Professor Susan Robertson, who explained that the statue was erected as a 'symbol of resistance to far-right attacks on education.' Professor Robertson was referring to then-President Bolsonaro's attempts to stop left-wing teachers indoctrinating Brazilian school children with 'Marxist garbage' because, not unreasonably, he thought that an education system should produce 'citizens and not political militants'.[10] This turn of events worried Professor Robertson a great deal. While she conceded that these 'aggressive attacks' were unlikely in the UK, she remarked that the faculty was 'alarmed' by what it saw as the serious threat of 'a consciously over-simplistic positioning of academics and educators as distant and out of touch'.[11] In other words, she was worried that the general public may be waking up to the fact that what goes on inside university education faculties has remarkably little to do with education.

Readers might also be curious as to why the University of Cambridge, or any university for that matter, pulls out all stops to erect a statue of a notorious Marxist revolutionary gifted to it by a Latin American, Communist-adjacent, militant group which steals land from the farmers. And above all, what does this say about the current state of academic priorities? They are not only reasonable questions to ask, they are also important questions to ask.

The Freire episode is important because it shows just how much Western universities have shifted away from the pursuit of truth and rigorous debate towards ideological indoctrination. It represents all that is wrong with the modern university: The abandonment of truth-directed inquiry in favour of the collectivism of identity politics and the moral relativism of postmodernism have dealt a fatal blow to our institutions of higher learning. It has degraded academic standards to a point where the university has become a parody of itself. Efforts to decolonise, debates over cancel culture, and clashes around free speech reflect a campus landscape increasingly polarised by ideological conformity. What is more, the deranged ideas about sex and race dreamt up in the humanities, previously confined to lecture halls and academic papers, are taught in kindergartens and schools around the West.

Historically, their role has been as custodians of knowledge and repositories for the collective wisdom of past generations. Academics working in the humanities were tasked with the preservation of the canon of Western thought: literature, philosophy, history, art, and the sciences, ensuring that this body of knowledge was passed on to future generations. The mission was not complicated. Academics had to transmit a well-rounded cultural and intellectual heritage to individuals and to society at large.

However, during the 1970s and 1980s, academics in the humanities decided to abandon their mission. They rejected their original purpose, which was to make sense of and understand the world through the treasure trove of the Western tradition of culture and philosophy. Instead, they adopted a range of 'new humanities' subjects constructed entirely around postmodernist critical theory in which everything had to be approached in terms of the societal power struggle of class, race, gender, and deconstruction. In essence, they embarked upon a destructive program of postmodern cultural critique, which has thrown our society into a state of cultural confusion.

The seeds of rebellion were sown in the 1930s when a group of intellectuals collectively known as the Frankfurt School fled Nazi Germany and set up shop at Columbia University in New York. The critical theory sold by Max Horkheimer, Theodor W. Adorno, and Herbert Marcuse to their American counterparts was more reconstructed Marxism than it was theory. They proposed that Western society was rotten to its core, framing capitalism, religion, patriotism, family, and individual liberty as oppressive forms of power from which people needed to be 'emancipated'.

In the 1960s, mainly French philosophers took this cultural critique to the next level by proposing that the cornerstones of civilisation: truth, reason and knowledge, were also oppressive tools of power to mask political agendas. Among the most notorious members of what Sir Roger Scruton termed the Parisian 'nonsense machine' were Michel Foucault, Jacques Derrida, Jean-François Lyotard, Louis Althusser, and Jacques Lacan. They started throwing about words such as 'hegemonic', 'metanarratives', and 'discursive structures'. They confounded their most ardent supporters but also each other. When Althusser (who later murdered his wife) tried to read Derrida's thesis, he gave up, saying, 'I can't grade this; it's too difficult, too obscure'. Althusser then passed it on to Foucault, who declared it either an 'A or an F'. He could not tell.[12]

By the 1970s and 1980s, post-structuralism and deconstruction were wildly popular among academics, many of whom had proclaimed themselves as Marxists in the 1960s and were itching for a cultural revolution. Perhaps their enthusiasm could also be attributed to what C.S. Lewis termed 'chronological snobbery', which was the notion that anything in the past was inherently inferior to the present, simply because it was in the past and thus outdated.[13] During these decades, some academics in the humanities lost interest in meaning, beauty, or historical insight and started to use their chosen fields as platforms for political critique and deconstruction. This was the era of 'false consciousness' and 'embourgeoisement', when Shakespeare's *The Taming of the Shrew* had to be read exclusively through the angry feminist perspective to expose patriarchal oppression in the literary tradition.

It was the era in which philosopher and classicist Allan Bloom wrote *The Closing of the American Mind,* lamenting that Plato, Aristotle, and Shakespeare were being devalued or replaced by modern ideological readings and that his colleagues' fascination with relativism, nihilism, and political correctness was leading to a generation of students who were intellectually and morally adrift. He wrote, 'The humanities are the repository of the books that are at the foundation of our religion, our philosophy, our politics, our science, as well as our art… only here are the questions about knowledge, about the good life, about God and love and death, at home in the university.'[14]

During the 1990s, the Parisian nonsense machine went into overdrive. Academics began to see themselves as having a higher purpose, ready to change the world by embedding feminist theory, post-colonial theory, gender theory, Critical Race Theory, queer theory, intersectionality, decolonisation, disability theory, and even 'fat studies', into their scholarship.

This brings us to the mid-2000s, when a worldview emerged, known as Critical Social Justice or 'wokeism'. This perspective is now the dominant ideological worldview in Western universities. Subjects that were once examined from a balanced standpoint are increasingly interpreted solely as examples of systemic oppression. Proponents of the Social Justice movement claim that its goal is to expose hidden biases and unequal power structures in society, thereby liberating minorities, women, and LGBTQIA+ individuals from what they view as the oppressive legacy of the white male patriarchy.

Not wishing to pick on the University of Cambridge, but the Faculty of Education is exemplary in its dedication to Social Justice. It is illustrative of the shift in academic priorities which has abandoned the pursuit of knowledge for the pursuit of political activism. Among its many research groups is a body called 'Knowledge, Power and Politics' in which students and academics discuss the 'formation of, and resistances to, classed, raced, patriarchical and colonial modalities of racial domination and coloniality in education.' This is done by tackling the following themes:

- Education and new productions of race
- Decolonising knowledges, social movements and pedagogies of resistance
- Youth identity and educational practices of everyday bordering
- Postcolonial politics of education and international development
- Representations of racialised, gendered, and classed childhoods in education and migration, displacement and the production of the 'preferred' citizen-subject
- Promise of social mobility, social integration, intergenerational justice [15]

It would not be unreasonable for someone outside the university to ask why it is that the education faculty is talking about decolonising knowledges, racial domination and intergenerational justice. A sensible person might not only question the faculty's statement that 'none of the defining issues of our time – such as climate change, global inequality, or how to rebuild after COVID-19 – can be addressed without recognising that education is part of the solution',[16] but they might also query the assertion that these are the greatest problems that our era can muster.

A sensible person might also ask why in January 2025, the Policy Institute at King's College London, a serious institute at a serious university, appointed lingerie model and asexual activist Yasmin Benoit to a two-year research fellowship. Benoit's preferred means of communication is to appear on Instagram posing in sexually alluring outfits whilst explaining what asexuality is not, but not much about what it is. Perhaps this is the enigma that she and her fellow researchers at the Policy Institute will resolve during her fellowship.

Again, an unsuspecting visitor to the University of Cambridge's one hundred and forty-year-old Museum of Classical Archaeology's Cast Gallery might be surprised to learn that the museum was offering a 'Bridging Binaries LGBTQ+ Tour'. This tour promised to educate and entertain with a 'personal selection of fascinating stories which challenge[d] binary approaches to gender and sexual identity through a range of lesbian, gay, bisexual, transgender and queer-related objects related to Ancient Greece and Rome.'[17] This is the best collection of Greek and Roman sculpture casts in the world and includes Michelangelo's *David,* Trajan's Column, and Ghiberti's

Gates of Paradise, yet in 2025 it was reduced to the lowest possible common denominator: who is sleeping with whom. If these are the waters in which the most prestigious universities in the UK swim, then we might as well just give up and go home now.

When it comes to the lowest common denominator, the Ivy League universities excel. Yale University offers a course dedicated to R&B singer Beyonce entitled, 'Beyonce Makes History; Black Radical Tradition History, Culture, Theory & Politics through Music'. Students are taken on a journey to 'explore landmark Black Studies scholarship and Black freedom struggle scholarly and cultural texts (in history, Black feminist theory, philosophy, anthropology, art history, performance studies, musicology, political science, sociology, dance, American Studies, religious studies, archival studies etc.) that directly resonate with Beyonce's sonic, visual and live performance endeavors.'[18]

Not to be outdone, Harvard University offers 'Taylor Swift and Her World' to undergraduates studying English, with the promise that they will 'learn how to study fan culture, celebrity culture, adolescence, adulthood and appropriation; how to think about white texts, Southern texts, transatlantic texts, and queer subtexts.'[19] Channelling the lyrics of Swift herself, lecturer Stephanie Burt said of the course that she had intentionally selected works about 'being looked at and having to incarnate femininity' that also engaged with societal expectations that women face to 'be hot for men, love yourself and make your own decisions.'[20]

But when it comes to absurdity, nothing comes close to the heights to which the academic journal article can soar. Take volume 39 of *Hypatia: A Journal of Feminist Philosophy* (2024), which published 'An Ecofeminist Politics of Chicken Ovulation; A Socio-Capitalist Model of Ability as Farmed Animal Impairment' by Australian academic Yamini Narayanan. Using a 'combined ecofeminist, and critical disability philosophical analysis of the commodification of female farmed animal reproduction,' Narayanan shows that 'Patriarchal farmed animal capitalism relies on the idea of naturalized ability of farmed females to be hyper-reproductive/hyper-ovulatory/hyper-lactative.' In one particularly memorable passage, the author describes her encounter with a chicken called Lila. 'Lila did not look quite right,' she observed. 'The gentlest and quietest of our hens rescued from an egg farm, she seemed more reticent than usual, and her face seemed screwed up in discomfort, perhaps even pain. Was it possible for a chicken's face to get screwy in that way? Did chickens even have facial expressions?'[21] Sadly, Narayanan does not elaborate on whether hens can grimace or, if after managing her discomfort, Lila was able to cross the road successfully.

Meanwhile, in volume 31 of *Gender, Place & Culture* (2023), you will find 'How we fuck: assembling intimacy-as-method to research trans sex practices' by University of Brighton PhD student H Howitt, whose pronouns are 'H'. 'Using my body as both a fertile site of knowledge production and an instrument for intimate analysis,' H writes, 'I articulate an approach to 'intimacy-as-method' within an assemblage framework to provide new ways of engaging in empirical sex research.'[22] H appears to be labouring under the impression that a wild Saturday night or two in Soho's *Heaven* not only constitutes scholarship but also interests other people.

Unfortunately, these mad musings masquerading as serious scholarship are not sitting on the fringes of academia. They are academia. Their authors are not being politely tolerated in academic circles as outliers whose commentary on grimacing chickens and their own sex lives are harmless and inconsequential. They are accepted and encouraged by their peers, who, judging from this list of articles published in the last ten years, have lost their collective grip on reality.

- Queer ecologies of home: heteronormativity, speciesism, and the strange intimacies of crazy cat ladies[23]
- Bitch, Bitch, Bitch: Personal Criticism, Feminist Theory, and Dog-writing[24]
- Trans objects: materializing queer time in US transmasculine homes[25]
- Homemaking and perpetual liminality among queer refugees[26]

- The unspeakable whiteness of volunteer tourism[27]
- Feline Entanglements: Feminist Interspecies Care and Solidarity in a Post-Pandemic World[28]

While the layperson will undoubtedly find these titles amusing, the academic community most certainly does not. This was demonstrated with the Grievance Studies Affair (2017–18) when three academics, Peter Boghossian, Helen Pluckrose and James Lindsay, could not take it anymore. Together, they wrote, submitted, and had accepted several satirical papers using postmodern jargon to reveal the ideological bias and low academic standards of the humanities. Among the twenty or so papers submitted, seven passed the review process and were accepted unquestioningly, wholeheartedly and presumably enthusiastically by the editorial boards of various journals. Some of the titles which made it through were 'Human Reactions to Rape Culture and Queer Performativity at Urban Dog Parks in Portland, Oregon', 'Super-Frankenstein and the Masculine Imaginary: Feminist Epistemology and Superintelligent Artificial Intelligence Safety Research' and 'An Ethnography of Breastaurant Masculinity: Themes of Objectification, Sexual Conquest, Male Control, and Masculine Toughness in a Sexually Objectifying Restaurant'.

This public humiliation might have elicited a modicum of self-reflection from within the academic community. But instead, it doubled down, resorting to tribalism and *ad hominem* attacks but without actually addressing the fact that it is possible to publish absolute nonsense. Boghossian's employer, Portland State University, even initiated a research misconduct inquiry against him because he had conducted human subject-based research without approval and was accused of fabricating data. In 2021, Boghossian resigned, calling the university a 'Social Justice factory'.

Death by Open Letter

Academia's response to the Grievance Studies Affair reveals that universities are dominated by an ideological and political monoculture. From the moment they set foot on campus, staff and students alike are compelled to navigate a cabal of left-wing, neo-Marxist academics, administrative staff and activist students who demand ideological conformity through control of expression, language and thought. In the first week of your compulsory politics major at the University of Melbourne, you are more likely to hear 'I'm a revolutionary Marxist, and if you're not one by the end of Semester I haven't done my job properly' from your lecturer than 'Perhaps you might want to read what J.S. Mill has to say about government overreach in *On Liberty*.' And on that note, you are also likely to hear your classmates refuse to read Mill on the grounds that he is 'an old dead white guy'.[29]

It has become very apparent to those on the outside that those on the inside think the same thoughts and have the same opinions. From the Vice-Chancellor down to the person working at the IT helpdesk, the singular acceptable worldview is that which is traditionally associated with the progressive left. Survey after survey probing into the political inclinations of the academics come back with the same conclusions: Our universities have well and truly been colonised by left-wing progressives who naturally vote for left-wing political parties.[30]

This is hardly a new state of affairs. Left-oriented individuals have been inhabiting the faculties of American universities since World War II, with one study finding that 78 per cent of academic departments in the top 50 institutions now have zero Republicans.[31] Sociologist A.H. Halsey surveyed British academics over three different time periods (1960, 1976 and 1989) and noted a gradual decline in support for the Conservatives over the last half-century.[32] Before the 2019 election, academic staff were asked how they would vote, with 77 per cent opting for left-wing parties, that is 54 per cent for the Labour Party, 23 per cent for the Liberal Democrats and five per cent for the Green Party, while only eight per cent were planning to vote for the Conservatives.

In 2022, the UK's Legatum Institute conducted a worldwide survey of 650 academics in law, history, sociology and economics faculties at elite universities in Canada, Australia, the US and the UK. The picture this survey paints is not a happy one for the right-wing academic. When asked about their political orientation,

76 per cent self-identified as left-wing. But within that group, 21 per cent said that they were far left, which means to say that their intellectual heroes are Marx, Lenin, Trotsky, Che Guevara and Mao Zedong and that the main problem with Communism is that it just hasn't been properly implemented yet. The survey also found that large numbers of academics, 70 per cent, to be precise, openly disliked those who did not conform to the dominant left-wing ideology. The feeling, however, was not at all mutual. Most conservatives said they do like their left-wing colleagues, while just 36 per cent said they did not.[33]

This means that if you are someone who happens to hold positive views about Donald Trump or Brexit, you will need to keep those views to yourself. A 2021 survey of academics and PhD students found that nine in ten Trump-supporting academics and eight in ten Brexit-supporting academics say they would not feel comfortable expressing their views to a colleague. Meanwhile, four in ten academics in Canada and the US said that they would not hire supporters of Trump, with one in three in the UK openly discriminating against Brexiteers.[34] In no single discipline did right-wing academics outnumber or even come close to balancing their left-wing counterparts. As Thomas Sowell says, 'The next time some academic tells you how important diversity is, ask how many Republicans there are in their sociology department.'

It is still possible to find a conservative or two whispering about Milton Friedman's belief that economic freedom is a precondition for political freedom in various economics faculties in Britain. And as Professor Nigel Biggar, then Regius Professor of Moral and Pastoral Theology at the University of Oxford, discovered, it is still possible to hold seminars (albeit under the cloak of secrecy) about the ethics of the British Empire, even though the mob has come after you for daring to suggest that this period of history was not all oppression, exploitation and self-deception.

None of this conjures up images of university departments brimming with *bonhomie*, where robust but respectful conversations about a wide range of topics take place over wine and cheese on a Friday evening. Academic life in the humanities and social sciences seems to be one in which a posse of hard-left activists make life a misery for everyone else, doing everything in their power to silence, intimidate and even destroy the careers of their colleagues. Often, this is done by publicly discrediting their work and mischaracterising what they have written or said, especially if it is about 'race' or 'trans'.

The academic landscape is strewn with the bodies of academics who the mob has intellectually defenestrated. One such individual was Professor Geoffrey Blainey, Australia's greatest living historian. In 1984, twenty-four staff members of the University of Melbourne's history faculty ended his university career by publishing a letter in *The Age* newspaper accusing him of being racist. What had he done to provoke the ire of his fellow historians? He had given a talk in which he dared to show empathy with mostly white working-class Australians who were having to compete for jobs with large numbers of Asian immigrants during a time of high unemployment, whilst simultaneously coming to terms with the changing demographics of their suburbs. This letter was not only career-ending, but it was nearly life-ending. After being threatened with violence, Blainey had to hire private security to guard his home, and someone planted a real bomb on the lawn of the wrong Blainey. The right Blainey finally quit in 1988, utterly fatigued by the hostility.

Another more recent victim of the open letter was Noah Carl, a young sociology PhD student at Cambridge, who was called a racist by an angry mob of 1400 tenured dons and junior academics. This mild-mannered and kind young man committed the unforgivable crime of questioning the critical social view of race as a social construct and lost his precious and hard-won junior research fellowship. With all the academic rigour she could muster, signatory Dr Antonia Ruppel (classics post-doctoral researcher at Oxford) said 'Before signing the letter, I googled Noah, and what I found online convinced me to add my signature to the letter.'[35] It is likely that 'gender critical' feminist philosopher Professor Kathleen Stock might not have imagined that one day she too would be the recipient of an open letter and hounded out of her teaching position at the University of Sussex in a way that she likened to a medieval style 'ostracism'.

Anonymous testimonies gathered in 2021 offer a revealing glimpse into the current state of the humanities and social sciences, where academics report being penalised for not aligning closely enough with far-left ideologies. One account features a self-described 'Very Left' Canadian anthropologist who was dismissed from her role as undergraduate programs chair due to her view that sex is biological and immutable. We hear how because a 'Centrist Remainer' failed to mention a large photo of Jeremy Corbyn on his manager's desk, he was immediately removed from the program he was running. We hear how a 'Left Labour Leaver' avoids making political statements and that their head of department actively prevents them from doing specific research.[36] A further account from a Canadian 'Centrist' classicist revealed that the administration's recent shift toward punitive measures against outspoken staff has led many to tread carefully, relying on collective agreements to shield themselves from potential disciplinary action.

Collectively, these accounts paint a picture of an academic environment increasingly marked by self-censorship and fear of reprisal. None of us wants to find ourselves at the sharp end of the university's disciplinary apparatus, yet this is precisely what is happening. Our universities are stacked to the rafters with activist administrators who are pursuing ideological purity through the controversial vehicle of Diversity, Equity, and Inclusion (DEI). Social justice has been elevated to an institutional goal, but this transformation is far from enjoyable for many. DEI advocates assert that universities are irredeemably marred by racism, sexism, and bigotry, and, therefore, must be purged of these evils. In the US, this mission is driven by an ever-growing corps of Diversity, Equity, and Inclusion Officers. By 2025, their numbers had swelled dramatically, with many earning salaries that surpass those of the average American and even much of the academic faculty. In the early 2020s, approximately 200 colleges were operating what they called 'bias response teams', presumably to handle misgendering misdemeanours and other such emergencies.

But DEI is much more than just a box-ticking exercise: it's wholesale indoctrination under pain of expulsion. Nearly 70 per cent of American universities, both public and private, will not allow their students to graduate unless they take an ideologically suspect course.[37] At the University of Minnesota, students can opt for *Queer Kinship: Undoing the American Family*, which teaches them that heteronormative families and patriarchal heteronormative structures impact minorities, while Princeton's students have to sit through hours of lectures on how white people are inherently racist in *Body, Culture, Power*. At Monash University in Australia, fee-paying students face the same rigid mandate: they will not be allowed to graduate unless they complete an online course detailing how the British stole land from the Aboriginal Australians.

A sceptical employee at University College London (UCL) who might resist being re-educated is warned that non-compliance during the probationary period could lead to failure, permanently hinder any chance of promotion, and even trigger disciplinary proceedings. The warning doesn't stop there: Honorary staff and Emeritus Professors are also under pressure. Should they remain non-compliant after reminders and discussions with their line managers, their titles or assignments may be revoked. One can't help but wonder: has HR already had to discipline a significant number of recalcitrant professors, or is this a pre-emptive strike in anticipation of a faculty rebellion?

These troubling developments correlate directly with the growing numbers of administrative staff and the overwhelming surge in policies resembling the protocols of a totalitarian regime. University bureaucrats are incentivised to hire more staff to justify larger budgets, resulting in the expansion of departments and the creation of new tasks that indirectly justify their growth. This cycle, often described as administrative bloat, fosters an environment where excessive rules proliferate and some of those excessive rules, which have been proliferating faster than you will be deplatformed for saying that there are only two genders, are free speech policies.

The trouble is that the more policies there are, the less free speech there is. Without a shadow of a doubt, there is a full-blown free speech crisis on Western campuses, although left-wing media outlets such as *The Guardian* and *The Conversation* will tell you otherwise. They'll claim it's a fake crisis, a 'right-wing myth' manufactured by conservatives to increase political power.[38] But the vast majority of academics, themselves left-wing, are telling us that they self-censor because they fear being targeted by fellow academics and students.[39] Even the militant University and College Union members say that there is a free speech problem, with 68 per cent of universities beset by some sort of censorship controversy on campus.[40] As we have seen, open letter writing and petitions are popular, with over half using these methods to cancel staff, students or visiting speakers in 2020.[41] In Australia, one university has banned 'man', 'ladies', 'mothering/fathering' and 'wife'. At the same time, another prohibits typing out a post in upper case because it is construed as shouting. Or should I say SHOUTING? [42]

There has been rather a lot of real shouting on American campuses of late. More than a decade ago, there were just two events where students shouted down speakers. However, in 2023 and 2024, there were 53 substantial event disruptions, which is a 26-fold increase. There has been so much deplatforming turmoil on campuses that records have been broken, with 167 in 2023 and 172 in 2024, which is the equivalent of one deplatforming attempt every other day or every day during term time.[43] This has been accompanied by a surge in violence and vandalism because students have been programmed into believing that words are able to cause physical harm, which then justifies violence.

We saw biology professor at Evergreen State College, Bret Weinstein, and his wife being threatened by students after he criticised the 'Day of Absence' which decreed that all non-whites absent themselves from campus. We saw swimmer Riley Gaines being assaulted by a man in a dress at San Francisco State University then barricading herself for three hours from a mob of transgender-rights protesters who stormed her speech about protecting women's sports. Political scientist Charles Murray and Allison Stanger, professor of politics and economics at Middlebury College in the US, were attacked by a group of protesters at Middlebury who began pounding and climbing on the car. Stanger went to hospital with a concussion, saying afterwards that she had feared for her life. In 2024, an Oxford Union debate 'Israel is an Apartheid State Responsible for Genocide' was constantly interrupted by students who hurled insults, cursing and screaming at the four panellists on the Israel side. And of course, we saw Charlie Kirk being shot and killed at Utah Valley University on 10 September 2025.

With record-breaking levels of fear and loathing, as well as the possibility of being concussed, it is remarkable that anyone even contemplates appearing on a university campus. Comedians gave up a long time ago. Jerry Seinfeld famously said he didn't play colleges because they were 'too PC'. Chris Rock, too, gives them a wide berth 'because they're way too conservative. Not in their political views – not like they're voting Republican – but in their social views and their willingness not to offend anybody.' When humour is considered too harrowing for delicate sensibilities, chances are the battle for hearts and minds is lost.

(Nearly) Everyone is a Victim

We have demonstrated that the average Western university exhibits a level of diversity of thought and academic freedom comparable to what one might expect from a theology faculty at Kabul University, if such a faculty even existed. We have shown that a cabal of far-left social justice activists within the academy is actively terrorising and silencing dissenting colleagues. Moreover, these revolutionaries appear to be working in tandem with a bloated bureaucracy which enforces campus-wide mandates through stringent Diversity, Equity, and Inclusion policies, as well as a suite of free speech codes that, paradoxically, restrict rather than promote open dialogue. And we have seen that Critical Social Justice has turned scholarship into grievance studies.

But what effect does this environment have on the students? First and foremost, they are increasingly taught to view themselves as either guilty of oppression, or as perpetual victims. They have been fed Critical Race Theory, a novelty invented in the law faculties of American colleges in the 1970s. CRT claims that race is a social construct created by white people to mask their privilege and supremacy. It simply remakes the old Marxist dichotomy of oppressor and oppressed by replacing the worker with black people and the bourgeois oppressor with white people. But, as Christopher Rufo points out, 'the basic conclusion is the same: in order to liberate man, society must be fundamentally transformed through moral, economic, and political revolution.'[44]

And in the 1990s, this attempt to transform society was helped along by Professor Kimberlé Crenshaw who invented the caste system otherwise known as 'intersectionality.' Crenshaw claimed that there were intersecting axes of oppression, such as ageism, racism, sexism and social class. She offered a demonstrably false, yet at the same time rather seductive premise that all white males are living lives of privilege, while everyone else scrabbles about in poverty, misery and failure. Professional intersectional sociologists, of which there are many, enthuse that 'Intersectionality as an analytical tool gives people better access to the complexity of the world and of themselves.' Common sense will tell you that intersectionality creates a permanent class of Untouchables as a form of determinism which traps people into their identity groups based on their skin colour and other immutable traits. It will also tell you that a black man was the President of the United States, and millions of white men died in the trenches during World War I. But as Douglas Murray so aptly puts it, 'Anybody hoping that intersectionality would dissolve amid its own inherent contradictions cannot have seen the myriad of contradictions a Marxist can hold in their head any one time.'[45]

By the time they finish their arts degrees, most graduates will be able to hold a number of contradictions in their heads at any one time. They will be able to tell who the oppressors are according to the Wheel of Power and Privilege (white, slim, able-bodied, neurotypical, rich, English-speaking, heteronormative men) versus the oppressed (dark, trans, intersex, lesbian, pansexual bi, large, significantly neurodiverse with mental health issues).

And many will no doubt have thoroughly unpacked and repacked educator and activist Peggy McIntosh's invisible knapsack of white privilege.

Some are taught by Kehinde Nkosi Andrews, Professor of Black Studies in the School of Social Sciences at Birmingham City University, that 'whiteness is a form of mental illness' which 'induces a form of psychosis framed by its irrationality, which is beyond any rational engagement.'[46] Geology students at Queen Mary University of London have been pondering Kathryn Yusoff's musing on how the study of rocks and fossils is enabling racism and that geology 'continues to function within a white supremacist praxis', which then leads to the creation of white supremacy and 'geotrauma'. However, it's not clear if it is the rocks or the geologist who are suffering from geotrauma.

Students studying Ancient Greece and Rome at the University of Cambridge are informed that reading Aristotle's *Politics* in Ancient Greek contributes to systemic racism because 'Classics as a discipline and departments of Classics have both historic and current problems regarding diversity and racism' and that 'the idealisation of Greece and Rome, and the embedding of that idealisation in education, has featured significantly in the development of modern Western racism.'[47] That said, the faculty's fear that it is a vector of racism is not preventing it from charging £10,000 per year to complete a BA in Classics. The University of Oxford's Faculty of History has a Race Equality Statement and a Race Equality Action Group. One wonders how anyone gets around to actual historical research and teaching. Similarly, one wonders if the then Law Faculty Dean, Mindy Chen-Wishart, had much time to educate students in contract law in between calling for anti-racism training and managing her #RaceMeToo Twitter campaign to 'fight prejudice faced by BAME academics and students'.[48]

All this is why one of the least surprising things to have happened in 2024 was the appearance of 'pro-Palestinian' encampments on university campuses across the Anglosphere. After years of being made to feel guilty about being white, being told that they have 'white privilege' and that they are the oppressors, these young people have realised that they too can finally shed the burden of guilt and join the ranks of the oppressed. At Columbia University, students set up the first 'Gaza Solidarity' encampment on the beautifully manicured lawns of their college grounds. Up went the tents, on went the keffiyehs and out came the yoga mats, as the students demanded that the university cut ties with Israeli companies, that there be a permanent ceasefire in Gaza and that the US withdraw military assistance for Israel. How they thought their college administrators might be able to bring about a ceasefire in the Middle East remains a mystery. Even their language was straight out of the Critical Theory Justice handbook: 'We envision a free Palestine. We necessarily envision an entire world free from colonialism and imperialism, and from the inter-related systems of oppression that uphold them.'

The movement quickly spread to other universities in the Anglosphere. In Australia, students waxed lyrical about how events in the US had brought a flame of inspiration and radicalism. By May, thirty-six universities in England, Wales, and Scotland followed suit. One student protestor who camped in the University of Oxford's 'Liberated Zone' had found the whole experience quite invigorating. 'The action we've taken has had clear results', he commented. 'The last hundred days have been completely transformative for me,' he added, thus reinforcing the stereotype that his generation suffers from extreme solipsism. By the end of the academic year, the encampments had vanished, some more dramatically than others. In the US, thousands of students were arrested, suspended or forcibly removed from their tents by police.

Perhaps the most thrilling denouement occurred where it all began: Columbia University, where the most committed barricaded themselves into Hamilton Hall's administrative offices. Footage of student leader Johanna King-Slutzky demanding 'humanitarian aid' so that her peers would not 'die of dehydration and starvation' adding 'Like, could people please have a glass of water?', did not exactly help the cause. Unsurprisingly, King-Slutzky is a graduate of the School of Arts and Sciences whose dissertation, 'On the Fantasies of limitless energy in the transatlantic Romantic Imagination 1760-1860' examines 'theories of imagination and poetry interpretated through a Marxian lens'. Even less surprisingly, her bio informs us she also worked as a 'political strategist for leftist and progressive causes'.[49] Images of mask-clad 'gluten-free warriors' weakly attempting to hold the line against the local constabulary were widely derided by those who also wondered if the irony that they were illegally occupying a building to protest 'illegal occupation' was lost on them. In the UK, a combination of legal threats and the siren call of the summer holidays saw tents packed down as quickly as they were erected. It turns out that liberating Gaza with your university chums was not worth sacrificing two weeks in Ibiza. Trying to get a good night's sleep in a tent on a lawn in the middle of East London also has its challenges.

In what appeared to be a giant game of cosplay, students everywhere dressed up as Palestinians and acted out a scene in which they had been displaced from Gaza. By wearing keffiyehs, eating Middle Eastern food and greeting each other with *al-salamu alaykum*, they simply acted out as the 'other'. In this way, they could finally join the ranks of the victim, whose status had been consistently glamorised by professors in the lecture theatres.

But as it turns out, their professors had been both glamorising and participating in the demonstrations, and it is fair to say, egging them on. Consider this piece entitled 'At Columbia and beyond, disobedience for Palestine becomes a duty' by Ayça Çubukçu, Associate Professor in Human Rights at the London School of Economics, who returned to her alma mater and made the following observations from the encampment:

> While I was there, the encampment felt quiet if not tranquil, there was the calm before the storm. Except for the occasional use of the people's mic — initiated with a loud injunction to "repeat after me!" — and excellent teach-ins on the geography and botany of settler colonialism in New York and Palestine, students were mostly lounging around, arranging food, doing homework, making art, speaking in tongues.

On Friday, at *Namaz* time, when the *Azaan* was heard at the centre of the encampment, a group of Muslim students began praying together, now on their feet, then on their knees, encircled by two rings of students shielding them from view with banners and blankets.

After observing the ritual in enchanted disbelief, I had a conversation with a colleague and a student at the encampment who was reading a book from 1968, *Difference and Repetition* by the French philosopher Gilles Deleuze. Seemingly removed from politics, we discussed the intimacy between philosophy and theoretical mathematics and thought about why 1 is no longer considered a prime number.[50]

While Associate Professor Çubukçu was fantasising about Deleuze and prime numbers, Dr David Ludden, retired professor of history and 19 other staff were arrested after forming a ring of protection around their truly 'amazing' students at New York University.[51]

During the height of the outbreak of Gaza fever amongst students at the University of Oxford, over 500 staff members from the law, music, anthropology, geography, philosophy, physics, and chemistry faculties, as well as librarians, archivists, computer boffins, admin staff, and keepers of the University's collections, encouraged the 'Gazans' with a letter of support.[52] Gender guru Judith

Butler cheered Hamas as 'progressive', having previously waxed lyrical about 'Hamas and Hezbollah' being 'social movements that are progressive, that are on the left, that are part of a global left.'[53] Meanwhile, a senior lecturer at Birkbeck University had tweeted 'Sometimes partying on stolen land next to a concentration camp where a million people are starved has consequences.'[54] This was the ultimate dramatic expression of their adopted victimhood and ideological posture.

Somewhat less dramatic but of equal ideological posturing was the reaction of Harvard's former President, Claudine Gay, to her handling of the pro-Palestinian protests. During what has become an infamous Congressional hearing on campus anti-Semitism, Gay could not bring herself to say that calling for a genocide of the Jews was a violation of Harvard's code of conduct. It would, she said, depend on the context. In her letter of resignation following accusations of plagiarism, Gay claimed that she had been 'subjected to personal attacks and threats fueled by racial animus'.[55] Similarly, when Ibram X Kendi, author of such bestsellers as *Anti-Racist Baby* and *How to be an Anti-Racist* was unable to explain why his $55 million Centre for Antiracist Research at Boston University had produced almost no anti-racist, or even just plain old research, as well as his sacking of staff by Zoom, he blamed the 'racist ideas' of the racists, rather than any personal shortcomings.[56] But despite their respective and very public failings, Gay is still employed by Harvard as a tenured professor, while Kendi has decamped, *sans* Antiracist Centre, to Howard University in Washington DC. The victim card still has the highest value in the deck.

With such examples, it is hardly surprising that students have taken up victim ideology like champions. They are, however, not exactly winning. While they have been dressing up as Gazans, pretending to be victims, these young people are entirely unaware that they are already real victims. They are victims of years of indoctrination by identity-obsessed academics who have succeeded in completely unmooring them from reason, truth, beauty, reality, and even humour. This unmooring was recently epitomised at the University of Sydney when it undermined its purpose with its 'Unlearn Campaign' aimed at prospective students. 'We live in a post-truth world, where everything is true, and everything is false', it told them. Under the guise of promoting research and its role in changing the world, students should 'challenge the established and question the accepted'. Forget any preconceived ideas that you might have about such things as 'truth', 'love', 'medicine' and 'criminal', it said. Out with the old and in with the new. When the university's founder, William Charles Wentworth, first proposed the idea of Australia's first university in 1850, he envisaged an establishment in which all Australians from every class would be given the opportunity to 'become great and useful in the destinies' of this country.

But the chances of an Australian, or a British, or an American student from any class being given the opportunity to become great and useful in the destinies of their respective countries are becoming slimmer and slimmer by the day. University students are not being given a positive formation. Instead, they are being taught a narrow, one-dimensional view of the world, seen through the prism of class, gender, and race, over a curious and inquiring three-dimensional view of the world that opens the mind. They are being led down the path of un-enlightenment and un-education. They are not being offered new approaches or new ways of looking at the world.

However, they are being given a giant safe space where they are coddled and protected from jokes which offend them, words that make them anxious, and ideas which make them feel uncomfortable. They have trigger warnings which alert them to all sorts of imaginary dangers lurking in the pages of Jane Austen or criminal law lectures on sexual assault. They are even being given trigger warnings about trigger warnings. Unsurprisingly, the only thing that trigger warnings do is make them incredibly anxious. If anything, universities should carry a health alert: by the end of their degrees, students will be far more confused, anxious, and brittle than when they first enrolled.

Thanks to a heady combination of identity politics, Critical Race Theory and the phenomenon of the 'microaggression', they will also feel more paranoid. The microaggression generally takes place entirely in the head of the supposed victim, who will see malicious intent in every interaction no matter how innocent. As a black student at the Art Institutes of California explained, 'I began to see myself through the lens of being black and a woman. If I saw someone coming up with their dog and the dog is barking at me, I could interpret that as a racist microaggression on behalf of both the dog and the dog walker. The world was a lot darker than I thought it was…I thought, I am paying a lot, so they are definitely teaching me the golden rules for life.'[57] Dogs, you see, can be racist too.

As it turns out, she, like so many others, is paying a lot of money to be taught some inordinately rotten rules which are darkening their worlds with the clouds of anxiety, paranoia, and distrust. Some of these rules, which Greg Lukianoff and Jonathan Haidt call 'The Great Untruths' in *The Coddling of the American Mind* are identified as: 1) what doesn't kill you makes you weaker: 2) feelings are a reliable guide to truth, and: 3) difference of opinion is simply a battle between fundamentally opposed groups.

We now have students attaching 'good and bad' to knowledge and opinions. But they do not have the tools to make those distinctions other than with the ideology infused into them. This has resulted in the worst combination of arrogance and ignorance in an individual who is lacking in charity and empathy and who is unwilling to consider even for a millisecond that they might be wrong.

We are also producing young people who think that resorting to violence is perfectly acceptable. According to FIRE's 2025 College Free Speech Rankings, student acceptance of political violence has reached record levels. In 2020, about one in five students said it was acceptable to use violence to silence a speaker; by 2025, that figure had climbed to one in three. While students on the far left remain the most likely to endorse such measures, the share of Republican students who say violence is fine has also more than tripled in four years. As FIRE concludes, support for political violence is no longer confined to one side of the spectrum: 'a rising tide of acceptance of violence has raised all boats.'[58] Meanwhile, a YouGov poll of the public taken after Charlie Kirk's assassination found that 20 per cent of American 18- to 29-year-olds said political violence is sometimes justified.[59]

We are producing generations of people who are highly opinionated and highly vocal, but who do not have the wherewithal to defend their opinions. This is why they resort to shouting, abuse and violence. One particular interaction between Kirk and a student encapsulates what a university education can do to the more susceptible individual:

> Student: 'Fuck you, I hate you. I think you are a fucking arsehole. You are just an awful person. You just want to energise your crowd of racists.'

Kirk [Smiling]: 'Can you say anything that is racist? When have I ever said anything that is racist?'

Student: 'Fuck you'

Kirk: 'That is the American left in one picture, everybody. Lots of rage and no wisdom.'

It is not only the wisdom function of the university that is lost in the maddening miasma of postmodernism; the very foundation of intellectual life is crumbling, as institutions are deprived of all five intellectual virtues identified by St. Thomas Aquinas: understanding, science, prudence, art, and wisdom itself.

This stripping of the intellectual essence has a profoundly dehumanising effect, striking at the very core of university education. It is here that we return to where this chapter began: the hijacking of the humanities by postmodernist critical theory. The humanities once equipped students with the tools to interpret the world critically, engage empathetically with others, and contribute creatively to society. But now, the 'human' part of the 'humanities' has disappeared altogether, leaving us with nothing but the '-ies' – gender studies, black studies, queer studies, and fat studies.

Once, disciplines such as History, English Literature, Political Science, and Philosophy provided students with a means to examine the entirety of the human condition, to grapple with the complexities of life, and to develop a deep appreciation of, and empathy for, humanity. Today, however, these fields no longer foster a shared human essence that binds us together. Instead, they have been systematically dismantled and reconstituted into ideological battlefields, where division is enforced along immutable lines of identity. What was once a pursuit of knowledge that uplifted and united is now a mechanism of fragmentation, reducing education to little more than a politicised exercise in grievance and power dynamics. It's no wonder that everyone is anxious.

As I reveal in this book, the dehumanising process does not begin at the university level, it starts much, much earlier. Universities now serve as the final stage in an indoctrination pipeline, sealing the fate of students with radical theories and progressive educational methods against which they stand little chance.

2

Decolonisation

If you wanted to weaken someone's mind, strip it of certainty, of knowledge, and tradition and leave it vulnerable, where would you start? You'd probably start by telling them that there is no such thing as objective truth. You'd insist instead that there are multiple truths, all equally valid and all equally unverifiable. You certainly wouldn't mention Aristotle's Law of Non-Contradiction, which states that contradictory statements cannot both be true and false at the same time. Nor would you bring up the fact that truth cannot be multiple if it contradicts itself. It's either true or false. And because they now believe that nothing can be objectively true, they would be left unsure as to how to distinguish reality from fiction. They'd stop believing their own eyes. Of course, these ancient insights would be easy to dismiss, because you would have already consigned them to the intellectual graveyard, filled to the brim with the so-called 'dead white males' of their ilk.

And naturally, you'd ignore warnings that moral relativism will leave that person unable to distinguish between right and wrong, telling them instead that everything is just a matter of perspective, and that those perspectives are equally valid. By doing this, you'd leave them completely vulnerable to ideological manipulation, adrift in a world where the difference between right and wrong was not merely blurred but obliterated altogether.

Next, you would tell them that the accumulated knowledge and culture of their civilisation – science, philosophy, art, literature – was invented purely as an instrument of oppression by white men, and that the only reason why their ancestors composed, designed, invented, organised or built anything at all, was because of power. Power to dominate, power to exploit and power to tyrannise, driven by a sociopathic desire to see everyone else suffer.

Finally, you would convince that person that for these historic and present wrongs to be righted, for all the pain and suffering in the world to end, the entire civilisation must be swept away, buried deep, and never spoken of again. You would also insist that there is no difference between cultures, except, of course, that their culture is uniquely evil because it claims to rise above the rest. And you would do all of this under the noble-sounding banner of equity and inclusion. This is exactly what is being done to millions of children in the West. And it all begins with decolonisation.

In 2014, Australian philanthropist and businessman Paul Ramsay died, leaving an A\$3 billion (£1.6 billion) endowment, of which a much smaller portion was allocated by his executors to educate Australians about the foundations of Western Civilisation. The duly named Ramsay Centre for Western Civilisation was established shortly thereafter and began seeking partnerships with universities to deliver a degree shaped by Homer, Aristotle, Plutarch, Augustine, Luther, and Calvin. Students would engage with Descartes, Locke, and Wollstonecraft by day, and listen to Gregorian chant, Beethoven, Mozart, and Wagner by night. It promised a truly enriching education, and a much-needed alternative to the identity politics-obsessed humanities departments of Australian universities.

This, naturally, was treated as a scandal by the universities. Professor Leigh Dale, former Head of an English Literature Department, lamented that a focus on the great texts of the West would be a disaster, damaging the university's reputation as a centre of feminist and post-colonial literature. She was aghast at the thought of dead white males displacing live (white) females such as Robin DiAngelo and Judith Butler.

But it was at Australia's oldest and most prestigious institution, the University of Sydney, that opposition was at its fiercest. Academics launched a campaign to 'Keep Ramsay out of USYD', as if the centre were planning to distribute *Mein Kampf* while recruiting students into the Nazi Party. One PhD candidate described the curriculum as 'structurally, institutionally, morally and epistemically violent to other knowledges,'[60] while a faculty letter declared it 'White supremacy writ large'.[61] Senior lecturer in English and Linguistics, Nick Reimer, went further. In 2019, he penned an article linking the study of the Western canon to the mass shooting of 50 Muslims in Christchurch. Writing in an Australian newspaper, he claimed, 'There is a clear analogy between thinking that European books belong together and thinking that European people do too', concluding by urging Ramsay's academic supporters to 'reflect seriously on how the Ramsay curriculum validates the worldview behind [the] massacre.'[62]

Most people would struggle to reconcile a fictional scene written in 1797, in which Mr Darcy takes an afternoon dip and is surprised by Elizabeth Bennet, with the slaughter of innocent people some 220 years later. And yet Reimer's extraordinary claim was not laughed out of the university. It wasn't laughed out, because for reasons that continue to baffle outsiders, Reimer's belief that Western Civilisation's entire record is just an expression of white people's supremacy is not a fringe belief. It is the prevailing view in Western humanities departments, upon which many academics have built their careers. It is one thing to critique Western Civilisation whilst being paid to preserve it, but it is another thing altogether to use your privileged position to discredit it as 'racist' and then dismantle it in the name of 'equity'.

What makes the Ramsay story so important in the context of this book is that this same attitude, the visceral hostility to the West, the belief that its legacy is oppressive and its knowledge illegitimate, has now made its way into your child's schooling. Across the Anglosphere, primary and secondary students are being taught to see the traditional curriculum not as a neutral or objective body of knowledge, but as a manifestation of 'whiteness' which is morally tainted and politically dangerous.

Decoding Decolonisation: Post-Colonial Theory

As the saying goes, or should go, 'behind every bad education project is a strong postmodern theory'. In this case, that strong theory is post-colonial theory, and it is behind the project to decolonise education. At its heart, this theory is an elaborate intellectual framework built to justify the dismantling of Western Civilisation. Post-colonial theorists throw around terms like 'alternative epistemologies', 'strategic essentialism', 'hybridity', 'subaltern', 'othering' and 'knowledges' to bamboozle the rest of us into submission. But beneath the jargon lies the claim that Philosophy, English, History, and Science are structurally racist and must be dismantled and then rebuilt from non-Western perspectives. They do not challenge the ideas of Western Civilisation on their merit because they say that the ideas were never legitimate in the first place. Truth is defined as domination, knowledge as violence, and civilisation itself as a centuries-long con played by 'dead white men'. But if it hadn't been for those 'dead white men', post-colonial theory would not exist, and there would be no civilisation for them to dismantle.

These seeds were planted over fifty years ago by Algerian-born French psychiatrist Frantz Fanon who produced *The Wretched of the Earth*, the formative work on decolonisation and post-colonial theory, in 1961. Fanon's central thesis was that colonisation dehumanises the colonised, and that violent resistance is essential to protect mental health and self-respect. It was, he argued, imperative to disrupt and reverse the colonial mind-set and worldview that had been forcibly imposed. In his infamous foreword to Fanon's book, Jean-Paul Sartre put it more bluntly: to 'shoot down a European is to kill two birds with one stone' and that 'it is possible to destroy an oppressor and the man he oppresses at the same time; there remains a dead man, and a free man.'[63]

While Fanon was no postmodernist, his intellectual successor, Edward Said, Professor of English and Comparative Literature at Columbia University, certainly drew heavily on post-structuralist theory. Born in Jerusalem in 1935 to wealthy Christian Arab parents, Said was educated at Harvard and Princeton. In 1978, he launched the field of Post-colonial Studies with his seminal book *Orientalism* in which he took the idea that colonisation is a dehumanising force, and applied to it the post-structuralism and the 'power-knowledge' of

Jacques Derrida and Michel Foucault. Said argued that the West (especially Britain and France) had, for centuries, created a false and patronising image of 'the East' or what he called 'Orientalism'.

But if it had not been for countries like Britain and France, Edward Said would neither have had a career, nor a reputation, nor an intellectual legacy. When scholars from around the world gathered at the University of Sydney in 2018 to venerate Said as a beacon of light in a world of colonial darkness, it is unlikely that anyone pointed out that their hero wielded the tools of Western scholarship: close reading, theory, philosophy, and even the university itself, to attack the West. Indeed, Said finds himself in the company of postmodernist saints Paulo Freire and Antonio Gramsci and thus is beyond reproach.

Edward Said's *Orientalism* found an especially receptive audience in English literature departments, which were already submerged in the waters of post-structuralism, Marxism, and critical theory. Scholars could not wait to 'dispel the Anglophone imperial spectre'.[64] Nor could they resist his charge that their own disciplines were complicit in the structures of imperial control.

Said fired the starter gun in what was to be the Great Decolonisation Race. Faculties across the humanities lined up to divest themselves of their 'Westernness', clamouring to distance themselves from the cultural and intellectual inheritance that they had been tasked to preserve and were supposed to love, as if it were a disgraced relative who had committed an unspeakable crime and must now be scrubbed from the family history and never spoken of again. Comparative Literature, Cultural Studies, and Anthropology took the lead, followed closely by History, Political Science, International Relations, Sociology, and even Geography. Bringing up the rear were the Education faculties, which began integrating 'decolonising' frameworks into curriculum design and classroom practice. By the 2000s it had become a moral imperative for educators to dismantle what they termed as 'Eurocentric content' and replace it with 'alternative epistemologies', 'marginalised voices', and 'culturally responsive pedagogy'. Decolonisation shifted from being a fringe idea to educational orthodoxy.

Today, decolonisers are turning on the university itself. We find the most egregious examples in the Antipodes, where academics at the University of Melbourne are so far down the decolonisation path that they published a book about the university's own guilt. In *Dhoombak Goobgoowana: A History of Indigenous Australia and the University of Melbourne - Volume 1: Truth*, the authors make the case that the University of Melbourne was complicit in colonialism, scientific racism, and the marginalisation of Indigenous knowledges.

They tell us that *Dhoombak Goobgoowana* translates as 'truth-telling' in the Woi Wurrung language of the

Wurundjeri Woi Wurrung people, 'whose unceded lands host several of the university's campuses'.[65] If the university acknowledges its complicity in colonialism, and believes its actions were unjust and restitution is owed, then that claim invites scrutiny as to how far the university is willing to go. Will it hand over its multi-billion-dollar property portfolio to the descendants of the Wurundjeri Woi Wurrung people? I suspect that we might have to wait until *Volume 2: Even More Truth* is released before we find out.

In 2025, the University of Sydney announced a hiring spree to 'Indigenise the curriculum' over the coming years. What this actually entails is as vague as the job description for the person who will oversee the indigenisation, which reads like a masterclass in jobspeak: 'provide expert guidance to stakeholders, identify scope, and plan multiple projects'. But if the Australian National Curriculum is anything to go by, where children now learn to count through Aboriginal dance, we might speculate that in the future, third-year medical students will study pulmonary disease by foraging for witchetty grubs in black wattle trees!

Decolonisation in Action

Among the many criticisms we could make of decolonisers and their methods, a lack of imagination is not one of them. Purging, it seems, can take many forms. In London, Philosophy lecturers at the School of Oriental and African Studies (SOAS) have been issued with a 'decolonising toolkit' because they are told that all that philosophising they do is part of the problem. 'Much academic philosophy in the UK, US, Australasia, and continental Europe' they are informed, 'masks its structural antagonism to everything that is not white, bourgeois, male, heteronormative, and able-bodied.' Philosophers and their kind are described as 'the institutional gatekeepers of Anglo-European academic philosophy' and warned that they 'will not take kindly to precisely this critical point.'[66] The document gleefully charges ahead anyway, damning the entire field as inherently racist, which is untrue.

Meanwhile, at the University of Liverpool's Centre for Education, students are shown an animation in which white people are depicted as mosquitoes. Their questions about culture, identity, or background are represented as mosquito bites. Friendliness is redefined as microaggression, and politeness as violence. And then there's Professor Kehinde Andrews, Chair of Black Studies at Birmingham City University, whom we encountered in Chapter One, informing students that whiteness is a form of mental illness, echoing Fanon's revolutionary zeal, and arguing that white people must be 'reborn' by confronting their complicity in oppression. 'The aim,' he says, 'is to make them reborn as allies to the dark oppressed people of the world.'[67] I can't imagine the banter flows freely in those classrooms.

It is equally unlikely that there would be much banter among the experimental psychologists being taken on 'uncomfortable walks' around Oxford, purportedly to help them reflect on just how irredeemably racist everything is. Especially the Ashmolean Museum, with all its artefacts and knowledge. This is a sentiment the Ashmolean itself seems to share, solemnly confessing that 'We acknowledge the Eurocentrism and lack of diversity in our institution and the fact that as a result the narratives from the perspective of other cultures and people have often been silenced or marginalised and we accept our responsibility to challenge and change colonial mindsets.'[68] Students who have embarked on Business degrees at the University of Birmingham are also herded around their city in walks of shame, so they can start 'interrogating, exploring and dismantling the systems that they no longer want to sustain',[69] such as entrepreneurship, capitalism, and meritocracy. Perhaps they should be taken on a tour of the back streets of Mogadishu to balance things out a bit.

In 2014, a collective of BAME (Black, Asian and Minority Ethnic) students at University College London asked: *Why is My Curriculum White?* to nobody and everybody, and then promptly answered their own question with absurdities such as: 'Because if it isn't white, it isn't right (apparently)'; 'the white curriculum is based on a (very) popular myth'; and 'because its power is intersectional'.[70] Remarkably, *Why is My Curriculum*

White? soon spawned a number of spinoffs, such as *Why is My Philosophy Curriculum So White and Male?*, *Why is My Psychology Curriculum Eurocentric?*, and *Why is My Art History Curriculum White?* If you sign up for a Fine Arts degree and are offended by Botticelli, Caravaggio, or even Damien Hirst, perhaps it indicates that you are not actually interested in art. Perhaps it means that you are more interested in activism and contemporary issues.

One could also ask the same question of the University of Cambridge students who, having enrolled to study English Literature, proceeded to write an open letter demanding that they be compelled to read less English literature. The faculty caved and launched a formal review to ensure that its curriculum included more 'post-colonial thought' and black and minority ethnic authors. Current undergraduates such as Shameera, who we learn has a 'highly diverse background', were delighted to discover that 'strong efforts [had] been made by students and researchers to break our fortified 'canonical' under-standing of English.'[71]

At Yale, the English Department famously dropped its once-compulsory 'Major English Poets' sequence, featuring Chaucer, Spenser, Donne, Milton, Pope, Wordsworth and Eliot, in favour of more 'inclusive' offerings. The stated goal was of course, to 'decentre' literature, which is just code for ditching white male poets. Harvard's English degree encourages students to focus on 'ethnic literary traditions' and 'the dynamics of power and resistance'. At Cornell, you can take courses in 'decolonial poetics' before ever encountering the King James Bible or Homer.

This truly is a race to the bottom, and it shows. At an American campus event in 2025, Charlie Kirk was approached by a fourth-year English Literature student who had taken particular umbrage at Kirk's statement that university is a scam. The student, however, was unable to name his favourite Charles Dickens novel. And when pressed to nominate his favourite Jane Austen work, he admitted, 'I don't know who that is,' before taking a wild stab and guessing, 'Harry Potter?' Amid the jeers from the gathered crowd, Kirk's retort was blunt: 'You are proving that college is a scam.'

Speaking of Dickens, Sir Jonathan Bate, knighted in 2015 for his services to literary scholarship and higher education, remembers that 40 years ago, he was able to say to both his British and American students, 'This week, it's Dickens, please read *Great Expectations*, *David Copperfield* and *Bleak House*.' In contrast, his current students struggle to get through one novel in three weeks. Bate attributes this to shrinking attention spans fuelled by smartphones. But he also blames the obsession with diversity and access in elite British and American universities, because 'those students come from disadvantaged schools where the teachers' main task is crowd control, and so the demands in terms of reading long books are just not there.' He continues, 'You only have to look at the thinning of the GCSE and A-level syllabuses and the tendency to prescribe works because they're shorter. I think of it as the "John Steinbeck: *Of Mice and Men* effect" – they would never prescribe *The Grapes of Wrath* anymore, but *Of Mice and Men* is nice and short.'[72]

Decolonising School Curricula

As it so happens, being short has not saved *Of Mice and Men* from the wrath of a Welsh exam board, which has placed Steinbeck on the 'not very nice list' on account of the racial slurs contained therein; slurs which it presumes would offend black students. One might wonder, though, whether the portrayal of Lennie Small as a knuckle-dragging imbecile might also affect white students with disabilities. The board has also dispensed with Harper Lee's story of tolerance and bravery in *To Kill a Mockingbird*, because the current Children's Commissioner, Chilean Rocio Cifuentes, thinks it is 'psychologically and emotionally' harmful to black children.[73] If we were to apply the same logic consistently, then no child could ever read anything, because literature is full of flawed characters, suffering, injustice, and painful realities. Should children who are being bullied be protected from *Lord of the Flies*? What about children with depression? Are they to be subjected to *Hamlet*?

Should children who have been sexually assaulted be protected from Bernardine Evaristo's *Girl, Woman, Other,* in which a number of protagonists are sexually abused and harassed? Some at the Cambridge OCR think they should not. This is presumably why they have put Evaristo's novel on the A-level reading list. Children will follow the fictional lives of twelve British black women, at least two of whom, Carole and LaTisha, have survived sexual assault by the same perpetrator. Other characters with a range of issues include Amma, a radical lesbian theatre director; Dominique, who moves to a lesbian commune in the US; and, last but not least, Morgan/Megan, a non-binary social media influencer.

Given that you'd be hard-pressed to find a more deceased, whiter, and more masculine genre than poetry, the OCR is excising centuries of mellifluousness from the syllabus as one might remove a tumour. Out go John Keats, Robert Browning, Percy Bysshe Shelley, Wilfred Owen, Thomas Hardy, and Seamus Heaney. In come poets with suitably 'diverse' backgrounds, whose interests in politics, identity, migration, race, and post-colonial struggle are expressed in poems such as Caleb Femi's *Things I Have Stolen:*

> From the highest shelf
> my tiptoes could reach me
> I stole a Mars bar & Haribo sweets.
> It wasn't a big deal: Mum said
> their prices were a robbery anyway.

Or in Fred D'Aguiar's *Letter to America (An Abecedary)*

> Who gave those uniforms permission to storm
> School car parks, automatics drawn? Finches ask
> Robins, who, channeling Auden, whistle —
> Bang! WTF!
> *Bang, bang, Lulu,*
> *Lulu gone …*
> The calypso worked its juju
> On my digital radio.

It's clear the decolonisers at the OCR and other organisations have developed an insatiable taste for this kind of literary surgery, but how much of it can the students take? Not very much, it seems. In 2013, approximately 83,000 students enrolled in A-level English Literature. By 2023, this number had fallen to around 54,000, representing a substantial decrease of about 35 per cent over ten years.[74]

Some might argue, and indeed they do, that this mass exodus is a result of too much Shelley and not enough Femi. Others might suggest that students are leaving because the diversity lacks diversity, and they are simply bored. Perhaps they understand that there is more to life than intersectional feminism, or intersectional anything. They might well be fatigued with the language of postcolonial theory, switching off when their teacher insists that *Girl, Woman, Other* is about 'how stigmatization and oppression are manifested through gender, race, social class and sexual orientation, which causes their invisibility in society and increases social injustice.'[75] And who can blame them. This is a monochrome world that forces students into a narrow presentism in which every story has to mirror their own experiences or identity.

Before despairing over what A-level students are ingesting, spare a thought for their Australian counterparts in the state of Victoria, who are not permitted to sit their final English exams without first ploughing through *Things Fall Apart* by Chinua Achebe. Set in precolonial Igboland, this work is described in some circles as the definitive study of 'the intrusive and overpowering presence of Western governments and beliefs,' a depiction of the damage wrought when a 'belligerent' civilisation imposes itself on another out of arrogance and ethnocentrism.[76] Also on the list is Matt Ottley's depressing hybrid of graphic novel, picture book, novella, and musical composition, *Requiem for a Beast*. The story follows a young man's attempts to 'reconcile his family's and his nation's shameful history of violence against Aboriginal Australians, while also coming to terms with his own suicide attempt.'[77] Uplifting this is not.

At this formative stage in their lives, children should be uplifted. Everyone should be exposed to the great books and poems which speak to each and every one of us about the human condition. The ideas and themes treated in great literature are universal, not particular, and they have endured, and will continue to endure for generations because of their universal appeal. Indeed, one of the best expressions of that common humanity is found in Shylock's speech in *The Merchant of Venice:* 'Hath not a Jew hands, organs, dimensions, senses, affections, passions; fed with the same food, hurt with the same weapons, subject to the same diseases, healed by the same means, warmed and cooled by the same winter and summer as a Christian is? If you prick us, do we not bleed?'

The decolonisers are ensuring that students will never read those words, and it is becoming increasingly unlikely that they will hear them at university. No longer are they engaging deeply with the great minds of the past or wrestling with the moral weight and universal themes of classic works. They are not being encouraged to ask profound questions that we should all ask. What is it to be human? What is our purpose? Why are we here? The answers to these serious questions are not buried in poetry about stealing chocolate bars or Haribo sweets. Nor are they likely to emerge when individuals are no longer obliged to test their own intellects or think beyond the mindless script of navel-gazing, victimhood and identity politics.

Instead, they are being fed the intellectual equivalent of gruel. Bland, predictable and lacking in nutrition. There are few times in life that afford us the opportunity to sit down and read a novel from beginning to end. And one of these is when we are still at school, gloriously free from adult responsibilities. That these organisations are using this precious time to impose a selection of identity politics-obsessed novels which are indistinguishable from one another, is unforgivable.

Indigenise Everything!

When it comes to decolonising, the New World is leaving the Old World for dead. Educationalists in the US and Australia are no longer content to merely 'diversify' reading lists; they want to remove everything, from science and maths to art and even sport. Consumed by the guilt of being so-called 'colonial settler societies', they are determined to atone for the supposed wrongs of the past by stripping away Western knowledge and replacing it with 'Indigenous knowledges' or 'ways of knowing'.

Their reasoning stems from an embrace of the postmodern knowledge principle, which insists that objective facts, like the Earth being spherical or hydrogen powering the sun, are themselves oppressive. In this worldview, we must speak of 'knowledges' in the plural, because to speak of 'Western knowledge' implies it is *the* knowledge, thus demeaning other ways of knowing. Likewise, 'ways of knowing' is now mandatory, since 'knowing' alone implies some kind of singularity, an unforgivable offence in the eyes of the postmodernist decolonisers.

In several US states, this takes the form of the mandatory inclusion of Native American perspectives from kindergarten onwards, while schools across the country increasingly prioritise 'Indigenous ways of knowing' as a counterbalance to Western epistemology. Teachers are trained to deliver these lessons using decolonised methods that reject objectivity as a Western imposition. Indigenous science is taught alongside biology and ecology, and mathematics is increasingly presented through tribal number systems and seasonal logic.

In 2015, Washington state mandated that the curriculum *Since Time Immemorial: Tribal Sovereignty in Washington State* be integrated into all Washington public schools from K-12. This means that science is taught through a series of tribal stories told by Roger Fernandes, who is a member of the Lower Elwha S'Klallam Tribe. Children learn about classification of flora through stories such as 'Coyote and Bear' and 'Beaver and Field Mouse'. And it means that 'The Coming of Slahal', a tale about a debate between humans and animals over who should be the predator and who the prey, resolved by a game using carved bones, is used as a device to teach them about the 'Structures of Life'.[78] At one point, when the animals think they might be winning, they sing 'Ho, ho, ho, he-o, ho, ho, ho, he-o, ho, ho, he he-o, ha, ha, ha, ha, e-o, ha, ha, ha, e-o,' which closely approximates the protest song 'Hey, hey, ho, ho, Western Civ has got to go!' led by Jess Jackson at Stanford University back in 1987. Cause or correlation? We will never know.

Occasionally, decolonisation takes us far beyond stories about beavers and field mice. In 2021, a new California public school curriculum which has a reach of 6.2 million children, incorporated pagan prayers and chants to five Aztec gods and a 'divine force' of the Yoruba religion. The curriculum explained how to honour and praise this deity by 'invoking their respective names, followed by the mention of various attributes and principles relating to these Aztec gods.' Children were taught to recite prayers for 'beautiful knowledge', to be 'more realized human beings', and to have 'strength that allows us to transform and renew'.

In the lawsuit filed by Catholic parents on the basis that it violated the state's Constitution, they pointed out, not unreasonably, that the Aztec gods were 'worshipped with brutal human sacrifice, including ripping the beating heart out of a victim', that 'Aztec worship is associated with black magic, cannibalism, bloodletting and the flaying of victims' bodies to provide a skin suit worn as 'golden clothes' by Aztec priests.'[79] All this of course, is factually correct. The California Department of Education and the State Board of Education agreed to remove these religious chants from the curriculum. This is not to say that all American schools are in the business of recruiting children into pagan cults. It merely serves to illustrate just how far 'indigenising' the curriculum in the name of decolonisation can go.

While Australian children are not instructed to pray to Aztec gods, they are similarly inducted into the world of Aboriginal mythology via 'The Dreaming'. In Australian classrooms, 'The Dreaming' is not treated as folklore or mythology; it is presented as a living cultural framework and as a key to understanding the known world.[80] Educators have taken pains to integrate it across all subjects, through 'songlines', also known as 'Dreaming tracks', which are described as 'the path across the land (or sometimes the sky) which marks the route followed by ancestral spirits during the Dreaming (the mythic time of creation).'[81] Children are taught about the rainbow serpent who shaped the landscape, creating rivers, mountains, and valleys as it moves. There is also 'The Dingo and the Moon', which tells of how the moon was once a man who was tricked by the dingo (or wild dog), and 'Tiddalik the Frog', about a giant frog who drinks all the water, causing drought.

In biology classes, teachers are instructed to emphasise that 'for millennia, First Nations Australians have sensitively cared for the living things in their Country/Place and have implemented sustainable practices to maintain environmental balance.'[82] While there is no mention of Linnaeus or Mendel, children are given to understand that stewardship of the earth's flora and fauna was well in hand long before they even started thinking about taxonomy. The construction of fish traps constitutes proof that Aboriginal and Torres Strait Islander peoples had already mastered the multidisciplinary principles of modern science. And Aboriginal Australians were the first astronomers due to 'thousands of years of unbroken observations of the night sky' using star maps to navigate the continent, predating Copernicus by several millennia, if not entirely displacing him.[83] This is not an education in science, but social engineering, where children are presented with mythology and scientific facts as if they are equally valid in terms of how the material world functions. In doing so, the lines between fact and fiction are deliberately blurred, and the very idea of a hierarchy of truth is swept away.

Indeed, trainee teachers in Australian universities are constantly directed away from Western knowledge as if it were inherently harmful. At the University of Melbourne, Master's students 'will engage in critical discussions and activities that enable them to reflect on the impacts of settler colonialism, racism, and unexamined bias on First Nations educational sovereignties, as well as build their understanding and awareness of Indigenous knowledges and strategies for working towards decolonisation.'[84] Some are led to believe that it is no longer sufficient to talk *about* Aboriginal knowledge; they must be able to talk about Aboriginal knowledge *in* Aboriginal, though no one specifies which of the 120 surviving languages they are meant to master. In more extreme cases, students are told that they must also be proficient in 'abolitionist, futurist, and Indigenist thinking'.[85] This sounds unhappily dystopian to me, but then again, I'm rather fond of Western knowledge.

There is, of course, nothing wrong with teaching children about Aboriginal history and culture. It should be part of every Australian child's formation. But when it is done not to enrich knowledge but to replace it, when every subject is filtered through this ideological lens, then we have gone too far. When 'The Dreaming' is taught in lieu of science, then we are in trouble. When students cannot properly form a sentence but can recite land acknowledgements, we are no longer talking about inclusion; we are talking about politicisation. When teachers are trained to view knowledge itself as a colonial weapon, it is not education, it is a soft revolution. It is children who will bear the cost.

Every age has its prophets. Often, their prophecies are deeply unpopular with the very people to whom they are addressed. In the late 1970s, E.D. Hirsch Jr. (who, incidentally, at the time of writing is 94 years old), an American educational theorist and English lecturer, warned of an enormous knowledge deficit among the students turning up at the Virginia community college where he was conducting literacy tests with colleagues from the University of Virginia. Even though these students had grown up where much of the Civil War was fought, they had never heard of Robert E. Lee or Ulysses S. Grant. Hirsch realised that even if these students were technically literate, their lack of historical knowledge meant they couldn't understand what they were actually reading. He concluded that children need a shared body of knowledge, particularly of Western history, literature, and civic culture, to become fluent readers, thoughtful citizens, and fully formed individuals.

In *Cultural Literacy: What Every American Needs to Know* (1987), Hirsch introduced fellow Americans to the concept of a 'core knowledge' curriculum: a set of shared facts and cultural touchstones everyone should know. He included an appendix of about 5,000 essential facts, ranging from capital cities and historical figures to common idioms. He thought, for example, that every American should know what $E=mc^2$ means, be able to tell you what Homer's *Odyssey* is about, know what happened at Pearl Harbor, and be able to understand sayings such as 'The pen is mightier than the sword' if someone casually threw it into conversation.

While *Cultural Literacy* became #2 on the *New York Times* bestseller list, many in academia considered the idea of cultural literacy a travesty. It completely undermined their progressive theories of education, such as John Dewey's 'child-centred' learning and constructivist teaching. Followers of Paulo Freire thought the whole thing was a ghastly show of Eurocentrism that would marginalise children with an outdated, hierarchical view of knowledge: one that failed to validate other 'knowledges'. Scholars in postmodernist and decolonial circles continued to argue that Hirsch's work simply reinforced white, male, Western power structures. Some even suggested that prescribing a fixed set of knowledge could lead to indoctrination because children would not be exposed to 'diverse' viewpoints or 'critical discourse'.[86]

Recently, however, Hirsch's work has been vindicated by a long-term study in Denver, where researchers followed more than 2,300 children from kindergarten through sixth grade, comparing those taught with Hirsch's Core Knowledge sequence to their peers in standard public schools. The results were stark: the Core Knowledge students gained approximately 16 percentile points in reading achievement, which was enough to eliminate altogether the gap associated with poverty.[87]

Hirsch's central insight is simple but devastating to the postmodernist project: reading comprehension and language fluency depend not on vague 'skills and strategies' or culturally affirming stories, but on a storehouse of shared knowledge, cultural references, history, literature, and context that the literate takes for granted. Far from being oppressive, this knowledge is the very means by which children can participate in the civic and cultural life of their societies. Cultural literacy is the glue that holds a society together. Without it, people cannot understand references in daily conversation, participate in civic debates, or even in the democratic process itself.

Ultimately, Hirsch's work underscores just how destructive this project to decolonise the curriculum really is. It paves the way for ideological capture of the mind by stripping away the core knowledge and shared moral framework that once anchored students' thinking.

By rejecting the idea of objective truth and presenting multiple truths or 'knowledges', you take away the child's ability to differentiate between fact and fiction, myth and reality, right and wrong. And when you deprive them of the great works of the past, of philosophy, literature, and history, you are denying them a kind of intellectual immune system against bad ideas. And when you frame knowledge itself as a tool of oppression or as a form of 'violence', you prepare the way for ideologies that promise to put an end to that oppression and violence. These are the radical collectivist solutions we will tackle in the next few chapters, beginning with race, where children are no longer taught to see one another as individuals but as members of racial categories locked in an endless power struggle.

3

Anti-Racist Racism

Part of the broader ideological climate in education today is an intense focus on race and racism. Schools across the West have embraced the idea that a key part of a child's formation is learning how not to be racist; an aim that is, of course, laudable. This mission has, however, taken the form of anti-racism training, in which advocates argue that without it, racism will run rampant in the classroom and the playground. Teachers, as the key drivers of this work, must examine their own unconscious biases to create 'more equitable and inclusive learning spaces'. Anti-racist educators promise that non-white students will be empowered by this training, as it openly acknowledges the structural barriers to their success.

Yet in practice, anti-racism training and its curricula are going far beyond promoting tolerance or fairness. They are imposing a rigid ideological framework that divides children into crude racial categories (oppressors or victims) and replaces the idea of individual moral character with collective racial identity. This is because the training is informed by Critical Race Theory (CRT), which we discussed in Chapter One. CRT claims that race is a social construct invented by white people to preserve their privilege and supremacy. At the heart of this ideological shift is the assumption that white children are inherently privileged. Instead of creating just and equal classrooms, anti-racism training risks turning education itself into a battleground of racial grievance and division.

It's important to acknowledge that in some local contexts, these dynamics might not be as visible or immediate. This chapter is about a much broader trend in education policy, teacher training, and national curriculum guidance that shapes what is taught in schools across the country, even if it manifests unevenly. National-level policies, such as the NEU's Anti-Racist Framework and Brighton and Hove City Council's 'Racial Literacy 101' training, show that teachers are explicitly trained to see whiteness as structural advantage, whether or not they apply it in a classroom where all the children are white.

What does CRT-informed anti-racist training actually do to the mind? Its advocates insist that it will produce children who are more open, more tolerant, and less prejudiced. But in practice, it does the opposite. It turns the child's mind inward, forcing them to view themselves and their future entirely through the lens of skin colour.

In this zero-sum game, no one wins. The white child is burdened with inherited guilt, warned that success may itself be a sign of oppression. The non-white child is told they are already a victim, that the system is rigged, and the odds are against them from birth. Before they can speak, they are told who they are, and who they are not. Why strive, if failure is assumed? Why celebrate success, if it is deemed unjust? This is not empowerment. It is a radical doctrine of predestination which strips children of agency, promise, and hope. It is, at its core, deeply nihilistic, and the cost is incalculable. How many young minds will be held back, not by lack of ability, but by an ideology that insists their destiny is already written in their skin? CRT claims to liberate, but in truth, it enslaves.

The white child is taught to feel inherited guilt; the black child is told that success is impossible in a system rigged against them. In this schema, white-skinned people are the problem, and everyone else is morally pure by default, unless, of course, you're Asian and doing well. Asian pupils, after all, outperform every other ethnic group in GCSEs. In that case, they're conveniently re-categorised as 'white-adjacent', a term used in social justice discourse to describe non-white groups seen as benefiting from whiteness or aligning with white privilege.

This ideology has been packaged up as anti-racist training, giving it a veneer of dinner party respectability.

Since the death of convicted criminal George Floyd, educational establishments outside of the USA have been falling over themselves to import racially polarising CRT, the slogans of the Civil Rights era, and Black Lives Matter. From kindergartens in remote corners of Tasmania to the hallowed halls of Eton, it has taken hold faster than you can say *Why I'm No Longer Talking to White People About Race* by Reni Eddo-Lodge, the bestselling British author who, ironically, is doing rather well in the society she insists is rigged against her.

Pointing out that dividing children by race invites outrage from the usual suspects. Christopher Rufo, who has done more than anyone to expose the truth in the US, is accused of stoking a non-existent culture war. Former Governor of Virginia Ralph Northam said that it was a dog whistle being used by Republicans to frighten people, whereupon he was promptly voted out and replaced by Glenn Youngkin, who then invited concerned parents to report when their children were taught topics related to systemic racism or current and historical inequality.

In the UK, the now Leader of the Opposition, Kemi Badenoch addressed Parliament to argue that teaching white students about white privilege and inherited guilt was unacceptable, she too came under fire from teachers. They believe that without anti-racist training, their white students will grow up to become the next generation of oppressors. They believe Western nations are built on white supremacy, and that all our institutions, including schools, are merely camouflages for racial domination, embracing the idea of collective guilt and insisting that white people must atone for the sins of their forebears.

Yet, proponents of anti-racism training do not worry about its miasma of contradictions; that race does not exist, but it also explains the meaning of life (which, disappointingly, is not 42). That race is a social construct with no biological basis, yet everything must be seen through a racial lens. That race is not real, though white children must reflect on their whiteness, meditate on their unconscious bias and ponder their collective guilt.

The concept of 'unconscious bias', which is the idea that people harbour automatic, hidden prejudices that shape their behaviour, was popularised in the 1990s. Yet, it has come under increasing scrutiny. Numerous scientific critiques have found that unconscious bias tests are unreliable and that training to reduce it has little impact on real-world behaviour. Despite this, the idea has become embedded in education policies and teacher training, where it is used to justify ideological frameworks that treat whiteness as inherently privileged and racial hierarchies as unchangeable. In truth, these psychological theories are far from settled, and their prominence in schools is driven more by ideology than by evidence.

As Douglas Murray notes in *The Madness of Crowds*, 'race' is one of the new cultural tripwires, and children are stumbling over it daily. In one UK school, a four-year-old was reported to the headteacher for racism after he described another child who had been misbehaving as having 'brown skin and black curly hair'. His words were recorded, the incident logged, and the parents were formally notified.[88]

While anti-racist training is not mandatory in British schools, it might as well be. The DfE allows schools to implement it, provided they adhere to guidelines on political impartiality. These guidelines, outlined in the *Education Act 1996* and expanded upon in 2022, require that balanced views are presented on politically contentious issues. In practice, however, these guidelines are often vague, inconsistently applied, or simply ignored when it comes to topics like race and identity, where activists and some teachers insist that the ideological stance of 'anti-racism' is beyond politics altogether. But for many schools, guidelines and impartiality are mere irritants in the way of teaching students that they are privileged 'by virtue of being white'. It's primary home in schools is in Personal, Social, Health and Economic (PSHE) Education, which is taught from the early years, all the way up to secondary school.

The ideological justification for this comes from the top. In its *Framework for Developing an Anti-Racist Approach,* the National Education Union says that 'young people's ideas about race must be explored and discussed within educational contexts – if not within education, where?'[89] Home, one might suggest, would be a good start. Unless of course parents use a resource produced for Barbie manufacturer Mattel by a BBC educational consultant, which suggests that white children playing Monopoly should start the game with more money, avoid jail time, and get first dibs on property. Parents are also advised to encourage activism, show children the petitions they're signing, and point out possible racism in bedtime stories. And if their home's decor or family members are 'too white', the guidance warns that they're 'complicit' in racism.[90]

But the NEU appears to have little interest in families discussing race. After all, they believe that 'colour blindness', treating people equally regardless of skin colour, is a retrograde idea that ignores the realities of racial injustice. In the eyes of progressive educators, this approach is not a virtue, but a refusal to see and challenge systemic oppression. The NEU's ambitions don't end with classroom conversations. It doesn't just want children to be 'anti-racist', it wants anti-racist leadership, an anti-racist curriculum, anti-racist discipline, anti-racist staffing, and an anti-racist student experience. It might as well demand anti-racist racism. This is not a vision of education; it is a totalising ideological framework. In practice, it replaces critical thought with political conformity. And in doing so, it violates not only common sense but also Section 406 of the *Education Act 1996*, which explicitly prohibits 'the promotion of partisan political views in the teaching of any subject'.

The National Association of Head Teachers (NAHT) has gone even further, publicly calling for mandatory anti-racism training for all staff in order to 'safeguard children from racist rhetoric' in schools, which is a remarkable phrase, unless it means protecting some children from being told that they're racists. NAHT thinks that even three-year-olds are guilty of racial bias, and teachers who fail to address the 'mechanics of racism and all othering' are effectively giving 'implicit consent'.[91] In other words, even in kindergarten, silence is violence.

Teachers are not merely encouraged to view race through a postmodernist lens, they are trained to do so explicitly. Materials used in teacher education draw heavily from CRT and the writings of American activist Ta-Nehisi Coates. In one widely circulated training resource designed for five-year-olds, teachers are told that 'race is a social construct – an idea invented by humans rather than an essential fact,' and that 'there are no biological differences between different groups of people. They are informed that 'Ta-Nehisi Coates argues that we have come to accept race as something real, but it is a flawed concept,' that 'race is the child of racism, not the father' and that 'the notion of race was created by Europeans in the sixteenth century as an attempt to justify the dehumanisation of groups of people, colonialism and slavery.'[92]

Should a particularly attentive five-year-old ask the awkward question 'Can a black person be racist towards a white person?', the teacher is instructed to explain that while black people can be 'racially prejudiced' towards white people (and that this is wrong), this is *not* racism. Racism, they are told, is 'prejudice plus power'. And since white people in the UK hold the cultural power and are more likely to be the judge, headteacher, or prime minister, it follows that only their prejudice can have systemic consequences. So: yes, black people can be racist. But also, no, they can't. And if that same child then comes back with 'I don't see the colour of people's skin so I'm definitely not racist', the teacher must thank the small interrogator for bravely sharing their thoughts but add that it's 'important to recognise people's skin colour as this could suggest you are ignoring a part of them that makes them who they are.'[93] If the pupils weren't bewildered at the start of the lesson, they certainly will be by the end of it.

As ideological training has spread through classrooms and staffrooms alike, it's easy to overlook another key influence shaping this landscape: local councils, perhaps the most quietly powerful players of all. While they no longer directly control school curricula, local authorities do fund teacher training, issue guidance, and endorse third-party organisations (3POs) that deliver ideologically loaded anti-racism programs. According to Don't Divide Us, a grassroots coalition that came together in 2020 to contest the idea that Britain is systemically racist, these 3POs, are pushing materials which embed concepts like white privilege, systemic racism, and lived experience as unquestioned truth. In its 2023 report *Who Are the Experts?*, Don't Divide Us found that 88 per cent of local authorities in their sample were found to have used or endorsed 3POs promoting CRT in schools. And it's not just ideology on offer, it's profit. These providers work on budgets ranging from a few thousand pounds to millions, with 28.6 per cent operating in the £1 million-plus band, the largest segment of the industry.[94] Apparently, there's serious money in telling children they're racist.

For the last 25 years, schools in England have been obliged to report all 'hate speech' incidents to local authorities as part of the 2000 Race Relations Act. In 2010, more than 20,000 under-11s were punished for racist and homophobic behaviour in schools, which was about the equivalent of around 100 primary school pupils a day.[95] In some cases, pupils were reprimanded for calling each other 'gaylord' and 'broccoli head'. And yet, with all this anti-racist training, the numbers haven't improved. In 2022, 11,619 pupils were suspended for alleged racist behaviour, up from 9,452 the year before that.

In 2024, 15,191 pupils were suspended for racist behaviour, 2,485 of whom were primary school children, and five of whom were aged between four and five.[96] Predictably, campaigners will say they pick up this racism at home, or from the media. Dr Shabna Begum of the Runnymede Trust says children are simply reflecting the hatred embedded in political discourse. Daniel Kebede, General Secretary of the NEU, echoes the sentiment, blaming the divisive, hateful language from politicians and press for fostering a toxic environment in schools.

But there also remains the distinct possibility that many of these alleged incidents are just simply childish playground chatter. Only the most zealous of anti-racist educators could think that a nine-year-old boy telling an eleven-year-old girl, 'You're a Turkey from Turkey', and then flapping his arms like a bird, is racist.[97] She might be a victim of a bad pun, but she's not a victim of racism. Similarly, a female pupil calling a male pupil 'white trash' whilst playing football, another child arguing with two other children and then calling them both 'chocolate bars' and Bangladeshi children calling other Bangladeshi children 'Kala bander' (black monkey), do not necessarily live up to expectations. Likewise, 'You're a toad on drugs with an arse on your face', impersonations of Donald Trump and one child saying to another, 'You're going to get roasted, toasted and burned' during a netball match are not exactly racist slurs.[98]

According to the DfE's own data, the ethnic group with the highest proportion of exclusions for 'racist abuse' was Asian students, followed by Black students, Black Caribbean, and Mixed White/Black Caribbean students, with White British students coming last. While White pupils, by virtue of being the majority, account for the highest absolute number of exclusions, proportionally they are not the worst offenders. These figures do not give us the full context behind each case, but they decisively undermine the narrative that racism in schools flows in one direction, from white children towards everyone else. In reality, the picture is far more complex, and considerably less convenient for those building school policies around inherited racial guilt.

Another area in which the narrative and the DfE's data do not quite match up is the question of attainment gaps. While anti-racism training in schools is often justified by citing attainment gaps among ethnic minority pupils, a closer examination of the data reveals a more nuanced picture. Government statistics indicate that White British pupils eligible for free school meals (FSM) are among the lowest-performing groups in the education system. Government figures from 2022 show that while 56 per cent of Black pupils eligible for free school meals (FSM) achieved a grade 4 or above in English and Maths,[99] only 36 per cent of White British FSM pupils did so, making them the lowest-performing major ethnic group in the country.[100] In 2024, only 18.6 per cent of white British FSM pupils achieved a grade 5 or higher in English and Maths GCSEs, compared to a national average of 45.9 per cent.[101]

This underperformance is not confined to boys; disadvantaged White British girls also lag behind their peers. These statistics challenge the assumption that systemic racism is the primary driver of educational disparities and suggest that socio-economic factors play a significant role. Furthermore, White British FSM boys, in particular, have the lowest rates of entry into higher education, with just 12.7 per cent progressing to university by age 19.[102] And on that note, research also finds higher aspirations among ethnic minority children at 14 years old compared with white children. White boys gave themselves an average probability of going to university of 60.9 per cent, while for White girls the estimation was higher, at 68.3 per cent. Compare these numbers with Black African boys and girls – 81.7 per cent and 88.8 per cent respectively.[103]

This data challenges the idea, which is often embedded in anti-racist education, that children of colour inevitably see themselves as powerless victims of systemic racism. In fact, the aspirations of Black African, Indian, Pakistani, and Bangladeshi children show a remarkable optimism and belief in their own ability to succeed. They do not appear to have fully internalised the narrative that skin colour alone dictates one's life outcomes. Instead, their ambitions reflect a sense of agency and hope that stands in sharp contrast to the doctrine of racial determinism being taught in many schools today.

Yet, national policies and third-party interventions remain fixated on narratives of white privilege, ignoring the fact that the children most likely to leave school without qualifications or prospects are often the ones accused of 'systemic advantage'. Anti-racism training in schools is therefore based on a false premise: it scapegoats the very children most in need of support, while ignoring the uncomfortable truths about which groups are truly disadvantaged in today's educational landscape.

CRT-derived content remains deeply embedded in British classrooms, and curiously, almost no one has bothered to ask parents what they think, let alone whether they wanted it taught to their children in the first place. What we do know is telling: only 24 per cent of UK adults believe Britain is 'structurally racist', while 53 per cent actively disagree, suggesting that CRT's core assumptions are at odds with public opinion. Meanwhile, exposure to Critical Social Justice content, including CRT and radical gender theory, is not just widespread but escalating: 68 per cent of 20-year-olds, 74 per cent of 19-year-olds, and 79 per cent of 18-year-olds report being taught these ideas.[104]

Compared internationally, British students are now absorbing between two-thirds and three-quarters as much Critical Social Justice content as their American peers which, frankly, is a lot. Nevertheless, its quiet and rapid spread through schools continues almost entirely unnoticed, and with gathering pace. Australian students too, are absorbing CRT like sponges. I cannot begin to do justice to the sheer volume of time and money now funnelled into anti-racism training resources available for Australian teachers and schoolchildren. Yet somehow, it's going largely unnoticed by the broader public. It has been embedded in the dreaded National Curriculum, where it sits under the Aboriginal 'cross-curriculum priority'. This framing insists that Australia was founded on white supremacy and racial oppression. The country, we're told, is systemically racist, and Aboriginal Australians, by virtue of their race, are the perpetual victims.

What students are not taught is that while society did indeed shun and exclude Aboriginal Australians in the past, this is no longer the case. Today, Aboriginal and Torres Strait Islander people enjoy full legal equality and, like every other group in society, some individuals do well while others struggle. Far from being neglected, the federal government spends billions of dollars each year on Indigenous-specific programs. As of October 2025, there are 11 Aboriginal members of the Australian Parliament, meaning they are slightly over-represented relative to their share of the national population. This marks a dramatic change from the past, when they were either entirely absent from Parliament or represented by only a handful of individuals. This reality certainly challenges the prevailing narrative of systemic oppression and reveals that society has moved on from exclusion to inclusion, with significant investment in, and representation of this sector of society.

What's more curious is that this re-education campaign finds its most vigorous expression not in history class, but in Physical Education. The experts have decided that anti-racism training is most effective when children are dangling from monkey bars or charging across football fields. As they do, they are encouraged to reflect on 'the impact systemic racism and discrimination have had on Australian First Nations Peoples,' and to investigate 'strategies that promote truth-telling and build cultural awareness to develop empathy and respectful relationships.'[105] There's a time and place for everything. Hanging upside down by your knees is not one of them.

Meanwhile, the New South Wales Department of Education mandates that all new staff complete hours of anti-racism policy training, which begins with the gentle presumption that they are racist. Students, for their part, are shepherded through the 'Racism. No Way!' program; an endless parade of cartoonish scenarios and moral lectures. In the same breath, they are told that telling Irish jokes and wearing swastikas to school belong to the same moral category.[106] According to the luminaries behind 'Racism. No Way!', training cannot start too early, so they have developed a series of anti-prejudice classroom activities for kindergarten children. In 'Understanding Prejudice' they are read *The Sneetches* by Dr Suess and then asked to discuss 'discrimination which exists between the two groups as well as its effects'.[107]

By the time these Australian children reach secondary school, it's all about 'white privilege'. In the lesson 'Got White Privilege?', students watch a film called *You don't have to be racist to have white privilege* which is made in the US and features a feisty woman of colour explaining that from the moment a white person is born, they are afforded certain privileges. 'One thing is consistent' she says, 'if you're white, society be like, you out here winning.'[108]

And although Australia has no historical legacy of slavery, its teachers have nonetheless become devout disciples of the Black Lives Matter movement. At a Sydney primary school, 10-year-olds proudly decorated their classroom with signs reading 'End White Supremacy', 'White Lives Matter Too Much', and 'Stop Killer Cops'. In high schools, things have taken a darker turn. One youth worker reportedly forced fifteen-year-old boys to stand before their peers and apologise for being white, male, and Christian.

In the US, people *have* noticed. They've noticed because the very public argument about how race should be discussed is now taking place inside classrooms. And they've noticed because school libraries are awash with picture books about white supremacy, aimed at members of the polis who have not yet learned to speak. Ibram X. Kendi's fabled *Antiracist Baby*, a firm favourite, and by some accounts already a classic, is the most obvious example. In cheerful rhyming prose, Kendi explains to his infant readership (via their adult interlocutors) that they are not only implicated in systemic racism, but that being three months old is no excuse. There is no such thing as innocence when it comes to race.

Antiracist baby is bred, not born. Antiracist baby is raised to make society transform. Open your eyes to all skin colors

Antiracist baby learns all the colors. Not because race is true. If you claim to be colour-blind, you deny what is right in front of you

Use your words to talk about race. No one will see race if they stay silent. If we don't name race, it won't stop being so violent.

That some parents willingly introduce the concept of violence into their babies' moral universe gives you a fairly good sense of how deeply this particular ideology has taken root. And if their children are too old for *Antiracist Baby*, they can always pick up a copy of *Stamped: Racism, Antiracism, and You* [109], in which Kendi will guide their twelve-year-olds through how to identify and stamp out racist thoughts in their own lives. As the Amazon blurb declares: 'RACE. Uh-oh. The R-word'. We too might echo that sentiment. Uh-oh indeed.

Americans have also noticed the rise of institutions such as Woke Kindergarten, a New York-based 'anti-oppressive early learning ecosystem' that aims to give 'power to the lil' people!' (And no, they're not using a politically correct term for dwarfs.) In between naps, the 'lil' people' will be introduced to revolutionary concepts such as 'So You Want to Free Palestine? A Resistance

Guide for Kids' and 'Five Ways to Understand Abolition in Early Childhood'.[110] Americans will have heard Department of Education contractors claiming that the education system is designed to harm brown and black children, or they might have heard one white teacher talking earnestly about 'trying to force' her white daughters to 'reside in reality' by pushing 'through all of the white fantasy that is part of what it means to grow up in a white supremacist society', because 'whites have a lot of fantasy about what it means to be white.'[111]

What is a fantasy is the idea that your character and your success or failure in life is somehow dictated by your skin colour. And because most people recognise it for what it is – fantasy – they are rejecting it. This belief, central to Critical Race Theory, insists that racial identity is the overriding factor shaping every aspect of a person's life: their opportunities, their moral worth, and even their inner character. But this is not how most people actually live or see the world. Polling consistently shows that a majority of people in both the UK and the US reject the idea that race alone determines someone's destiny. They understand that family environment, education, personal choices, and social class play far greater roles in determining whether someone thrives or struggles. This is why the anti-racism agenda, rooted in the idea of fixed racial determinism, feels out of step with people's lived experiences. It is also why it is being met with growing resistance: because it turns life's complexity and human potential into a one-dimensional story of racial power and victimhood. And most people, regardless of their politics, instinctively know this story isn't true.

A 2023 national survey found that 69 per cent of American voters with an opinion on the issue believe that CRT curricula are further dividing young people. Additionally, 70 per cent of these voters expressed the view that public schools should prioritise teaching core subjects like math, science, and grammar over cultural curricula such as CRT and discussions on sexual identity and transgenderism.[112]

In fact, the backlash has been so significant that it has reached federal level. In 2020, President Donald Trump issued Executive Order 13950, banning federal agencies, and by extension, federal contractors and grant recipients, including schools, from promoting race-essentialist concepts such as collective racial guilt, inherent bias based on skin colour, or the idea that the United States is fundamentally racist. Although the order was later revoked by President Biden, it marked a turning point: CRT was no longer an academic abstraction, it had become a frontline political issue.

And in 2025, with Trump's return to office, Executive Order 14190 was introduced, expanding the original ban to explicitly cover K-12 schools. The order directed federal agencies to investigate schools suspected of promoting CRT or gender ideology, with the threat of revoked funding for those that refused to comply. Whether or not schools eventually comply with the new guidelines or legislative threats is a matter of policy and politics. But the more pressing question is: what damage has already been done to children?

The Damage Done

In 2006, former teacher and filmmaker Adrian Hart was hired to create an educational film as part of the 'Watch Out for Racism!' project, which was implemented in Essex primary schools. The project was funded and overseen by local educational authorities in Essex, with creative input and support from Greenwich and Lewisham Young People's Theatre (GLYPT), a group known for producing educational and community-based drama resources.

His brief was to investigate the problem of racism among 10- and 11-year-olds in primary schools in Essex. But, after visiting a number of schools, he found no evidence of racism. Yet the schools pressed ahead with race-awareness workshops regardless. As Hart noted, these sessions were entirely at odds with the children's real concerns and behaviour. In the playground, they were carefree, colour-blind, and open-minded, until the workshops encouraged them to see themselves and their friends through the prism of race.

And this prism is not just teaching them to believe the central tenets of critical theory, it's teaching them to become critical theorists, and to think like critical theorists. A thirteen-year-old was shocked when his father, in an effort to explain the difference between Nelson Mandela and Lord Nelson, described the former as being black. 'Oh, my God' the child gasped. 'You can't call him black. That's so racist.… 'You need to say he's got a black skin tone.'[113] Or consider the young American girl being raised by progressive parents, who, in what sounds more like an examination of conscience than the diary of a little girl, writes 'Sometimes I do have an unfortunate bias. If I am walking my dog down the street and I see an African American male, I sometimes notice myself pulling my dog a bit closer and preparing my body for certain circumstances. I am very disappointed in myself, but I also realize this is how lots of society was taught.'[114]

The idea that children are born racist is the dubious foundation upon which school-aged anti-racism training rests. For Foucault, childhood, race, and even truth itself, are just social constructs shaped by power. Thus, a child is never 'innocent' in a political sense, because they are already part of power structures such as whiteness, colonialism, or heteronormativity. CRT scholars like Richard Delgado, beloved by education faculties, explicitly reject racial innocence in white children.

The belief is that white children benefit from systemic racism, even if they don't express individual prejudice. This view comes directly from the postmodernist suspicion of universalism: race, like truth and morality, is seen as socially constructed and politically contested. And children are not exempt. 'In the United States' writes a member of the CRT cult 'a lot of us believe that children, especially white children, are racial innocents – completely naive, curiously fragile with respect to the realities of race, or both. The truth is that well before their teen years, the vast majority of children are well aware of prevailing biases, and most kids, of all racial stripes, have taken on a bunch of their own.'[115]

But empirical evidence and common sense both tell us that three-year-olds are racially innocent. They are neither racist nor do they harbour 'unconscious bias'. They do not oppress one another based on skin colour. White children are not guilty of 'othering' their peers, nor do they need to 'check their privilege'. No child is participating in a fantastical postmodernist system of racial oppression dreamt up in the feverish imaginations of critical race theorists.

Children are colour blind in the truest sense: they see differences in skin colour, but they do not attach moral weight or social hierarchy to them. Research has shown that 'children's prejudice is not innate – it develops from environmental cues and social learning,'[116] while 'prejudice emerges in childhood only as a reflection of the attitudes children encounter in their families, schools, and communities.'[117] Even as they learn to categorise people by race in the preschool years, children 'do not naturally assign worth to these categories.'[118] It is only later, under the influence of their social environment, that children begin to absorb the prejudices and divisions of the adult world.

And because they are not racists, they do not need to be remade into anti-racists at school. As Thomas Sowell observed, 'Much of the social history of the Western world over the past three decades has been a history of replacing what worked with what sounded good. In area after area – crime, education, housing, race relations – the situation has gotten worse after the bright new theories were put into operation.'[119] Anti-racist training in education is a solution in search of a problem. And when the problem doesn't exist, the 'solution' inevitably does more harm than good. Teachers in both the UK and the US have reported that interracial friendships have been strained by lessons that frame whiteness as inherently oppressive and blackness as synonymous with victimhood.

In the US, schools have become so ideologically splintered that they now implement 'affinity groups', which are racially segregated spaces where pupils are encouraged to discuss race in isolation from their peers. This reinforces separation rather than integration. One teacher in California, a self-described black Christian, conservative, saw the effects in her classroom. Her students, who were learning English as a second language, 'didn't need to be taught to check their privilege' she said. 'It's hyper-race focused. And whenever there's hyper race focus, racism will follow.'[120]

In the UK, some white children have reported feeling ashamed or anxious about their race, especially in primary school, where they lack the maturity to understand these concepts. At one London school, every subject, from maths to music, was so heavily infused with 'race' that some students felt unable to speak freely. In addition, the school was running racially segregated after-school clubs, where children only mixed with their own ethnic group.[121] A teacher at one of the most elite high schools in New York City, who had studied Derrida at college, said he was alarmed when Critical Race Theory arrived at his school, albeit in a mutated form. 'I started seeing what was happening to the kids. And that's what I couldn't take. They are being educated in resentment and fear. It's extremely dangerous.' Another teacher in Los Angeles, teaching prep school, said 'It teaches people who have so much to see themselves as victims. They think they are suffering oppression at one of the poshest schools in the country.'[122]

And one of the worst aspects of all this is that many of the people imposing it on the children know exactly the effect it is having on them. Douglas Murray relates the story of the maths teacher who, after noting that anti-racist training caused white students to feel like 'oppressors', while others responded with 'dependency, resentment, and moral superiority,' was formally disciplined for pointing this out. But in a private conversation, his principal admitted that the material was demonising white children and punishing them 'for nothing they are personally responsible for' and that it was making them feel 'less than'. He later attempted to retract his statement, but the damage had already been done.[123]

A UK report suggests that this atmosphere of anxiety is not isolated. Students exposed to concepts such as 'white privilege', 'systemic racism', and 'unconscious bias', were significantly more likely to report being afraid of being shamed, punished, or expelled for expressing controversial views. And when asked how comfortable they would feel criticising a black classmate, white and Asian students said they would feel highly uncomfortable. Black students, in contrast, showed no change in comfort level based on CRT exposure.[124] These findings suggest that far from fostering open dialogue, anti-racist education may be training students to censor themselves or worse, to believe that honest conversation with certain peers is off-limits. One Los Angeles mother disbelievingly related how her son was told by his friend, who was black and a multi-millionaire, that he was 'inherently oppressed'. 'My son said to his friend: "Explain it to me. Why do you feel oppressed? What has anyone done to make you feel less?" And the friend said: "The color of my skin."' This, she said, blew her mind.[125]

This discomfort was on full display in Channel 4's abominable 2021 documentary *The School That Tried to End Racism*, which was later exported to Australia. In the UK version, a red-headed schoolboy and his excited classmates were taken to a field and told they'd be competing in a race. But it wasn't a race of speed, it was a re-enactment of Peggy McIntosh's infamous 'Privilege Walk'. With every question about their home life or family background, the more privileged children were told to step forward. Unsurprisingly, the ginger boy who was pale, freckled, and raised in a stable home, ended up at the front of the line. He had 'won' the race, and he promptly burst into tears. The burden of white privilege, it seemed, was too heavy for his childish shoulders. A few years ago, this same boy might have been mocked for his hair colour. But now, yesterday's victim has become today's oppressor.

What these children went through however, was nothing compared with the abuse that children suffered at the hands of African American 'race' consultant Glenn Singleton who, through Pacific Educational Group (PEG), has made millions of dollars embedding radical ideas into K-12 schools across the US through what he calls 'Courageous Conversations'. In 2009, he hired a group of actors who took children from their classroom in an overwhelmingly white area. They were then chained together, blindfolded, and driven to a park, released and then chased by an angry Singleton. When finally caught by the actors, the traumatised children were forced to write down the things that they loved, only to have the pieces of paper then taken away from them. This technique was apparently meant to teach them 'tolerance'.

Unsurprisingly, parents had no idea about that their children were to be put through such as an ordeal, as they were not asked to sign a permission slip. One history teacher, completely devoid of empathy, attempted to explain that some of the children 'got really emotional right away' because they were 'feeling cultural empathy'.[126] Perhaps it was more to do with the sheer terror of being chained, blindfolded and chased by strangers through a park.

These ideological frameworks, built on concepts like 'white privilege', 'white fragility', and 'unconscious bias', create an educational climate where whiteness is seen as a problem in itself. Even if white children in some schools do not directly experience this as personal shame, the very fact that their teachers are steeped in these frameworks inevitably shapes how they are taught and how they understand themselves in the world. And this is precisely the problem: many teachers or schools don't notice these ideological frameworks because they are embedded as common sense in words like 'diversity', 'inclusion', and 'anti-racism', yet they reframe curriculum priorities and diminish the cultural authority of the Western canon. This is not about claiming that every white child in every classroom feels guilty or ashamed, it's about recognising the cumulative effect of these ideological frameworks: a quiet but profound shift in how children are taught to see themselves, their nation, and their civilisation.

4

Gender Ideology

Most people hope that when their children grow up, they will carry with them happy memories of early childhood in kindergarten – morning naps interspersed with songs, finger painting, and playing in the sandpit with other children. But many future adults will remember something else entirely: being accused of transphobia and thrown out of kindergarten. Yes, you read that correctly.

In the United Kingdom today, official DfE data show that small children, including a toddler, have been suspended for 'abuse against sexual orientation and gender identity'.[127] Ten children in Year 1 and three in Year 2, none older than seven, were also suspended on the same grounds.[128] The official statistics do not give individual case details, but journalists using freedom of information requests have revealed that even nursery-aged children have been caught in this net. Their crime? Failing to repeat the slogans about gender and sexuality demanded by the new orthodoxy, even though they do not know what a slogan is, or what orthodoxy means, or even have much awareness of the difference between boys and girls, let alone the concept of transgenderism.

This is not a scene from some far-off dystopia. This is Britain in the 2020s. This injustice is being inflicted on thousands of innocent schoolchildren and their parents by ideologically motivated bureaucrats in the DfE, which has decided that 'abuse against sexual orientation and gender identity' constitutes a formal offence and is meticulously documenting how many children are committing it. In England, suspensions and exclusions for what the DfE calls 'abuse related to sex or gender' have been rising steadily. In 2022-23, a total of 178 pupils across all schools were suspended or expelled for homophobic or transphobic behaviour, including 94 pupils in primary schools.[129]

What exactly constitutes this 'abuse'? In law, crimes must meet clearly defined legal thresholds. Not so at the DfE which has gone all postmodernist and does not wish to be constrained by oppressive power structures such as 'definitions' and 'thresholds'. So, one school might punish a child for calling a peer by their pre-transition name. Another might deem the question 'Why is that boy wearing a dress?' a heinous act of transphobia. Or a pupil might be chastised and given a detention by their transgender teacher for using 'Miss', instead of 'Mx' and then make matters worse by confusedly asking what 'Mx' actually means. The interpretation of the supposed crime is fluid, changeable, and highly subjective, much like the radical ideologies about men, women, and sexuality that it is determined to enforce. Life imitating art, as it were.

How is it that the DfE, whose portfolio includes child protection, is not just failing to protect children from this pernicious ideology, but actively persecuting them for refusing to conform to it? Why did primary school teachers put down *The Very Hungry Caterpillar* and pick up *Who Are You? The Kid's Guide to Gender Identity*, instead?[130] Why are children being taught that 'some girls have penises' as objective fact by educators who simultaneously believe nothing is objectively true? Why are they being told there are a hundred genders?[131] Why is it that little boys are being told that their very essence – their maleness – is problematic? And what effect is this having on the children who are being fed this ideology, day after day, year after year, from kindergarten until they finish school?

The Scavenger Ideology

It is astonishing that radical fringe theories, once confined to niche academic circles, have become standard educational fare. Children across the West are being indoctrinated with a confusing blend of queer theory, radical gender theory, and intersectional feminism. This is a fatal cocktail of concepts that casts biological sex as irrelevant, identity as sacred, and masculinity as inherently toxic.

It's an ideological minefield because it is contradictory, anti-scientific, and at times utterly deranged. Of course, it is not presented to parents in those terms. It's sold to parents as a necessary part of their children's development, packaged up in harmless sounding programs such as 'Consent Education', 'Respectful Relationships' or 'Relationships and Sexuality Education' which we will cover later in this chapter. They tell parents that their children need to be in an 'inclusive environment' where they are encouraged to develop their own identity. But make no mistake. These programs are a Trojan horse for an incoherent, disordered ideology which has no place in a sane society, let alone in a kindergarten. To understand how we arrived at this point, we need to examine the ideological pillars, beginning with queer theory.

Queer Theory

If queer theory had a slogan, it would be: 'Trans women are women'. Queer theory emerged from the dark corners of academia before the 1990s, inspired by the postmodernism of Foucault and Derrida and their rejection of objective truths, fixed identities, and stable meanings.[132] Its core beliefs are that gender and sexuality are fluid, socially constructed and performative. One of its high priestesses is American philosopher and gender theorist, Judith Butler, who currently identifies as non-binary and who unleashed her ideas into academia in 1990 with *Gender Trouble: Feminism and the Subversion of*

Identity.[133] Drawing on postmodernism, Butler argued that identity categories such as 'man' and 'woman' are not natural but 'the effects of a certain kind of power, and… sites of necessary trouble.'[1] She then went even further and insisted that sex itself is socially constructed.

Another key figure is Gayle Rubin, a white middle class academic who is a spirited opponent of 'normativity', and remarkably candid about the political motivations behind these theories, asserting that 'we should believe sex, gender and sexuality to be social constructs, not because it is necessarily true, but because it is easier to politicize them and demand change if they are social constructs than if they are biological.'[134]

Over the past three decades, these concepts have infiltrated education faculties, activist NGOs, and school curricula. When your children are taught that their true self lies in how they 'identify', and not in their biology, that's Butler and Rubin. When teachers claim that 'gender is a spectrum' or 'boys can be girls if they feel it inside' that's Butler and Rubin again. Butler's latest book, *Who's Afraid of Gender?* is a dig at those who err on the side of science and reality. It should be renamed *Who's Afraid of Queer Theory?*; not everyone is, but everyone should be.

The ultimate goal of queer theory is to 'liberate' society from normativity in sex, family, relationships, and behaviour. These are seen as oppressive structures that must be dismantled. The majority of the population, those who are heterosexual, biologically aligned in sex and gender, and not morbidly obese, are now labelled with pejoratives like 'hetero-', 'cis-', and 'thin-'. They even have their own verb, which is 'to queer.' But what is it 'to be queered'? It is 'allowing someone to be simultaneously male, female, or neither, to present as masculine, feminine, neuter, a mixture of three, and to adopt any sexuality.'[135] It is no wonder this theory 'does little to encourage its accessibility with most people, who rightly see it as being quite mad.'[136]

Still, queer theorists are pushing ahead with their project. In the Great Queering, no stone is to be left unturned, including the stones. This includes Shakespeare (To Queer or Not to Queer?), architecture, classical music, brunch, the wilderness, science, babies, and children.[137] Childhood is to be queered. And one of the ways in which this is being done is through the phenomenon of the Drag Queen Story Hour. Once a form of adult entertainment where men dressed as glamourous, sexualised women, drag queens are now often found reading picture books to small children in public libraries and schools across the Anglosphere. Billed as harmless fun, and a way of inspiring 'a love of reading', Drag Queen Story Hour is nothing of the sort. It is a live action application of queer theory's core principle which is that 'heteronormativity' should be disrupted, destabilised and deconstructed, starting with children.

Its proponents could not be clearer about their goal. Harris Kornstein, University of Arizona lecturer and celebrated author of the semi-autobiographical work *The Hips on the Drag Queen Go Swish Swish Swish*, is one such individual. In *Drag Pedagogy: The Playful Practice of Queer Imagination in Early Childhood,* co-written with a fellow academic, Kornstein, aka 'Lil Miss Hot Mess', proposes that drag queens reading to toddlers is about teaching them 'how to live queerly'. Drag is not merely about exposing children to diverse lifestyles but a way to 'engage in embodied inquiry into queer/trans ways of being'. They dismiss traditional instruction and instead praise drag pedagogy for fostering environments in schools, which they claim are 'more hospitable to queer knowledge and experience'. Finally, they ask: what potentialities might be unlocked by the convergence of children and drag queens?[138] They didn't have to wait long to find out. The result was not just potentialities, but a raft of actualities in the form of protests from outraged parents who saw Drag Pedagogy for exactly what it is: an ideological project targeting their children.

What is a Boy?

A great deal of school policy and teacher training is fixated on radical gender theory. While queer theory questions the very existence of fixed identities, radical gender theory insists that internal gender identity is innate, unchangeable, and must override biology in all contexts and at all times. Where queer theory revels in ambiguity, contradiction, and subversion, gender theory polices identity with authoritarianism. It enforces pronoun use, affirms self-declared identities in children without question, and labels dissent as hate. And as we have seen, one of the DfE's projects is to label dissenting children as haters with a rigour absent from most other areas of schooling.

A key architect of gender theory was Dr John Money, a New Zealand-born psychologist and sexologist working at Johns Hopkins University in the 1960s. He was one of the first to coin the term 'gender identity' and insisted that biological sex had nothing to do with being male or female. To prove his theory, he conducted a now-infamous experiment: persuading Canadian parents Janet and Ron Reimer to raise one of their twins, David, who had suffered a botched circumcision, as a girl named Brenda. Money's methods were grotesque. In an interview with *Rolling Stone*, David reported that during visits to his gender identity clinic, he reportedly asked the twin boys graphic questions about their sexual preferences, showed them pornography, and instructed them to examine each other's genitals, sometimes in front of up to six colleagues.[139] This was not therapy. It was abuse.

The result was profound psychological trauma and, eventually, suicide. David, despite years of being raised as a girl, always knew he was male. The experiment was a devastating failure, yet Money, blinded by ideology, declared it a success. As *Spiked* writer Lauren Smith notes, 'Without Money, it's unlikely that trans ideology... would exist today in the way that it does.'[140] Indeed, trans ideology is the activist arm of queer theory, the part that has left the university and entered the school system and which is now taught to children as unquestionable truth.

Intersectional Feminism and Toxic Masculinity

Another ideology now taught to schoolchildren as truth is the idea that masculinity itself is toxic. By extension, if masculinity is toxic, then all boys and men must be too. This idea originated with the aforementioned caste system of intersectional oppression invented by legal academic Kimberlé Crenshaw in the 1990s which demonises all straight white males as oppressors, regardless of their individual behaviour. By the late 2000s, intersectional feminist-inspired misandry had not only become acceptable in elite circles but *de rigueur*, epitomised in 2018 by Suzanna Danuta Walters, editor of the feminist journal *Signs* who published an op-ed in the *Washington Post* asking, 'Why can't we hate men?'[141] If the same question had been posed about women by a man, all hell would have broken loose.

In schools, this message is not framed so bluntly. Instead, it is couched in the language of masculinity, more specifically, 'hegemonic masculinity', a concept developed by Australian sociologist and gender theorist Raewyn Connell who transitioned from Robert to

Raewyn in later life. To put it simply, hegemonic masculinity is the dominant cultural ideal of manhood, defined by power, control, emotional restraint, and heterosexual dominance. It is said to uphold male supremacy. Given that Connell's notion of hegemonic masculinity was a result of a 'synthesis of ideas about masculinity from psychoanalysis, feminist theory, gay theory, and structural sociology,'[142] perhaps a more accurate term would be 'emasculated masculinity'.

This paved the way for the concept of 'toxic masculinity' popularised by psychiatrist Terry Kupers, who originally used the term to describe prison inmates, which is not exactly fair to the general male population. Today it is used liberally, uncritically, and without definition by politicians, media figures, teachers, and curriculum writers. While definitions vary, toxic masculinity is generally understood to include traits such as misogyny, aggression, homophobia, violence, and emotional repression. In practice, it seems to be deployed against men just for being men, and boys for being boys.

Helen Joyce, one of the few authors who was prepared to say that biological sex is real, says:

> 'There are many strange things about gender identity ideology. One is that it's internally inconsistent, picking up bits and bobs from here and there and without any attempt at coherence. It's a scavenger ideology. Internal contradictions, such as gender being fluid, and innate, and socially constructed all at the same time make no difference to the faith believers.'[143]

In this sea of contradictions, gender is a social construct unless it's your identity, in which case it's sacred and permanent. Masculinity is toxic and harmful, unless it's performed by someone identifying as female, in which case it's stunning and brave. Critics might ask, if sex is meaningless, why is it trans women are so often framed as victims because they are 'women' in a patriarchal society? Or if gender is just a construct, then why must everyone affirm another person's internal sense of it as a moral truth? And if 'trans women are women', then why are there still campaigns insisting they be allowed into women-only spaces, which have historically been defined by biological sex? These contradictions don't cancel each other out. Instead, they coexist in a kind of ideological détente, bound not by logic but by a shared refusal to accept biological reality.

Respectful Relationships and Ideological Capture

These theories are so riddled with holes that, were they a kitchen item, they'd be a colander. Yet in their infinite wisdom, Western governments have seen to make it compulsory for them to be taught in schools. By and large, this is done through seemingly benign sounding programs such as 'Respectful Relationships' or 'Resilience, Rights and Respectful Relationships' which purport to be about building healthy relationships, matters of consent, and the prevention of domestic violence. These DEI-inspired programs are sold to the parents as a critical part of their children's upbringing, which will teach them to live in a society where everyone is included and accepted, no matter their skin colour or sexual proclivities. It is often touted, not unreasonably, as a means by which schools will become fair and welcoming for all. And while there are some minor inconsistencies, such as being told to celebrate uniqueness whilst simultaneously insisting everyone is fundamentally the same, or that we must be both colour-blind and colour-conscious at the same time, these are unimportant in the grand scheme of things.

In reality, these programs are the vehicles for smuggling queer theory, radical gender theory, intersectional feminism and the idea of 'toxic masculinity' into schools. The story is identical in the UK, the US and Australia, where purveyors of such programs will strenuously deny that it is happening. Or, when faced with insurmountable evidence to the contrary, they will pivot and say yes, it is happening, but it is a necessary part of a child's education. In Victoria, Australia, the far-left government has taken to gaslighting the public by claiming on its website that gender theory in the curriculum is a myth invented by right-wing conspiracy theorists.[144] To suggest otherwise marks one out as a tin -foil- hat-wearing crackpot.

The Wild West of Sex Education

The UK's Relationships and Sex Education (RSE) was made compulsory for primary and secondary school students in 2020 by Boris Johnson's Conservative government. It is a perfect example of a mismatch between what RSE says it will do on the tin, and the actual contents contained therein. The Statutory Guidance written by the DfE for schools to follow, talks a great deal about respect and inclusion, age-appropriate content, even referring to 'British values' for added credibility. It promises a miraculous transformation of your child into the embodiment of 'honesty, integrity, courage, humility, kindness, generosity, trustworthiness, and a sense of justice, underpinned by self-respect and self-worth'.[145] If we were to take the department's promises at face value, then RSE would seem essential. Who would not want that for their children?

However, we are now several years into this social experiment, and it's safe to say that RSE has lifted the lid on a Pandora's box, unleashing chaos and confusion about biological reality and identity into young hearts and minds. This confusion has flourished because schools are attempting to make sense of the senseless, and because lacking clear guidance in the form of a curriculum, they have been improvising as they go. But mostly it is because schools have invited in well-funded, unaccountable lobby groups, non-profits, and charities whose methods and resources go far beyond the remit of the Statutory Guidance.

One of those organisations is Stonewall, which most people still associate with 1969 riots at the Stonewall Inn in Greenwich Village, or perhaps, as Sydneysiders do, with a lively three-storey gay bar featuring DJs, dancers, and drag shows. Fewer realise that taxpayer-funded Stonewall is now one of the most powerful drivers of queer theory in UK institutions, including schools, councils, and government departments.[146]

In 2019, Stonewall launched its *Creating an LGBT-Inclusive Primary Curriculum* guide, which looks at every subject through a queer lens. From Maths to Science, History to English, every lesson becomes a rainbow-washed platform. 'You'd be surprised at the opportunities for LGBTQ+ inclusion in your science lessons,' they inform us. Indeed, we would, and we are. In Science, children are asked to solve a problem for a same-sex couple, Dean and Ishmael, who have bought a holiday home in notoriously windblown Fuerteventura. Concerned about evaporation, they face the terrible dilemma of choosing whether to use saltwater or freshwater in their pool. One might suggest Dean and Ishmael could have avoided the conundrum by buying a place somewhere less windy or simply leave the pool empty and go for a dip in the Atlantic instead.

Meanwhile, in geography, students are to act as travel agents for newlyweds Simon and Pete who are planning their honeymoon. They are to research possible destinations whilst being 'aware that Simon and Pete might be worried about facing discrimination'. Surely, this is a trick question, for according to Stonewall, LGBTQ+

individuals are discriminated against everywhere in the world, even in the UK. Perhaps the children should simply advise Simon and Pete to stay home for their honeymoon. Over in Art classes, students are encouraged to paint Frida Kahlo-inspired self-portraits by using vibrant reds, greens, blues, and yellows, perhaps adding a monkey, a monobrow and moustache to their portraits for authenticity.

At the back of the curriculum, Stonewall has included a helpful LGBTQ+ glossary for the kiddies who, if not already exhausted after dealing with Dean, Ishmael, Simon and Pete's dramas, will certainly be by the time they get to this. 'G', they are told, is for 'Gender Identity':

> Everyone has a gender identity. This is the gender that someone feels they are. This might be the same as the gender they were given as a baby, but it might not. They might feel like they are a different gender, or they might not feel like a boy or a girl.

Then we have 'N' for 'Non-Binary' which is 'A word for someone who doesn't feel like they're a boy, girl, man or woman'. In this scenario, the child who points out that the 'N' contradicts the 'G' will likely earn them a 'B' for Bigot.

While the Stonewall curriculum invites satire, the broader story of this ideological influence is deeply troubling. One of the most controversial organisations also operating in schools is taxpayer-funded lobby group Mermaids.

Established in 1995 to 'support transgender, non-binary, and gender-diverse children and young people', Mermaids subscribes to the school of thought which posits that 'our gender is decided by other people when we're born, based on the way our body looks' and that 'a child born with male genitalia, for instance, will be assigned as "male" but may grow up to be a transgender woman or a number of gender identities'.[147] Astonishingly, between 2017 and 2019, the DfE funded Mermaids and sent employees into 40 schools to disseminate this Butlerian fantasy via training materials for teachers. In 2024, it came to light that the lobby group had been doing a little more than disseminating ideas. It had also been quietly disseminating chest binders to children as young as 13, without parental consent. Even though the Charity Commission's two-year inquiry found 'systemic failings' and 'mismanagement' mostly around the chest binders as well as its description of puberty blockers for children as being 'safe and reversible', Mermaids, whose annual income is £2.3 million, was cleared of misconduct and continues to offer resources and training to schools.

Finally, by way of another example, No Outsiders began life as a University of Sunderland research project written by Andrew Moffat, who posited that 'heteronormativity' in primary schools was problematic and that the concept of childhood innocence was both naïve and outdated. Unsurprisingly, socially transitioning primary school children features heavily in the organisation's 42 lesson plans, which draw from an inexhaustible supply of children's books about transitioning such as *Dogs Don't Do Ballet*, a story of a dog who insists on wearing a tutu and is told by adults that dogs can't be ballerinas, until, triumphantly, he masters the rond de jambe. In *You Need to Chill!* by activist Juno Dawson, a pre-pubescent child whose sibling has 'transitioned', defiantly, and some might say, insolently, exclaims 'You need to chill' to every adult who enquires about what has happened to her older brother, who went from being Bill to Lily.

Who knew that there were so many opportunists who want nothing more than to talk to other people's children about everything but inclusion? One of the most popular topics is sex – not heterosexual sex of course, as that would be far too 'normative', but any other type of sex. As one resource laments, 'penis in vagina sex can be a bit meh, or rubbish, for many couples'. At every opportunity, old-fashioned heterosexual sex must either be denigrated or, at best, squeezed onto equal footing with an endless parade of 'exciting alternatives'. In a lesson plan of an award-winning independent school, twelve- and thirteen-year-olds are asked what they 'know/think/feel' about the type of sex that 'heteronormative couples' and 'non-heteronormative couples' have. After being put into pairs and told to 'mind map the ways that couples can show intimacy' using pencils and cardboard boxes, the teacher prompts, 'What do you notice?' With any luck, the more observant among them will notice just how highly inappropriate this is and will be informing their parents about it in due course.

Even though RSE does not make one single mention of the subject of masturbation, it is being taught in schools as a vital component of the program. Among a number of resources is *Masturbation – A Hands on Guide*, which contains a passage which is not only totally unsuitable for children but sounds like something that you'd find on the shelves of an X-rated adult bookshop:

> Some people enjoy greasing themselves up with lubricant, oil, skin cream, or anything smooth, silky or sticky. You can taste and sniff your vaginal secretions, pre-ejaculate or sperm. Again, your home can be a source of inspiration. Take the contents of the fridge, for instance. Whipped cream, jam and yoghurt can enhance the pleasure of masturbation. Carrots and cucumber of various sizes can be used as dildos or anal plugs. Experiment with hot and cold sensations by using warm vanilla sauce and ice cream, by dripping warm candle wax onto your skin, or by rubbing yourself with an ice cube.[148]

In the olden days, the most risqué thing that children might pick up at school was how to roll a cigarette. Now it's how to use condiments for self-stimulation.

Pornography, like masturbation, is another topic which, naturally enough, is entirely absent from the RSE Statutory Guidance. Yet some providers, such as a crowd called Split Banana, have included it anyway, with resources such as *A Simple Guide to Great Sex-ed: How to Talk About Porn*.[149] Children, it says, should watch pornography because according to them, everyone of all ages does it anyway. While Split Banana thinks all children should watch pornography, the UK charity Tender Education and Arts, which uses drama to 'teach children about healthy relationships'[150], thinks that if boys watch 'revenge porn', it is a sign of toxic masculinity and will lead to the 'normalisation of violence'.[151]

But the charity also believes that the pre-game locker room banter of the Under-15 Boys' 1st XV, for example, is one of the most dangerous pre-conditions for genocide. In its 'Misogyny Resource' circulated to schools, Tender includes the 'Pyramid of Sexual Violence', at the base of which sits, among attitudes and beliefs, 'locker room banter', 'strict gender roles', 'objectification', 'bragging', and the familiar saying, 'boys will be boys'. According to the Pyramid, these cultural attitudes inevitably lead upward, through sexual harassment and assault, toward the apex: gang rape, femicide, and finally genocide.[152] In this worldview, casual teenage banter and centuries-old social norms are no longer harmless fun; they are the seeds of mass violence. That such a claim is taken seriously within the cloistered world of academia is one thing. That it is being taught as established fact to boys and girls is another thing altogether. Tender claims that its 'programmes are safe, enjoyable, age-appropriate spaces where young people can engage with sensitive topics and "rehearse" for real-life scenarios.' How Tender can claim that telling teenage boys they are only a heartbeat away from committing a violent crime is 'enjoyable' beggars belief.

War, it seems, has been declared on boys, using the language and objectives of intersectional feminism – the 'patriarchy', 'toxic masculinity', and the 'manosphere'. This socially destructive force has entered schools across the West with remarkable speed and little public scrutiny. Enter Prime Minister Keir Starmer. After watching the fictional Netflix series *Adolescence*, which depicts a thirteen-year-old white working-class boy murdering a girl from his class, Starmer declared it a must-watch for schools. Despite the show being fictional, Starmer appeared to take it as a form of documentary insight, insisting it be shown across the country because, as he put it, 'it shone a light on misogyny, on online content, and this sense of children, particularly boys, getting drawn in to this world'. Coincidentally, the charity involved in the promotion of *Adolescence* happened to be Tender, which was not only co-founded by Keir Starmer's ex-girlfriend, Phillippa Kaufmann, but which has also received £3.9 million in government grants since 2020. The government promised that before the end of the 2025 academic year, schoolchildren would be given lessons to counter misogyny in new RSE Guidance.

In Australia, educators believe that they have solved the problem of 'toxic masculinity' altogether. Men should just stop being men. All it will take is for teachers to provide 'opportunities for men and boys to explore and reflect upon their personal male privilege and power' and that everyone should 'move away from a binary notion of gender and invite men to loosen their attachments to notions of masculinity altogether'. But do not fear. 'These approaches needn't be thought of as mutually exclusive. Beginning with a focus on freedom from unhealthy masculine stereotypes can support a process of disruption that eventually moves away from binary notions of gender in the long term.'[153]

Meanwhile, beyond the worlds of government and NGO collaboration, and indeed the classroom, not everyone is on board with the terminology. A 2024 survey found that 60 per cent of British 16-to 24-year-olds had heard or read a lot about toxic masculinity, which interestingly is three times the proportion of those surveyed aged over 55, who finished school before this ideology took hold. And unsurprisingly, it's not a hugely popular concept among men, with 37 per cent of men aged 16 to 29 saying that 'toxic masculinity' is an unhelpful term –which is putting it rather politely. Meanwhile, nearly half of young women say they find the term very helpful. The survey does not elaborate on exactly how.[154] The data suggests that the concept of 'toxic masculinity' has been embraced enthusiastically by younger women, tolerated uneasily by younger men, and largely rejected by older men and women. It also hints at a broader cultural trend: the vilification of traditionally masculine traits is not a fringe academic idea confined to university campuses.

Your children, Our Agenda

You would hope that parents would not want their children having conversations about pornography at school and would prefer that the stigma surrounding it stayed exactly where it is. Similarly, it would be reasonable to expect that twelve-year-olds being taught 'anal sex top tips' by total strangers might be frowned upon. You would think that most parents might prefer that their children did not know what 'lube', 'pegging', 'mess', 'control', 'kink', 'BDSM', or 'Chemsex' even are.[155] But it seems that this is precisely what a significant cohort in Britain now supports. According to a 2024 YouGov poll, 61 per cent of respondents said that children should be taught that 'people can be non-binary / identify as a gender other than male or female' and that 'people can be transgender / change their gender identity'. Even more strikingly, 68 per cent were perfectly happy for their offspring to be exposed to 'explicit discussions of sexual acts'.[156]

While YouGov is regarded as a reputable polling organisation, and its methodology is considered sound, it is important to take into consideration that respondents may interpret broad terms like 'gender identity' differently, and that social desirability bias cannot be ruled out, particularly on highly charged topics such as this. Nevertheless, in general the results are entirely consistent with the country's political and ideological divide, and it will not surprise readers to learn that women, younger people, and Labour voters were firmly in Team Sexual Enlightenment, while their male, older, and Tory-voting counterparts stood more firmly on the side of shielding children from adult themes.

Across the Atlantic, however, the situation has taken a somewhat different turn. The American population at large is far less enthusiastic about this inexplicable obsession with sex and gender. We know this because several recent polls tell us so. A 2024 Pew Centre research report found that 68 per cent of US parents, along with many teachers and teenagers oppose teaching gender ideology in school.[157] But we also know this because we have seen it playing out in real time. For the past few years, the militant National Education Association, American Federation of Teachers, as well as the National School Boards Association, have been flooding schools with gender theory and explicit sexual material through Comprehensive Sex Education (CSE) and Social and Emotional Learning (SEL). Sixteen states now require teachers to promote gender ideology in schools, and because some of these states, like California and New

York, are so populous, this policy affects approximately 37 per cent of American students.[158]

As parents all over the country started to realise what was happening, they began turning up to the school board meetings to challenge the *status quo.* This did not go down so well because the last people that the boards actually wanted to hear from were the parents. In fact, they found it so objectionable that in 2021, the National School Boards Association infamously urged the Biden administration to treat protesting parents as Domestic Terrorists. In Loudoun County, Virginia, a father was arrested during a board meeting after protesting the school board's cover-up of his daughter's assault by a transgender-identifying student. In Katy, Texas, parents were vilified for objecting to books graphically depicting sexual acts. In Arizona, a Scottsdale school board president was caught compiling secret dossiers on rebellious parents. And in Fairfax County, Virginia, parents who opposed gender ideology in elementary classrooms were dismissed as bigots.

As one such 'bigot' explained to the board: 'You consulted the community, the community said no – and then you voted 16 to 0 to move forward anyway. That clearly shows you see parents not as partners, but as obstacles to your agenda. I have a really hard time looking at my son and saying, I'm handing you over to people who do not want to partner with me in how you're going to be raised.' The message was clear: education officials were no longer interested in dialogue. They were enforcing an ideology, but parents were standing in the way.

American parents are not alone in their reservations about handing their children over to strangers with a different worldview. Australian parents face the prospect of handing their two-year-olds to kindergarten teachers who think that teaching social justice in early years is an 'exciting' opportunity to explore issues around gender, sexuality, race, culture, and our environment. In 2024, the federal government-approved a syllabus designed for 0-5-year-olds called *Belonging, Being and Becoming*, which is compulsory in all kindergartens. Teachers are told that 'early childhood is a critical time for children to begin understanding and exploring gender', and that they should ensure that kindergartens are 'safe spaces where LGBTQI+ children and families feel welcomed, honoured, and supported'. They should do their utmost to resist 'heteronormative ways of working and ensuring rainbow families are meaningfully included and experience a sense of belonging'.[159]

As they grow up, Australian children are subjected to ten years of gender theory through the government mandated Respectful Relationships Education (RRE) which has been embedded into the Australian National Curriculum. If they have the misfortune of living in the State of Victoria, they experience twelve years of indoctrination, culminating, as they leave school for the wider world, in being taught that gender identities are not fixed, 'but come into being due to multiple influences', that 'regardless of whether people are cisgender or transgender, they will be influenced by the gender norms of their society, and they may be negatively policed if they fail to fit dominant norms,' and last but not least, that 'in Australia, there are no bathroom provisions for transgender people'.[160]

As it happens, public toilets were the unlikely focal point of the UK Supreme Court's ruling in April 2025, which stated that the word 'woman' refers to biological females under the *Equality Act*, thus making it illegal for men who identify as women to use women's facilities. In the days that followed, men identifying as women entered female toilets anyway, posting videos of themselves on social media with captions such as 'this woman will use female spaces' or threatening to 'p*** on the floor'. Toilet Wars aside, the ruling sharply contradicts the message many children are being taught in schools. That message now has no legal basis and directly conflicts with current law. While the full implications of the ruling are yet to unfold, the consequences for schools, teachers, and the parents who have long objected to this ideological capture may be considerable.

In 2023, the Conservative government announced a long-overdue review into RSE. An independent inquiry was promised, but it never came. When the Conservatives were voted out in 2024, the incoming Labour government made it clear there would be no rethink, and no review. Education Secretary Bridget Phillipson stated that her priority was to ensure schools were 'delivering high and rising standards for every child' which is a vague and meaningless reassurance that conveniently side-steps the question of what, exactly, is being taught. The inquiry has quietly vanished. And rather than curbing the ideological excesses of RSE, the government appears to be going in the other direction altogether. Given how high the level of ideological contamination already is, the mind positively boggles at the kind of material that children will be subjected to. If Keir Starmer's promise of new misogyny lessons is anything to go by, then Britain is in trouble.

And not just Britain, but Britons like fourteen-year-old Cynthia, whose testimony offers a startling glimpse of what it is already like at school:

> My friends don't know I disagree with gender ideology and I'm too scared to say anything that goes against the accepted norm in case I'll be targeted; I've heard what's happened to girls in other schools when they've spoken out – take "Kate", for example, she was spat on and harassed and ended up self-harming after bullying from her classmates after she said "I respectfully disagree" to a person who was talking about the topic of "trans rights". I feel like it is EXACTLY the same environment at my school, and it's basically like there's been this mass-radicalisation of today's youth in favour of a hateful

ideology which favours sexist, regressive stereotypes over biological truth.

I have "trans" and "non-binary" friends, and I love them to pieces, but if they find out I disagree with gender ideology I have zero doubt they'll abandon me (and probably turn on me) in the blink of an eye. There's this culture of absolute intolerance towards any notion of an opinion that differs from the politically correct norm, and it's clearly present at my school. So I just meekly agree and nod along while my friends rant on about how men can have cervixes; why "birthing partner" is an acceptable replacement for the word mother; why there's actually no reason for single-sex sport; why "neopronouns are the future!"; why JK Rowling is a "transphobic TERF" who deserves to die, etc., because I'm terrified of speaking out.[161]

Cynthia reports that after one girl in Year 7 announced she was 'transgender', almost every other girl in the friendship group promptly followed suit, each adopting a novel, often incoherent identity such as 'gender-fluid', 'non-binary', or other imaginative labels, along with new names and demands for alternate pronouns. Soon, children in other year groups began to mimic the trend. Outside schools, over the past decade or so, demand for NHS gender identity services for children has skyrocketed. In 2009, there were fewer than 50 referrals per annum, but by 2021-2022, they had exploded to over 5,000. This staggering surge, driven overwhelmingly by adolescent girls, sparked enough alarm to prompt the commissioning of the Cass Review, an independent investigation into what exactly was going on inside gender clinics.

Yet, amid the confusion and pressure to conform, something unexpected is happening. There are people like Cynthia who are refusing to accept the zeitgeist. In fact, a growing number are beginning to push back and rejecting the mantras around gender identity that is being taught to them. In April 2025, a recording from Rye College in East Sussex captured an extraordinary classroom exchange between students and their teacher during a discussion about gender identity. When the students expressed the view that there are only two genders, male and female, the teacher immediately accused them of being 'despicable,' threatened them with disciplinary action, and insisted that gender identity is 'not an opinion'. When one student pointed out that many people share their belief but are too afraid to say so, the teacher dismissed this and ordered the students to prepare statements to be handed to school leadership. The situation borders on the surreal, almost as if a *South Park* episode has broken loose in real life. Children calmly asserting that boys are boys and girls are girls, while teachers spiral into ideological meltdowns, demanding statements and threatening re-education.

The inversion is striking. In some cases, the students have more common sense than the adults charged with teaching them.

The Effect on Children

This brings us neatly the next question, which is how did things become so inverted that parents who want to protect their children from harmful material are placed in the same category as those who actually want to harm other people with violence, bombings or kidnappings? How is that, even in the face of opposition, bureaucrats in control of education are allowed to impose their agenda on other people's children? And what exactly do they hope will be gained from it all? In contrast, what of the many parents who now support this agenda? How is it those natural instincts to protect their children have been warped or so thoroughly suppressed that they now welcome the exposure of their children to indoctrination?

At the heart of this question lies the concept of childhood innocence itself: that brief period in life when children are pure, naive, and lacking in worldly experience. A time in which they are curious and impressionable, but not yet fully formed. This idea has long underpinned the way Western societies understand childhood. It is why we try to protect children from sexual content and why we normally shield them from adult political debates. Queer theorists, however, have spent decades challenging the very notion of childhood innocence, arguing that it is not a natural or universal stage of life but a social construct, deployed by adults to regulate and control children.

Unsurprisingly, Judith Butler is among them. In *Undoing Gender*, she says that 'childhood is not outside power; it is one of its primary sites' adding that 'It might, then, be necessary to rethink the prohibition on incest as that which sometimes protects against a violation and sometimes becomes the very instrument of a violation.'[162] Other theorists agree. Lee Edelman insists that childhood innocence is a repressive adult fantasy and a tool of power to be dismantled. Meanwhile, Professor Erica R. Meiners, argues that 'preserving innocence becomes a justification for excluding discussions of LGBTQ identities, erasing queer lives from children's realities and silencing their questions.' It is not unrelated that Foucault, Derrida and Lyotard were signatories on a 1977 petition to the French parliament to decriminalise all consensual relations between adults and children under fifteen. When James Bowen of the UK's National Association of Head Teachers protested that he found no 'evidence to suggest there is a widespread problem with pupils being presented with age-inappropriate materials' in RSE, he was being perfectly honest.[163] If childhood innocence does not exist, then everything is, by definition, age-appropriate.

Let us pause here for the sake of sanity to contrast this radical postmodernist view with the vision of Aquinas, just to see just how far Western society has strayed. For Aquinas, childhood innocence was a real and precious thing: not an 'adult fantasy' but a fragile state to be nurtured. Even though children are born with the seeds of reason, they still lack the full use of it, and so must be lovingly guided toward truth, virtue, and happiness. Education was, for him, a sacred moral act in which the young soul was ordered toward its highest good. In the secularist world of gender theorists, which is ordered entirely around the physical body, there is no room for discussions of the human soul, and thus importantly no room for discussion about morality and what is right or wrong.

Indeed, one of the most devastating consequences of this ideological education is that children are no longer being taught how to tell the difference between right and wrong. Children are taught that morality is relative. Postmodernist theorists like Foucault, Derrida, and Lyotard explicitly rejected the idea of moral universals. Foucault, in particular, argued that moral norms were nothing more than instruments of control, enforced by schools, churches, and prisons to preserve dominance. Derrida dismissed fixed definitions of justice, claiming that 'true justice' is always 'to come,' forever unknowable, and therefore forever out of reach. Lyotard urged 'incredulity toward metanarratives', which was a typically obscure way of saying that good and evil, justice and injustice, don't exist.

This is indeed dangerous territory. To tell a child that truth is subjective is to begin the slow unravelling of their mind. If there is no such thing as objective truth, only 'your truth' and 'my truth,' then there can be no shared reality, only competing narratives and power struggles. If we abandon the idea that things are objectively true, then we are leading young minds down a path of madness, where facts are opinions in disguise, and the concept of a knowable reality is done away with altogether.

5

Twisted History

Much of this book has explored the extent to which children are being inducted into a world that is far too political, far too ideological, and far too adult for their tender years. This should not be their world, but it is. Progressive educationalists, teachers' unions, and policymakers are working night and day to ensure that the politics of identity, intersectionality, and decolonisation are the cornerstones of education in the West. But there is another, equally insidious element in all of this: the distortion of school history in the name of diversity and inclusivity, all under the banner of making amends for past injustices in order to build a more 'inclusive' future.

British schoolchildren are being taught that the British Empire and colonialism were, and continue to be, wholly destructive forces. In the US, the *1619 Project* recast the entire American experiment as a four-hundred-year system of racial oppression. In Australia, children are constantly reminded that they live on 'stolen land' and that the arrival of the First Fleet in 1788 was not the founding of a penal colony which eventually became the modern nation of Australia, but the beginning of genocide and dispossession by British settlers who made the conscious decision to systematically wipe out Aboriginal Australians, destroy their culture and take their lands.[164] Genocide, in this context, is not framed as a tragic side effect of colonisation, but as its central goal. Dispossession, likewise, is taught not as a contested historical process, but as a one-sided theft that delegitimises the existence of the modern Australian state.

But what do these distortions of a nation's history do to young minds? Western children are increasingly taught to see being British, American, or Australian as something shameful rather than complex, heroic, or worthy of admiration. They are being led to believe that their countries are morally compromised, and this in turn breeds anger and resentment.

A curriculum that was once about understanding the past has become about dismantling it. The danger is a loss of intellectual rigour and a simple sense of history. Children are being taught to feel history rather than to understand it. The task of history should not be to erase complexity or to moralise the past through the lens of the present. It should be to help future citizens understand where they came from, what unites them, and why their nation, even with its flaws, might still be worth loving.

But the more they learn about their countries these days, the less they love. By downplaying a nation's heritage and denying any rooted connection between its history and its people, children are left with guilt, not pride; shame, not belonging.

None of this is happening by accident. Among the architects of this ideological shift are activist historians, post-colonial theorists, and critical race educators whose goal is, and always has been, to sever loyalty to country. This is because they are postmodernists who believe that national myths are lies, that patriotism is a mask for oppression, and that emotional attachment to country reinforces injustice. Everything has to be looked at through the lens of anti-colonial struggle. Critical Race Theory and post-colonialism are not just neutral about patriotism; they are explicitly opposed to it. Children are taught to view narratives *not* as a shared civic inheritance, but as tools of exclusion and control.

As Edmund Burke warned in *Reflections on the Revolution in France*, 'To make us love our country, our country ought to be lovely'. Patriotism is natural when the nation is seen as a source of beauty, meaning, and shared memory. Belonging to a nation gives people a framework of identity: a common history, culture, and set of values that root them in time and place. When these things are strong, they provide anchors in a fast-changing and uncertain world. Strip them away, and children are left unmoored, adrift in ideology, and vulnerable to whatever replaces it.

From Fact to Feeling

There are two things currently happening in schools when it comes to teaching the history of Britain, and both are equally dispiriting. The first is that it has become *fashionable* among the educational establishment to frame the British Empire solely as a system of racial violence and colonial plunder. No one these days is saying that the dark pages of British history should be ignored; the triumphalist version of pith helmet-wearing, tea-drinking missionaries bringing civilisation to the 'uncivilised peoples' has not seen the light of day for decades. For want of a less colonial term, the teaching of history has become a juggernaut of colonial guilt, racial injustice, and post-colonial grievance. The current narrative leaves no room for complexity or historical debate; it renders the entire imperial past morally illegitimate and, by extension, calls into question the legitimacy of modern Britain itself.

The second trend is the growing tendency to treat white British children as just another migrant group, no more 'rooted' in the nation's history than an Afghan child whose family arrived last week. First, you delegitimise the past; then you strip ownership of that past. In many classrooms, students are being led to believe that Britain's 'true' identity lies not in its ancient heritage, but in its rich multicultural identity. Increasingly, to focus on white British history as the history of Britain is, in some quarters, considered racist. Even acknowledging that much of Britain's past was shaped by white Britons is now treated as a moral failing. Again, nobody is suggesting that the role of migrants in shaping Britain's story should not be taught, but when migration becomes *the* story, rather than *a* story, it is a recipe for cultural confusion and national amnesia.

One of the more persistent claims surrounding the teaching of empire and slavery is the assertion that British schoolchildren are not actually being taught about empire or slavery. This charge is repeated so often that it has become a kind of folklore. Journalist Jonn Elledge, writing in *The New Statesman* in 2020, lamented that he learned more about imperialism from *Doctor Who* than from his school history lessons, and that its continued absence from the school syllabus 'means that racists are never confronted with the mindblowing irony of their whining about foreigners coming over here and nicking our jobs'.[165] Elledge was educated in the 1970s, a period when schools largely avoided Britain's imperial past, but things have changed a lot in 50 years.

A 2025 Policy Exchange report looking at how history is taught in English secondary schools has revealed that it's almost impossible for an English student to reach their fifteenth birthday without having heard about the empire and the slave trade. Of the schools surveyed, 99 per cent covered the transatlantic slave trade and Britain's role in the First World War, 96 per cent taught the abolition of slavery, and 89 per cent covered the British Empire and colonisation.[166] On paper, this inclusion appears positive. But as we shall see, even the abolition narrative is now framed less as a story of moral courage and political will, and more as a tale of national shame and reluctant atonement.

Yet it remains entirely possible for a child to leave school without ever hearing of Agincourt, Trafalgar, Waterloo, or Gallipoli, which were once staple reference points in the teaching of British history, but which have been quietly dropped from the curriculum. Admittedly, historical ignorance is nothing new. A 2010 poll found that one in twenty children believed Horatio Nelson was a French footballer, presumably captaining Marseille during the Napoleonic Wars, while others thought Winston Churchill was the first man to walk on the Moon.[167] Today, they are more likely to believe he was a genocidal monster responsible for the deaths of millions.[168]

This is not a case of omission, but of emphasis. Children are being saturated with content about Britain's imperial past. In England, the Key Stage 3 curriculum encourages schools to teach empire and slavery as key topics, and many schools have expanded these units considerably. For example, students might study the Atlantic slave trade, colonial exploitation in India, and anti-colonial resistance movements, often over multiple terms. The Cambridge OCR History syllabus includes optional units such as *Migration to Britain, Empire and the British People*, and *The Impact of Empire on Britain 1688-c.1730*. These units are widely adopted by schools and are supported by extensive resources that frame the British Empire primarily as a source of oppression, racism, and exploitation.

But the more pressing question, at least in the context of this book, is not *whether* these subjects are taught, but *how* they are taught. When it comes to the British Empire and its legacy, one would be hard-pressed to find classroom materials which dare to even suggest that despite its many flaws, perhaps colonialism was not all bad. As Nigel Biggar has argued forcefully in *Colonialism: A Moral Reckoning*, the empire was a morally mixed phenomenon, responsible for both exploitation and emancipation. British history, meanwhile, has been whacked over the head with the decolonisation stick and dragged into the world of presentism, identity politics, Critical Race Theory, post-colonialism, social justice, diversity, and equity and inclusion.

Since the death of George Floyd and the rise of Black Lives Matter, schools have been falling over themselves to 'diversify' and 'decolonise' their history curricula. By 2021, 83 per cent had already 'diversified' their Key Stage 3 history programs, typically by adding Black and Asian British history, migration, women's history, and LGBTQ+ themes. The top three motivations cited by teachers were: (1) a sense of social justice; (2) better representation in history; and (3) a direct response to George Floyd's death and the BLM movement.[169]

But what does a 'diverse' or 'decolonised' history syllabus actually look like? In truth, it looks less like history and more like a social commentary on modern-day grievances. And it's no longer about understanding what happened, but about how we feel about it *now*. But in the misguided effort to confront modern social issues through the history classroom, the past is being distorted. The result is a version of history so mangled by ideology that it's often unrecognisable.

The teaching of the transatlantic slave trade is an area where balance and nuance are a foreign concept. Among progressive educators, there is a marked reluctance to acknowledge that it was the British Empire and its much-maligned 'white saviours' like William Wilberforce, that ultimately abolished this appalling practice. Nowhere is this more clearly illustrated than in the free classroom resource produced by Liverpool's International Slavery Museum.

This resource leaves children with the distinct impression that Britain not only invented slavery, but that its eventual abolition came not from moral conviction or political courage, but from national shame. The key abolitionist figures are mentioned only in passing: 'The study of the slave trade should include the abolition of slavery and the work of reformers such as Equiano and William Wilberforce.' No context, no depth, just a perfunctory nod. The framing is lopsided throughout. When Europeans bought and sold slaves, it is unequivocally labelled as slavery. But when Africans engaged in the same practice, it is reframed as something resembling serfdom.[170] The British role in abolition, with its naval patrols, financial costs, lives lost, and moral leadership, is downplayed to the point where it is virtually invisible. But we should not be surprised. Even the museum café promotes grievance, offering visitors the chance to explore 'the complex and entangled histories of food and colonisation in the West Indies' through its curated 'diaspora dishes'. Not even the curried goat is free from the weight of colonial guilt.

The Black Curriculum

Another common complaint about the history curriculum is that it is too white, or too 'Eurocentric'. The rationale is that the historical picture taught in schools has been incomplete and, in some cases, untruthful. Advocates argue that the contributions of non-white individuals to British society have been grossly overlooked and that this historical neglect must be rectified. Furthermore, black students and teachers need to 'see themselves' reflected in the syllabus in order to feel fully engaged. Proponents also point to demographic shifts in the classroom, arguing that history teaching no longer reflects Britain's multi-ethnic society.

Others go further, arguing that the teaching of Eurocentric history results in marginalisation, alienation, and even racism. The Black Curriculum argues that the National Curriculum marginalises Black British history and contributes to systemic racism, claiming that a Eurocentric focus alienates students of colour. 'Yet with no mandatory place on a highly Eurocentric national curriculum, Black British history continues to be viewed as insignificant. We have seen the effects of this omission, which pose a number of serious and dangerous political consequences. It has seen the arbitrary deportation of UK nationals, and not least the preservation of racism in British society.'[171]

According to the Runnymede Trust's *The School Report: Race, Education and Inequality in Contemporary Britain*, the dominance of a white, mainstream cultural framing within the curriculum contributes to exclusion and systemic stereotyping. It stresses that 'educational success for minority ethnic groups... needs to address broader issues – cultural capital, role modelling... that affect not just children themselves, but broader minority ethnic families and communities.'[172]

Critics might point out that schools should be in the business of teaching historical events, not identity politics. They might also observe that in a country which is 80 per cent white, most historical figures will also be white, and that this is not racism, it's demography.[173] They might also say that it is spectacularly patronising to suggest that a person must be given their own separate history on the basis of their skin colour. After all, no one claims that a white child cannot learn about the Silk Road during the Tang Dynasty, because they don't 'see themselves' peddling porcelain in 8th-century China. Yet we are expected to accept that a black child cannot learn about the Norman invasion simply because they cannot see themselves marching in William the Conqueror's army. This narrative was reinforced with Netflix's latest series, *King & Conqueror*, which featured African Normans participating in the Battle of Hastings. The principle of universal human curiosity is quietly abandoned, replaced by the soft bigotry of low expectations.

At present, the loudest and most persistent voices calling for a de-Europeanised curriculum are leading us into the realms of fantasy and nonsense. As Professor David Abulafia warned, 'One of the first requirements of a competent historian is the attempt to be accurate. When arrant nonsense is taught in the name of "decolonisation", political ideology has taken over from history, and ignorance has triumphed over truth.'[174] We are witnessing in schools a wholesale rewriting of the past in which white children are being denied the truth of their own story, while being denied a unique cultural or ancestral claim to Britain. They are recast as simply another migrant group among many. The same reluctance to acknowledge any good in the British Empire also runs deep when it comes to the white British children's indigeneity.

This message is now being introduced at the earliest stages of education. In *Brilliant Black British History*, a book by Nigerian-born author Atinuke, primary school children are told: 'The first migrants to Britain had black skin. Yes, that's right! – the very first Britons were Black!' The book goes on to assert:

> Britain was a Black country for more than 7,000 years before the white people came – and during that time the most famous British monument was built: Stonehenge. Britain has been a mostly white country for a lot less time than it was a Black country – only about 4,000 years.

And the final blow for any white child reading: 'Every single British person comes from a migrant.' This book was awarded 'Children's Non-Fiction Book of the Year' by the British Book Awards in 2024. The most charitable interpretation is that someone behind the scenes got their categories confused.

Nor is this an isolated case. The Brilliant Club, an organisation that supports disadvantaged pupils in non-selective state schools, advises teachers to abandon 'traditional narratives'. So instead of the Vikings being a 'homogeneous community of blonde Scandinavians', they are a 'diverse group', some of whom, apparently, were even Muslim.[175] And we are now told by the same organisation that they were not violent raiders at all, but misunderstood refugees in search of a better life. All that raping and pillaging, we are assured, was mostly peaceful.[176]

This brings us to the theme of migration, which is an undeniably important part of Britain's story. But if one were to judge by the current curriculum, it is the *only* part. Not monarchy, not war, not Christianity, or industrialisation. Just migration. It has become so central to the Key Stage 3 history curriculum (ages 11–14) that some teachers now complain that other essential topics, such as medieval or Tudor England, are being pushed aside by wave after wave of, well, migration. A survey by the Historical Association found that 73 per cent of schools now teach some aspect of migration history, with 40 per cent making it a standalone unit rather than a passing theme.[177] Some schools even begin their history curriculum not with pre-1066 Britain, but with post-war immigration. The most taught period of migration history in Key Stage 3 is the twentieth century, especially post-war migration, the Windrush generation, and the end of the British Empire. These modern topics were cited by over 100 teachers, while foundational periods such as the Norman Conquest were mentioned by just 20. In some schools, only two eras of migration are covered at all: Saxon/Viking settlement and twentieth-century immigration. This shift in emphasis may come at a cost: students gain a politicised understanding of recent history, while missing the foundational knowledge necessary to make sense of Britain's long historical arc.

If we take the resource on migration put together by Cambridge OCR at face value, and many children will, we are left with the impression that Britain was built solely by migrants. The overarching narrative is both strikingly consistent and oddly contemporary: each period becomes the story of a minority group seeking a better life, only to be met with hostility, suspicion, and pork pie–eating Little Englanders. Well, not quite, but you get the picture. We learn that in Medieval England, 'immigration was constant and needed' and that while 'most migrants settled peacefully' they were 'not always welcomed' while 'ideas of who "belonged" and who did not often changed'. By the time we get to the Industrial and Modern periods, we discover that 'migrants experienced immigration controls, discrimination and organised racism and had to struggle for acceptance'.[178] What we are not being told is that a stable indigenous cultural community has been around from the Anglo-Saxon period through to the 20th century.

Ultimately, the message being conveyed to white children is that they don't belong. But the message to black children is that they don't belong either. Both messages are false, and both are cruel. Jason Arday, author of *The Black Curriculum* report and a prominent campaigner for curriculum reform, argues that the national curriculum 'systematically omits their histories and contributions, thereby reinforcing their exclusion'. For Arday, belonging is not something that black children inherit by virtue of citizenship, but something they must fight for, and which can only be granted once Britain has radically restructured the way it teaches its past. The implication is that until the curriculum is fully 'decolonised,' black children will remain outsiders in their own country'.[179] From Anglo-Saxon settlements to the Windrush generation, everything is filtered through the question: 'Who gets to belong?' The answer, it seems, is nobody. Is anyone really benefitting from their British history lessons? Not as they currently stand. History should not be used to sow alienation, resentment, or guilt. It should give all children a sense of perspective, continuity, and place. It should provide them with a shared story in which they can all find meaning, not a weapon with which to divide them.

Worse, they're not just being deprived of a shared story, but historical facts and the ideas of chronology, context, and complexity. According to one teacher, English children struggle to tell you who Edward II or Edward III are, and the only thing they know about the Victorians is that they were evil colonisers.[180] Another schoolteacher reports that 'the history curriculum at many schools may now feature the diversity of troops in the First World War, or the 1980s as a period of queer exploration. These are worthwhile subjects for an undergraduate essay but not substitutes for the basic building blocks of historical knowledge.' In a Year 8 lesson on the 'black Tudors', the teacher noticed that a student asked, 'Who were the Tudors?' because 'they hadn't thought to teach the Reformation before the racism.'[181]

Survey after survey reveals gaps in historical knowledge, some of which are surprising. Despite the heavy focus on the transatlantic slave trade, 27 per cent of 18-30-year-olds had never even heard of such a thing.[182] Meanwhile, the facts about World War II are obscured in a miasma of confusion and guesswork. One third of Britons did not know Winston Churchill was Prime Minister (after all, how could he win a war *and* walk on the moon at the same time?), while 37 per cent could not tell you when the war took place. Nearly half didn't know that Hitler's invasion of Poland in 1939 sparked the conflict.[183] In another survey, just 40 per cent of 18-24-year-olds knew that Germany was the enemy on D-Day, and just 32 per cent were aware that the United Kingdom and its empire contributed the most troops.[184] One can be forgiven for not knowing that King Rædwald son of Tytila, was the first East Anglian king to convert to Christianity in the 7th century. But not knowing that Britain fought Germany in a war still within living memory is verging on unforgivable.

These results suggest more than simple gaps in historical trivia. They point to a deeper erosion of collective memory and historical literacy among younger Britons. The fact that so many young people could not identify the most basic facts about one of the defining moments of the twentieth century speaks volumes about the state of history education. The past is being overwritten. As the curriculum shifts away from national narratives and shared milestones, a generation is emerging that knows far more about Britain's historical shame than its historical substance.

Under the current Labour government, the shift away from historical substance is set to be seismic. In the preface to the OCR's report, *Striking the Balance*, former Labour education minister Charles Clarke suggests that the school curriculum should be 'far more contemporary and forward-looking, including more content on digital skills and artificial intelligence and climate change' and 'focused far more on the world as it now is and is going to be than on the past.' The study of history, he opines in one short, dismissive sentence, is merely about 'acquiring the canons of knowledge which have been built up over centuries'. [185] As historian Professor Robert Tombs has noted, 'What remarkable self-assurance to assume an understanding of both the present and the future while demeaning knowledge built up over centuries – which is, of course, the only knowledge we have.' Clarke's vision of the future involves making climate change a central part of the curriculum. 'Education or indoctrination?'[186] Tombs asks. The answer, increasingly, seems to be the latter.

This does not bode well for the future of history in British schools. Clarke's formulation reveals a deeper worldview in which history is seen not as essential to the formation of national identity, moral understanding, or intellectual maturity, but as a dusty archive of irrelevant facts. The underlying assumption is that only the present and the future matter, and that the past is, at best, a collection of outdated mistakes and, at worst, a catalogue of crimes. In this vision, history is not something to be learned from, admired, or even debated but rather something to be overcome.

1619 and All That

What Britain has seen through post-colonial theory, America has experienced through the racial reframing of its founding story. For at least three decades, American children, especially in urban and progressive areas, have also been taught, like their British counterparts, to view their country with suspicion or outright shame. What began in the 1990s as the inclusion of African American history, Indigenous perspectives, race, gender, and class, has now morphed into the institutionalisation of a largely critical narrative of the US, where children are trained to critique whiteness, examine historical power structures, and understand America's past as morally compromised. And while this shift has not been universal (more traditional curricula persisted in many southern and rural states), it has laid the intellectual groundwork for what came next.

And what came next was the *1619 Project*, created and led by journalist Nikole Hannah-Jones in 2019 for *The New York Times*. Hannah-Jones started her career the way she intended to continue. Whilst at Notre

Dame University, she wrote a paper proposing that 'the white race is the biggest murderer, rapist, pillager and thief of the modern word', that 'Columbus and those like him were no different than Hitler' and that white people today are 'bloodsuckers in our community'.[187] After spending a 'career investigating racial inequality and injustice',[188] Hannah-Jones concluded that virtually everybody had been getting history wrong until now. In her view, the true founding of America was not 1776, but 1619, the year 20 African slaves first arrived in Virginia. The Declaration of Independence, the Constitution, and the ideal of liberty were not, in her telling, foundational aspirations but rhetorical cover for a racial caste system. Slavery, she claimed, was not a tragic contradiction within the American project, but its very origin and purpose.

Certainly, slavery was an integral and horrific part of early American society, particularly in the South, where it underpinned large parts of the economy.[189] The radical claim of the *1619 Project* however, was not simply that slavery existed, or even that it was profitable, but that everything in American life, from capitalism to traffic patterns, was born out of white supremacy.[190] It portrayed the American Revolution as a war fought not for liberty, but to preserve slavery.

This claim was widely rejected by leading historians across the political spectrum, such as Gordon Wood, professor emeritus at Brown University. 'The idea that the Revolution occurred as a means of protecting slavery – I just don't think there is much evidence for it,' he said, continuing that 'in fact the contrary is more true to what happened. The Revolution unleashed antislavery sentiments that led to the first abolition movements in the history of the world.'[191] James McPherson, professor emeritus of history at Princeton University stated plainly, 'I don't know of any colonists who said they wanted independence in order to preserve their slaves.'[192] Their objections were not to the inclusion of slavery, but, as McPherson said, a 'very unbalanced, one-sided account, which lacked context and perspective on the complexity of slavery, which was clearly, obviously, not an exclusively American institution, but existed throughout history.'[193] Ultimately however, Hannah-Jones was not concerned with facts. Her goals were to make sure that reparations bills were passed, and 'to get white Americans to stop being white.'[194]

The *New York Times's* longstanding motto 'All the News That's Fit to Print' may need to be updated to 'Never let the Truth get in the Way of a Good Story'. After the kerfuffle over its central claims, the team behind the *1619 Project,* with the blessings of the paper's editor Jake Silverstein, was discovered to have altered the online version of the project's text which put 1619 as the 'true founding'. When challenged, they said it didn't matter anyway, because the words 'true founding' were never meant to be taken literally, but metaphorically. But as

Timothy Sandefur, one of the projects most incisive critics, points out: 'The question the *1619 Project* posed was whether the American nation should be viewed as having its genesis not in the Declaration of Independence, with its covenants of equality and liberty, but in a commercial transaction for human flesh.'[195]

Why this matters in the context of this book is that many educators have embraced the 'human flesh' origin story. Despite the poor journalism and now-debunked historical claims, its narrative of foundational moral corruption is being taught to American children as truth. We are far enough into this tale of global educational misadventures to be only mildly surprised that the journalists behind the project claimed schoolchildren were victims of 'educational malpractice', deprived of the 'fuller truth' about slavery and racism. Naturally, they proposed a remedy: The *1619 Project* itself. To say it was swiftly repackaged for schools would be an understatement. The original magazine edition appeared in August 2019. In September, it had already been adapted into classroom materials, courtesy of a partnership between the *New York Times* and the Pulitzer Center. By 2021, the project had made its way into 4,500 classrooms across the United States. If one were inclined toward cynicism, one might conclude that this was always the endgame.

It is fair to say that the Pulitzer Center's *1619 Project* school resources are not for the faint-hearted. In fact, the Center offers some thoughtful advice to teachers bracing for impact: 'We anticipate that these notes will assist you in planning which tools to provide students to help them process big emotions, should they arise. Deep breathing, the opportunity to journal before speaking, and quiet fidget toys are a few examples we've seen be successful.'[196] Students will need more than a few fidget toys, however, to make it through the lesson based on 'Race', an essay by Dorothy Roberts, Professor of Law, Sociology, and African Studies. Together, teacher and pupil are invited to explore 'the history of racial classification in America', with particular focus on 'the need to both justify slavery and maintain white supremacy'.

They are asked to reflect on Roberts' claim that 'through a complex system of laws, policies, publications, programs, and myths, the American government, at both the national and local levels, has monitored and maintained a rigid racial hierarchy that permeates contemporary society.' Students are also encouraged to consider the 'exploitation and degradation of Black women throughout American history as a crucial component to privileging white men and disempowering Black communities.' The lesson covers themes such as 'institutionalised racism', 'misogynoir' (not to be confused with film noir), and reproductive justice, while students are expected to master vocabulary including 'eugenics', 'statutory', 'mulatto', 'miscegenation', 'licentious', and 'genome'.[197] The mind truly boggles.

In 2021, the US Senate weighed in on the *1619 Project*, introducing a bill to ban federal funding for schools which were teaching the project, while several states, including Iowa and Arkansas, have moved to either restrict or prohibit its use in classrooms. In some areas, especially urban or Democrat-controlled districts, children are taught to see American history not as a complex legacy of liberty and contradiction, but as an unbroken lineage of oppression. The Founding Fathers have been replaced by 'lived experience' and grievance narratives. That this explicitly ideological version of the past, shaped by Critical Race Theory, memory politics, and moral judgment, is now embedded in public education should concern anyone who believes that history should illuminate, not indict.

Australia as a Crime Scene

Australia's deeply progressive education establishment long ago abandoned the idea that history should illuminate young minds. Among academics, bureaucrats, and policymakers, there is now near-unanimous agreement: the story of modern Australia, though relatively short, is primarily a story of violence and genocide. They present the nation's past not as a complex history, but as a crime scene, but in this version, there's no mystery about the culprits. They lay the blame for the problems plaguing remote Aboriginal communities, fairly and squarely on the arrival of the British in 1788.

As theologian and ethicist Nigel Biggar notes: 'Certain historians have chosen to exaggerate the role of settler violence in causing such [native peoples'] extinction, and some have gone so far as to equate the actions of colonial authorities with those of the Nazis, casually deploying such emotive and provocative words as 'concentration camp', 'holocaust' and 'genocide' in describing British policies. In fact, the colonial authorities strove to avoid the extinction of native peoples. That they too often failed was not a sign of their covertly genocidal intention, but rather a manifestation in human tragedy.'[198]

No one today denies the profound injustices suffered by Aboriginal Australians as a result of colonisation. But to ascribe genocidal intent to the British, and to frame the entire national story as a one-dimensional tale of violence and dispossession, is both historically reductive and pedagogically damaging. In the current political climate, to suggest otherwise risks cancellation, deplatforming, and the ire of the academic establishment. It will make you deeply unpopular.

Yet some, such as Australia's pre-eminent historian, 95-year-old Professor Geoffrey Blainey, who has already been cancelled, are, in a sense, uncancellable. 'I myself believe that most Aboriginal Australians and Torres Strait Islanders are far, far better off today than if they were living in 1788,' he says. 'This land is infinitely more fruitful than it was in 1788, and most Aboriginals are now the gainers... Here in this continent arose a democratic society which, for all its imperfections, offers liberty in a world where liberty is not normal.'[199] By 'better off', Blainey means that by the end of the nineteenth century, the application of science and a pursuit of progress by the Europeans lifted the material standards of living above the impressive level achieved by Aborigines. Even quoting Blainey in this book, suggesting on balance that colonisation may have brought benefits, will no doubt provoke the wrath of the establishment.

For the moment however, it is this unnuanced history that is being presented to Australian children. Just as their American counterparts must atone for its original sin of slavery, so too are Australian children required to apologise for the sin of colonisation. In Australia, this is called 'reconciliation', and it starts in kindergarten. On government orders, teachers are expected to recruit their dummy-sucking charges into a battalion of 'active citizens' embarking on what is promised to be a lifelong 'journey of reconciliation'.

They are to decolonise early childhood education by 'reconsidering education spaces, acknowledging colonisation and its continued impacts, while seeking to disrupt and reconceptualise colonial understandings.' This is extraordinary language to use, and it comes across more like a treatise on post-colonial, anti-capitalist pedagogy than guidance for toddlers. Finally, teachers are to 'critically reflect' on existing curriculum resources, and practices, asking whether they serve to 'sustain or privilege colonial narratives – and how these might be reconfigured to prioritise Indigenous perspectives.'[200] But what does all this decolonisation and disruption and reconfiguration look like in practice? It looks a lot like Play-Doh, sandpits and *The Tiger Who Came to Tea* are being replaced by political action. Above all, it looks cruel.

Toddlers are being initiated into a world of collective culpability, asked to shoulder an impossibly heavy burden of guilt for actions committed by people who died three centuries ago. And this initiation is being orchestrated by their teachers, many of whom are motivated by a genuine desire to right historical wrongs. One particularly imaginative kindergarten teacher has offered her colleagues guidance on how to mark National Sorry Day, first established in 1998 to reflect on injustices committed against Aboriginal and Torres Strait Islander peoples. While she acknowledges that her methods might not be entirely age-appropriate, she presses on regardless.

First, she explains to preschoolers: 'We commemorate Sorry Day because many, many years ago, the people in charge of running Australia made some bad choices, and many Aboriginal families were hurt and became very sad. The people in charge realised they were wrong and said Sorry.' Then she escalates the lesson, directing the children to act out emotionally charged scenarios deliberately designed to make them feel 'sad, angry, frustrated, jealous, happy, excited or hopeful'.[201] In another classroom, teachers had a small group of children paint apology cards on National Sorry Day. The children proudly brought home their creations, bearing messages like: 'Sorry for hurting the Dharawal people. We will be kind now.' They were so visibly distressed that their grandparents had to comfort them, reassuring them that they had done nothing wrong, that it was all in the past, and that they were kind, innocent children.[202]

Remarkably, children are introduced to the concept of an invasion before they hear about something called the First Fleet. In Year 3, teachers explain that 'people have different points of view on some events that are commemorated and celebrated; for example, some First Nations Australians regard 'Australia Day' as 'Invasion Day'. It's not until an entire year later that they learn about 11 ships carrying convicts, marines and officers under the command of Captain Arthur Phillip, which marked the formal colonisation of the continent in 1788. But even then the focus is on the 'effects of contact with other people on First Nations Australians and their Countries/Places following the arrival of the First Fleet and how this was viewed by First Nations Australians as an invasion.'[203] Guilt runs through the syllabus like cracks in a façade, as Australian history is recast as single, unbroken narrative of 'frontier warfare, massacres, removal from land, and relocation to protectorates, reserves and missions'. Everything it seems, except nation-building.

But here's the kicker: children are also taught that no number of apologies, cards, or tears can atone for the sins of the past. The curriculum insists that not even 'reconciliation and truth-telling' can heal the deleterious effects of colonisation. Instead, they are told that 'Reconciliation is not a single significant event or change, but an ongoing process of truth-telling and healing between First Nations Australians and other Australians.'[204] This is reinforced by national observances such as National Sorry Day, National Reconciliation Week, and NAIDOC Week which are calendar fixtures which embed a rhythm of annual remembrance, contrition, and activism into school life. Children are thus trapped in a cycle of endless apology and inherited guilt, from which there appears to be no escape. As Douglas Murray notes, 'If there is no possibility of forgiveness, then apology is merely the first step in a process of permanent submission.'[205]

This sense of guilt has been amplified in recent years by Australia's very own version of the *1619 Project*: *Dark Emu*, written in 2019 by Australian author Bruce Pascoe, who identifies as Aboriginal. Pascoe claimed that Aboriginal Australians were not nomadic after all, but instead practised agriculture with techniques superior to those of the white colonisers who dispossessed them. According to *Dark Emu*, they lived in permanent settlements, managed the land with advanced ecological understanding, invented democracy, pioneered mankind's first complex fishing systems, and even baked the first loaf of bread. Like Nikole Hannah-Jones in the United States, Pascoe positioned himself as the discoverer of a long-suppressed foundational truth which supposedly over-turned everything Australians thought they knew about their past.

Pascoe directly undermined *terra nullius*, 'nobody land' or 'land belonging to no one', which is the idea that the land was unowned and uncultivated prior to British colonisation. If Aboriginal societies were, in fact, agricultural and sedentary, then the British claim to have settled an empty or primitive land collapses. The implication though not explicitly stated, is that the modern Australian state was founded on a lie. While this does not render the state null and void in a legal sense, it calls into question its moral legitimacy and strengthens demands for treaty and reparations. Pascoe's challenge even bolsters the argument that Aboriginal sovereignty was never ceded, for if Aboriginals had complex systems of land ownership and governance prior to colonisa-tion, then the moral basis of British sovereignty, that is whether modern Australia has a right to exist at all, is called into question. Australian courts, including in the landmark 1992 *Mabo* decision, have recognised native title (traditional land rights), but have stopped short of recognising Aboriginal sovereignty, which refers not to land ownership, but to the right to self-government and political authority.

Pascoe claims to have arrived at this revelation after immersing himself in the diaries of explorers. 'You have to read them in the original form' he said in an interview, 'without the editing, because in some of them there was a severe edit before they became public documents, and often the only stuff missing was the observations about Aboriginal use of land.'[206] The only problem is that Pascoe missed some pretty important 'stuff' himself. In 2021, *Dark Emu* was exposed as work of historical distortion. Anthropologist Peter Sutton, along with archaeologist Keryn Walshe, mounted a detailed rebuttal in *Farmers or Hunter-Gatherers?* demonstrating that Pascoe selectively uses colonial-era sources and misinterprets evidence to support the claim that Aboriginal Australians were agriculturalists. His book, they concluded, while well intentioned, sacrifices scholarly accuracy for a highly political narrative.

And this is precisely the key point. This is politics disguised as history. And despite having been thoroughly discredited, a simplified version of what is essentially a work of fiction, *Young Dark Emu: A Truer History*, published in 2019, has been widely adopted in Australian primary schools. Glowingly endorsed by education departments all over the country for its 'corrective' approach to history, and stocked in school libraries by enthusiastic librarians, *Young Dark Emu* presents children with a false version of the past in which Aboriginal people were an advanced civilisation of farmers, builders, engineers, and political organisers, wiped out by colonisation.

For children raised on Pascoe's narrative, national pride becomes difficult. So difficult in fact, that schoolgirls such as nine-year-old Harper Neilson, who made headlines around the world, no longer have the will to stand for the national anthem because she believes that it is racist. 'It says Advance Australia Fair and when it was originally written it meant advance Australia for white skin people,'[207] she explained. As one commentator writes, 'Unquestioning loyalty to Australia isn't necessary. Some loyalty to Australia, some unity and some pride in the country is enough.'[208] It's not that much to ask. But young Australians are increasingly less proud and less unified as the narrative of settler colonialism is further embedded in their education.

On Australia Day, many are far more comfortable waving the Aboriginal flag or the Palestinian flag around, (or even a hybrid of the two) or marching through the streets shouting politically loaded slogans such as 'sovereignty was never ceded' or 'always was, always will be'. But when asked if they would stay and fight in the event on an invasion, 48 per cent of Australian eighteen to twenty-four-year-olds say they would flee the country – presumably leaving the Aboriginals to defend themselves.[209]

Pride and Prejudice

The numbers are similar in the UK, where only 11 per cent of young people said they would be willing to fight, while 41 per cent said there were *no circumstances* under which they would take up arms for their country. The same number, 41 per cent, said they were proud to be British, and only 15 per cent believed the country was united. In contrast, two decades ago, 80 per cent of young people said they were proud to be British.[210] In every survey, older generations who benefited from a knowledge-rich, ideology-free education are far more likely to express pride in British identity, warts and all.

It is clear that patriotism and a connection with the past in the young is ebbing away. 'A teacher friend visited a school recently,' wrote one contributor to *The Secret Teacher* column in *The Times,* 'and heard its head of history describe the aim of their curriculum as the creation of "scholar activists". They said they wanted to turn pupils into radical agents of protest against a state they say is institutionally racist.'[211] They might not be producing scholars, but they are certainly producing pupils who believe Britain is defined by racism. In 2025, it was reported that nearly half of Gen Z educated during the post-2010 era of ideological reform, believe that Britain is racist and 'stuck in the past'.[212] The teacher also recalled asking pupils if they hated Britain. This in itself is an unusual question to ask children in any scenario, but we live in unusual times. Thirty students eagerly raised their hands to show how much they loathed the country. Most were from ethnic minority backgrounds, which is not an indictment of them, but of the education system itself, which no longer seeks to unify.

According to the Commonwealth War Graves Commission, 22 per cent of 18-24-year-olds find that commemorative events for the World Wars are unnecessary, with some calling them 'boring' or 'repetitive'.[213] The red poppy, once a universal, unifying symbol of remembrance, is increasingly rejected. 'I can't think of any of my friends who would buy a poppy now,' said one young woman. 'It feels too close to nationalism somehow. I have a lot of pride for my relatives who fought in the Second World War, but I'm not sure wearing a poppy just says we are commemorating that anymore. It feels a bit adjacent to hanging a St George's Cross in your window.'[214]

That this young woman is 'triggered' by the St George's flag, which is ostensibly the flag of England, is profoundly sad, but entirely logical given the ideological framing she receives at school. Indeed, for many teachers, patriotism has become a dirty word, or at least a dangerous one. A 2009 survey found that rather than teaching children that they can be proud of their country while still being honest about its failures, teachers are told to present patriotism as morally questionable, even dangerous. One history teacher expressed acute discomfort about addressing the topic at all: 'It has come as rather a shock to me that you would be thinking about this... Left to my own devices I wouldn't dream of covering it really, explicitly. To me it sort of reeks of the old British Empire.' Spoken like a true post-colonial theorist.

Others felt that any attempt to promote or support patriotism in schools would likely cause ructions in the classroom. One commented that 'praising patriotism excludes non-British pupils. Patriotism about being British in my experience tends to be a white preserve so divides groups along racial lines, when what we aim to do is bring pupils to an understanding of what makes us all the same.' In fact, most interviewees felt that the role of school was to promote more cosmopolitan forms of identification: 'We shouldn't be promoting patriotism, we should be promoting universal brotherhood.' Another added: 'I think we should identify as humans,'[215] which is rather an outdated point of view given that these days it's not unheard of for both teachers and students to identify as dogs or non-binary woodland creatures.

Some teachers appeared to regard all forms of values education as problematic. This is a bit rich considering many teachers' unwavering attachment to the modern 'values' of DEI. Interviewees were worried that 'if schools are allowed to give opinions on patriotism they run the risk of influencing young minds and/or supporting views which may be insensitive' and that 'schools should always be neutral – it is dangerous for teachers to put value judgments on opinions.'[216] But this is a clever way of saying: *we don't think patriotism is justifiable*.

Michael Taylor, history teacher at London's Michaela School, known as England's strictest school, has taken the opposing stance and thinks that teaching pupils to embrace a 'moderate patriotism' is the teacher's duty. This is, as we have seen, a highly unfashionable position to take these days. But he makes the point that if more pupils saw themselves as part of something bigger – community, family, and country – they are less likely to 'fall into the traps of selfish individualism, of social media, and the paths of crime and violence that are all too readily awaiting them outside the school gates.'[217]

These 'traps of selfishness' are also touched upon by Yuval Levin in *The Fractured Republic,* who observes that a collapse of national identity causes either hyper individualism or hyper group identity, both of which are equally corrosive. He believes that once patriotism disappears from schools and cultural institutions, it leaves a vacuum to be filled with ideology, grievance narratives and identity politics. The young, in particular, says Levin, need a civic memory and a national identity as stabilising forces in their lives. This deliberate erasure is leaving young people adrift, sceptical of loyalty, wary of pride, and with no anchor or compass.

And the same logic is applied to Christianity: once part of the moral and cultural foundation of British life, it's now filed under 'controversial issue' which is best avoided or downplayed. While there is a legal requirement under the *Education Reform Act* to provide religious education that 'reflects the fact that the religious traditions in Great Britain are in the main Christian, while taking account of the teaching and practices of the other principal religions represented in Great Britain,'[218] this is now often quietly ignored, diluted, or reinterpreted in favour of a pluralistic or secular model. Indeed, the now disbanded Commission on Religious Education (CoRE) 2018 report titled *Religion and Worldviews: The Way Forward* recommended the way forward for RE in schools was to move away from a Christian-centric model towards a 'pluralistic' model.

Christianity is now treated in schools merely as 'what some people believe', rather than as a cornerstone of Britain's legal, political, and cultural development. Children are not taught that Britain has been steeped in Christianity since St Augustine arrived in 597, nor that everything from parliamentary sovereignty to Shakespeare's metaphors owe something to the Christian tradition. They have no idea that Christian theology helped give rise to the very ideals of individual liberty, human rights, and democracy that define modern Britain. In being severed from this inheritance, they are also being severed from the past itself. When they encounter Britain's ancient churches and cathedrals, these monuments will signify nothing, for they will have no concept of who built them or why. They see them as merely assemblages of bricks and masonry that, if put to another use, will mean nothing to them. Schools are producing generations of Britons who are ignorant of the institutions, values, and beliefs that shaped the long historical development of their own society.

Even Ofsted, which is hardly a bastion of cultural conservatism, admitted in its 2024 report *Deep and meaningful?* that Christianity's cultural and historical significance is being sidelined in schools. It found that RE syllabuses were shallow, fragmented, and allergic to anything resembling depth, especially when it came to explaining how religious traditions shape civic life, morality, or even basic national identity. It also found that children are somewhat hazy on the fundamentals of Christianity. When one child was asked why God sent Jesus into the world, the child confidently replied: 'To be king, be kind, and pick up litter'.[219] While this is an unintentionally hilarious response – one imagines Jesus pondering over whether to put polystyrene in the red or yellow bin – it is also a damning indictment on how Christianity is being taught to children.

This intellectual and moral amnesia is not just religious or historical. It has consequences for how young people think, read, and participate in civic life. Here we return to the valuable insights of E.D. Hirsch, who argued that the erosion of historical and cultural knowledge extends far beyond the classroom and weakens society as a whole. He believed that dismantling shared cultural understanding dissolves the social glue that holds democratic societies together. The decolonisation movement's contempt for national narratives directly undermines this cohesion. As Hirsch argued in *Cultural Literacy*, a shared body of knowledge is essential for literate citizenship and mutual understanding among citizens. He also warned that individuals cannot function effectively without shared knowledge of the past.

Severed from the historical inheritance of their own civilisation, its religion, its literature, and its institutions, young people become easy prey for manipulation. They lose the ability to distinguish ideology from truth, or to recognise the slow, cumulative development of the democratic freedoms they now take for granted. In rejecting Shakespeare, British history, or Enlightenment principles as colonialist or white supremacist, decolonisers are not expanding young minds, they are closing them off from the very ideas that sustain liberal democracy. When history is reduced to a set of feelings, migration replaces Christianity as Britain's origin story, and Jesus becomes a recycling fanatic rather than the central moral and cultural force behind British history, children lose the conceptual tools to make sense of the society around them. The education system is no longer producing fully functioning citizens. Instead, what is emerging from the schools are young people who are being exiled from their own civilisation, and are now unsure what, if anything, they belong to.

6

Eco-Anxiety and
the Crisis of Civilisation

So far, the picture that is emerging, to borrow Orwell's understatement, is far from encouraging. Or in the words of Bertie Wooster, it's beginning to look a little bit blue around the edges. Children across the West have, it seems, become unwitting participants in a vast social experiment that even the most optimistic of individuals would struggle to describe as a success. They are being disoriented, ideologised, and burdened with adult political agendas.

But there is another aspect of this panoply of classroom failures that we have not yet addressed, which is a relative newcomer to the scene: climate change education. In just a few short years, education about climate change has evolved from a focus on science and environmental responsibility into a message increasingly shaped by emotional urgency, moral pressure, and political over-tones. Children are being gripped by a wave of anxiety now known as 'eco-anxiety', 'eco-stress', or 'eco-grief'. Many are being driven into a kind of existential paralysis, questioning whether they even have a future at all.

This alarmism is made all the more inexcusable by the growing number of well-credentialed scientists such as climatologists, physicists, atmospheric scientists, statisticians, and former IPCC contributors who argue that climate change is not primarily man-made or that it does not represent a planetary 'crisis'. Dr Richard Lindzen, Professor of Atmospheric Science at MIT, calls global warming 'hysteria' and 'political, not scientific'.[220] Dr John Clauser, who won the Nobel Prize in Physics in 2022, states, 'There is no climate crisis. Climate science has been corrupted by a false narrative', and that CO_2 is not a pollutant but beneficial for plant growth.[221] And Australian geologist Professor Ian Plimer repeatedly and persuasively argues that geological records show evidence of natural climate cycles long before industrialisation. Yet, as a collective, these esteemed individuals, along with so many others, are dismissed as 'climate deniers' and their arguments are never once presented to students inside the classroom.

Instead of being taught that the climate has always been changing, children today are taught to view every weather event, every dry summer, every cold winter, as a moral referendum on human behaviour. The great sin is carbon; the path to redemption is recycling and self-loathing. But they are also being taught that a 'sustainable' world cannot be achieved without a socially just world, and that the economic, social, and environmental systems of Western Civilisation are harmful both to the planet and to people. Climate activism is increasingly couched in moral terms: you are either a good person or a bad person, judged by the size of your carbon footprint. Children are not only told that the planet is dying, but that it is dying because of Western greed, capitalism, and inequality, and that they are, by inheritance, part of the problem.

The psychological consequences of this approach are profound. It is painfully apparent that children's mental health is under assault. But they are also being robbed of something deeper: a sense of gratitude for the world in which they live – a world which, in Western nations, is clean, safe, technologically advanced, and full of opportunity. That gratitude has been replaced with anger and resentment, a sentiment encapsulated by Greta Thunberg's famous 'How Dare You!' speech delivered at the Climate Action Summit in 2019:

> You have stolen my dreams and my childhood with your empty words. And yet I'm one of the lucky ones. People are suffering. People are dying. Entire ecosystems are collapsing. We are in the beginning

of a mass extinction, and all you can talk about is money and fairy tales of eternal economic growth. How dare you!

Climate Alarmism in the UK

There is no shortage of climate change resources available to UK schools. In fact, there are hundreds. Every major NGO, teaching union, curriculum publisher, and environmental charity has produced classroom packs, lesson plans, animations, and activity sheets, all designed to educate children about the climate crisis. It would be impossible to analyse them all here, nor is it necessary. They all say exactly the same thing. Pick almost any resource at random and you will find the talking points repeated with near-identical phrasing: that climate change is the greatest crisis of our time, that global temperatures are rising at an unprecedented rate, that the ice is melting, and that the future is uncertain. The tone is grave, the messaging urgent, and the emotional pitch unwavering.

Rather than catalogue dozens of resources, I will instead focus on just one, not because it is uniquely alarming, but because it is perfectly typical. One of the most widely used climate education providers in UK schools is the World Wide Fund for Nature (WWF). As you would expect from such a well-funded organisation, its free and easily downloadable classroom resources are colourful, attractive and enticing. But beneath the gloss lies a message that is doom-laden to the core. Its key learning materials include lessons titled 'The Climate Crisis Explained' and 'How Hot Will Earth Get?', with content that focuses almost entirely on irreversible tipping points, disappearing ice caps, species extinction, the displacement of millions and the total collapse of ecosystems.[222]

In one worksheet aimed at six-year-olds, we are told that 'globally, sea ice is diminishing faster than ever before. Some regions are losing sea ice faster than others, with terrible consequences for wildlife in those areas.' Small children are also informed that people who drive petrol cars are 'making the air we breathe dirty so that more people get asthma as a child, and people die earlier because of problems caused by air pollution.' And to complete the picture, the worksheet explains that 'when ice melts it will cause sea levels to rise so that millions of people and lots of wildlife could see their homes disappear below the waves.'[223]

Fear-Based Teaching

What a six-year-old with an underdeveloped frontal cortex but an overactive imagination is likely to hear from these statements is: 'the world is falling apart right now', and 'all the animals will die in my lifetime'.[224] The resources rely heavily on using imagination to elicit feelings. In one activity, children are asked to imagine 'what the world might look like in 100 years if nothing is done'.

In another, they are shown images of polar bears and penguins and asked to imagine what the animals would say to human beings if they could speak.[225] 'Have you got any fish?' will likely be considered the wrong answer.

With messaging like this, we can hardly be surprised that psychologists are reporting an increase in juvenile patients presenting with what the American Psychological Association defines as 'the chronic fear of environmental cataclysm that comes from observing the seemingly irrevocable impact of climate change and the associated concern for one's future and that of next generations.'[226]

'You come across it in children as young as three,' says a clinical professor of psychiatry at the University of Nevada School of Medicine. 'You find them on TikTok, sobbing about losing their teddy bears or sobbing that animals they loved got killed in an extreme weather event'.[227] An Australian psychologist reports a similar pattern. 'In recent years, I have witnessed an alarming trend; more and more young children are entering my clinic, gripped by fear that they will not live to see adulthood. They tell me with absolute certainty that the world is ending, that the government doesn't care, and that the adults around them have failed.'[228] Crucially, she comments that these are hardly isolated incidents, and that the rise in children with eco-anxiety, seen by herself and her colleagues, is linked to the way climate change is taught in schools.

In the UK, the Royal College of Psychiatrists explains eco-anxiety as a 'way of describing how people feel when they hear bad news about our planet and the environment. This can be things like warmer temperatures around the world, events like floods, fires or droughts or harm to animals and their natural habitats.'[229] Symptoms include, but are not limited to, being 'breathless, sweaty, sick, headachy, tense or fidgety, anxious, fearful, panicky, upset, tearful, irritable, negative, angry, frustrated, furious, guilty, hopeless, drained, on edge, numb,' and last but not least, 'withdrawn'.[230] Perhaps a more accurate name for the condition should be 'eco-despair'. Ben, a twelve-year-old who first learnt that the end of the world was imminent when he was in Year 3, might well agree. Now he is not only upset that 'animals and humans will become extinct' but he's worried that 'we don't have the space equipment to find another planet to live on, even if there was another planet out there.'[231] As children are wont to scribble on their placards these days, 'There is no Planet B!'

According to a major study conducted in 2021 and published in *The Lancet Planetary Health,* eco-anxiety is not just anecdotal. Nor is it confined to rare instances. After interviewing 10,000 young people aged 16 to 25 across ten countries including the UK, the US and Australia, researchers concluded that eco-anxiety among young people is endemic. It found that 59 per cent were very or extremely worried about climate change, and 75 per cent said, 'the future is frightening'. Over half (56 per cent) said that 'humanity is doomed', and 55 per cent believed they would have fewer opportunities than their parents. Nearly 40 per cent said their fears made them hesitant to have children.

Here we have wandered out of the fringes of fear and into the depths of despair. Forty-five per cent of respondents said that their climate anxiety was affecting their daily functioning. Worse, not only are they beset by a nihilistic ennui, but their days are filled with rage, with 57 per cent reporting feeling angry about the state of the world, and the lack of meaningful action by governments and leaders. An American psychologist who works directly with children and families warns that making climate collapse the only story can leave students asking, 'Why study – isn't the world going to burn anyway?'.[232] Another child, existentialist beyond their tender years, asks, 'Why do I have to live in a time like this with climate change? How can I help the planet and change the situation?'[233]

In 2024, the Department for Education (DfE) commissioned the Royal Meteorological Society to find out what people think and feel about climate change. The resulting Climate Literacy survey, which interviewed just 522 Year 11 school leavers in England, concluded that over half reported concern about climate change. Researchers were disappointed to discover, however, a shortfall in knowledge about net-zero, global warming levels, and greenhouse gases. 'Most school leavers are "fairly concerned" about climate change, but, for those communicating on climate change, it is worth noting that more are "not very" or "not at all" concerned about climate change than are "very concerned",' it stated.[234] But reading between the lines, it becomes clear that the DfE is less concerned with over-alarming children than with the possibility that some are not alarmed enough. This sentiment was echoed by the Royal Meteorological Society. 'We should...make sure that our focus is on making young people "concerned and hopeful" as only this will lead to effective...climate action.'[235]

The implication is clear: if children are not sufficiently anxious and ready to be activists, the education system has failed. This no longer bears any resemblance to science. It's psychological conditioning, and it borders on policy-driven emotional manipulation. The end justifies the emotional means; children must be frightened into action, even if it comes at a price.

And what a high price it is turning out to be. In *The Lancet Planetary Health* survey, researchers also noted some of the young people they interviewed expressed 'hopelessness to the point of suicidal ideation', though this was not always explicitly recorded as clinical diagnoses.[236] In a 2024 study published in *Frontiers in Psychology*, researchers found a positive correlation between the intensity of eco-anxiety and suicide risk scores in adolescents. Interestingly, the link weakens once things like general anxiety and depression are factored in, which suggests that eco-anxiety might not cause mental illness on its own, but instead makes existing emotional struggles worse.

At this juncture, it would not be unreasonable for parents to hope that education departments, curriculum writers, and influential organisations such as the WWF might reconsider their heavy-handed approach, or that education departments might heed the growing warnings of a full-blown mental health crisis and protect those who lack the developmental tools to process existential fear. But such hope, sadly, appears to be misplaced. Rather than pause to reflect on the evidence, governments and curriculum designers are going even deeper down the alarmist abyss. Climate education is being rolled out not with greater care and caution, but with increased emotional urgency.

Hope or Activism?

During a Westminster Hall debate on eco-anxiety in 2021, MPs cited evidence that growing numbers of children felt 'betrayed, ignored and abandoned' by adults and governments, while psychologists urged age-appropriate, less catastrophic teaching.[237] The DfE's response? To double down. Rather than scaling back the panic, it decided that what children needed was not less anxiety-inducing climate change education, but more. Under its 2022 Sustainability and Climate Change Strategy, schools are now required to embed climate change messaging across the entire curriculum, not just science and geography. It also mandated that from September 2025 onwards, every education setting must have appointed a 'Sustainability Lead' as well as produce its own Climate Action Plan, even as head teachers struggle to staff maths and physics lessons.

One of the common refrains we hear in discussions about climate change education is that it will make children both hopeful and resilient. 'By empowering children on climate action, schools can contribute to building a generation of emotionally resilient, environmentally aware, proactive citizens', writes the DfE. Children must be sufficiently 'concerned and hopeful' because only this emotional combination will inspire the right kind of collective climate action to ensure a future for the planet. This is echoed by the WWF, which advises teachers that 'it is important to focus on hope to avoid eco-anxiety but also because there is cause for hope. That message is much more engaging and motivating for young people and gives them a better sense of how they can be part of shaping the future.' But having made this point, the WWF then fails to offer actual hope. Instead, it says teachers should encourage empathy, promote student activism, and make the issues feel more 'relevant', stressing that 'climate change affects everyone and everyone has a role to play'.[238]

Instead of being offered hope rooted in scientific progress, rational optimism, or even philosophical resilience in the face of uncertainty, children are increasingly being handed activism and protest as a remedy. We have organisations such as Teach the Future, which has an explicitly activist agenda to turn climate education into a vehicle for climate action by overhauling *every* subject area and level of schooling.[239]

In 2019, millions of school children around the world took days off school to 'Strike4Climate'. But instead of being castigated for missing school, many teachers encouraged their students. This is because, as one teacher points out, 'many teachers have been trained to believe in the goals Freire proposes'. And what are those goals? That pupils become activists, and that they rebel against teacher authority. 'The intrinsic (ie. non revolutionary) value of education was under assault, and so educationalists inspired by Freire celebrated.' Jeremy Corbyn, by way of illustration, was delighted, commenting that the youthful picketers 'had taught him a lesson about climate change', revelling in this 'inversion of teacher-pupil hierarchy'.[240]

Ultimately, it's not so much about changing the climate. It's about replacing the institutions and the values of Western Civilisation with something else. The authors of 'School Strike for Climate: A Reckoning for Education' published in the *Australian Journal of Environmental Education* tell us so. 'Across diverse places and platforms, school strikers are crying out for the world to 'change the system, not the climate' they write. 'What is needed is not techno-utopian market-based mechanisms of haphazard climate *action*, but socio-cultural, economic and political transformation for climate justice.' They go on to ask: 'What if education is not the solution, but part of the problem?' They clearly believe that it is, for then they suggest that it's time 'for a reckoning for education'.[241] The education system certainly needs a reckoning but it's probably not the 'burn it all to the ground' year zero sort that progressive educationalists have in mind.

Here we have another question: does missing school and attending strikes truly help young people in the long run? Some, like British teenager Lauren Jeffrey, think not. After attending climate protests, she noticed that her friends were becoming even more despondent, saying things she found 'quite disturbing', like: '"There is no future anymore," "We are basically doomed.", and "We should give up."' In an open letter to Extinction Rebellion, she warned: 'As important as your cause is, your persistent exaggeration of the facts has the potential to do more harm than good – to the scientific credibility of your cause, as well as to the psychological well-being of my generation.'[242] These are the words of a young person who sees the cost of emotional manipulation dressed up as engagement. If throwing tomato soup at priceless paintings doesn't shift policy, and if gluing oneself to a busy road delays commuters but not the rise of sea levels, then we must ask: is this really the right path for children? Or have we mistaken panic for purpose? Do children really have the cognitive maturity or historical perspective to lead climate discourse or are they being used, consciously or not, as vessels for adult political agendas?

Certainly, climate education as it stands is not building a generation of resilient individuals. There is no evidence that children are being made stronger, but everything points to the descent into a state of fragility. And what good is a generation of fragile individuals? As one teacher asks, 'Why, exactly, is it better for the scientists of the future to miss school? How could children claim to understand the data without a rudimentary grasp of statistics? How are they to deliver a convincing speech without studying the most persuasive writing penned in the English language?'[243] Surely the future will require strong, rational, well-informed, and emotionally grounded young people, not a cohort overwhelmed by anxiety and on the verge of despair.

If schools genuinely wanted to offer children hope and make them resilient, they might start by offering a more hopeful perspective. They might mention the countless apocalyptic climate predictions that never came to fruition. In 1989, a senior UN environmental official warned that entire nations could be 'wiped off the face of the earth' by rising sea levels by the year 2000. The Maldives, one of the supposed casualties, continue to expand their airports and luxury resorts. In 2007, Al Gore predicted the Arctic could be ice-free by 2013, yet as of 2026, Arctic summer sea ice still exists. While it has declined since the 1980s, it has not disappeared.

In the early 2000s, scientists at the UK's Hadley Centre suggested that Britain would develop a Mediterranean-style climate by 2020. In reality, Britain still has rain, clouds, and long grey winters. No vineyards have replaced the Lake District. And despite repeated predictions from media outlets and climate scientists that snow would 'soon be a thing of the past', the UK has experienced multiple severe snowfalls in recent years, including the notorious 'Beast from the East' in 2018.

It might also be worth telling children that the Earth is, by many measures, greener than it was several decades ago.[244] Above all, they might be told that the most recent IPCC Sixth Assessment Synthesis Report (Climate Change 2023) does not predict the imminent collapse of civilisation. It does not say that an apocalypse is inevitable. On the contrary, it speaks of a 'window of opportunity to secure a liveable and sustainable future for all', and outlines 'feasible and effective' solutions already within reach.

But they are not told any of this because in today's climate education, even basic balance is no longer tolerated. When BBC Bitesize, which is a key resource for schoolchildren, published a page outlining both the negative and potential positive effects of climate change, the response was swift and furious. Among the so-called 'benefits' listed were a longer growing season in Siberia, fewer winter deaths, and new shipping routes in the Arctic. These were not editorial opinions, but standard points found in older geography textbooks, and entirely appropriate for students learning to weigh complex environmental consequences. But the idea that climate change could produce any positive outcome, however marginal or temporary, was deemed unacceptable.

Activist and journalist George Monbiot, writing on X, author of *Heat: How to Stop the Planet from Burning*, called the page 'an absolute disgrace', adding: 'You could come away thinking: 'on balance, it sounds pretty good'. Stuart Lock, CEO of the Advantage Schools trust, insisted the material was 'flat wrong', and didn't align with curriculum standards. A spokesperson for Extinction Rebellion's South-East group claimed the guidance would 'warp and distort the truth'. In response, the BBC quickly removed the page and issued a statement saying it was 'amending the content to be in line with current curricula'.[245] In other words, only the *negative* side of climate change may now be shown to children. As one exam board put it, 'we do not advocate a positive viewpoint on this topic'.[246] You can say that again.

This is the crux of the matter. Climate change, once a scientific issue with multiple dimensions and outcomes, is now treated as a purely moral crisis. Any attempt to introduce nuance is accused of 'distorting the truth'. But the truth, by definition, includes complexity. In the name of preventing 'false balance', climate education has become a one-sided moral instruction. Indeed, when it comes to morality, children are being trained to look at climate change through a lens of right and wrong, as an element of behavioural conditioning is introduced into the classroom.

In a WWF classroom activity on 'carbon footprints', children are asked to judge the lifestyles of three characters called Anisha, Jaydon, and Nye, based on their supposed environmental impact.[247] Nye is a fairly ordinary rural teenager who goes by 'they/them', drives a small petrol car, eats meat, recycles, and has solar panels. Anisha is a frugal vegan who rides a bike, never eats out or orders takeaway, only buys second-hand clothes, and, one imagines, wears a hairshirt once a week. Not quite, but it's not much of a stretch. Jaydon is mostly vegetarian (though occasionally succumbs to a Big Mac), keeps the thermostat at 17 degrees in winter, goes on holiday but never offsets his flights, and sometimes forgets to turn off his computer.

The moral ranking is unmistakable. Anisha is morally pure and bound for climate heaven. Jaydon, a careless consumer, might scrape into purgatory. But Nye, despite the gender-neutral pronouns, is passive, polluting, and destined for eco-hell. Even the they/them won't save they/them. This is a simple and clearly appealing message. The smaller your carbon footprint, the greater your moral worth.

It is worth pointing out that none of these characters are living what could be considered luxurious lives. None, as far as I can tell, admitted to owning a private jet. But only the least Westernised, and most dull lifestyle is held up as ideal. Nye's lifestyle of living in the countryside, owning pets, eating meat, driving a car, occasionally buying things, is now cast as irresponsible and harmful to the planet. In some circles, this is known as 'carbon guilt'.

Children learn that those most affected by climate change are the world's poor, Indigenous peoples, and marginalised communities, and that those most responsible are wealthy, industrialised nations, especially their own. The issue is no longer framed as a shared global challenge, but as an historical injustice for which the West must atone. As a result, climate education becomes less about understanding the environment, and more about reinforcing a familiar narrative: oppressor and oppressed, guilt and reparation. 'Although climate change affects everyone around the world,' says the WWF, 'it is the poorest and most vulnerable people who will be hardest hit by climate change, even though they did the least to cause it in the first place.'[248]

Michael Shellenberger, however, thinks that poverty is the problem, not climate change. 'Poor communities are more vulnerable to natural disasters, but the reason is not that climate change is making things worse. The reason is that they are poor,'[249] he writes. He also notes that climate-related deaths have fallen by 98 per cent in the past century thanks to wealth and infrastructure, arguing that Western climate policies that restrict cheap energy development are more likely to harm the poor than help them. These facts do not make him popular amongst the climate change intelligentsia. And they certainly do not end up in school curricula.

Instead, the framing is often delivered under the banner of 'sustainability', a term which, as Joanna Williams points out, 'speaks to one approach to addressing environmental concerns that is often anti-growth and anti-development.' Rather than asking children to debate, for example, the benefits of fair trade versus free trade, or nuclear power versus renewables, all they have to do is talk about the recycling habits of the Nepalese. 'Through such processes', Williams writes, 'the interests of a small group of curriculum planners are recast as universal moral values.'[250]

The Met Office school resources for 7-year-olds frame this in an emotive, experimental way designed to elicit empathy and urgency. 'Your pupils will step into the shoes of people in other countries, finding out about their ways of life and how climate change is having an impact today, and into the future.'[251] What does this do other than make children guilty about living normal, Western lives?

This seems to be the intention of the *Let's Go Zero Climate Activity Pack* for Primary Schools, which is used by thousands of schools across the UK. It positions everyday behaviour such as having a bath, driving and eating meat as sinful and has a range of suggestions on how to change. 'Maybe today could be different?' it suggests cheerfully. 'Could you skip your bath today or share the bath water with a family member?' 'Go electric', it also suggests. 'Ask your parents to think about making their next car an electric one!' But until then, 'Don't idle – ask your parents to turn off their engines when the car isn't moving – you can let them know it's against the law to leave their car idling!'

By the end of the 60 pages of activities, the pack resembles a training manual for climate evangelists. In the final section, the tone shifts from informative to instructive, telling children how to 'spread the message' and respond to sceptics, in a manner uncomfortably close to religious proselytising. When confronted by someone who does not believe in climate change, they are to 'make it personable and relatable', and 'bring it closer to home'. If they love skiing, mention that many ski resorts might lose snow within the next decade. If they enjoy a café latte, let them know they'd better start getting used to herbal tea, as rising temperatures are threatening their global coffee supplies. If they voice concern about food prices, tell them that it's because extreme weather disrupts crops. And if, by some miracle, their interlocutor hasn't edged away from the conversation, the final piece of advice is 'know when to pause', because 'not every conversation will go perfectly. If someone is resistant or you're feeling overwhelmed, it's okay to step back.'[252] This sounds an awful lot like reprogramming.

We need to take a step back from all this and ask a few questions. How much valuable developmental time is being lost as children are made to contend with the terrifying scenarios presented to them by adults in the classroom? Too much. What effect can it possibly have on a child's psychological wellbeing to be told they may not reach adulthood? Untold harm. Parents should be deeply troubled that their children are not being prepared to face the future with hope, confidence, or resilience, but that instead they are being programmed with a new moral code which sets them at odds with their own lives, their own families, with their countries, and with Western Civilisation itself.

And speaking of severing ties with their countries, a recurring, yet somewhat puzzling theme in climate education is the idea that being British, Australian, or American no longer cuts the mustard when it comes to saving the planet. Over the last decade or so, UK education policy has increasingly linked climate change lessons with global citizenship. The DfE says that 'we will empower all young people to be global citizens through a better understanding of climate change and a greater connection to nature. Practical opportunities to participate in activities to increase climate resilience, reduce carbon impact and enhance biodiversity will enable children and young people to translate knowledge into positive action to improve their local communities, their country and the planet.'[253]

Only a global community of 'global citizens', whatever that means, is capable of halting rising temperatures and saving the polar bear from extinction. The message being delivered to children is that there is something parochial, even slightly embarrassing, about thinking of yourself in terms of national anthems, borders, and flags. This is of course the same rejection of nation they are being fed in history lessons. Being a citizen of a country is what your parents do, as they selfishly drive around in their petrol-powered, air-conditioned cars, picking you up from school.

It will not surprise readers to learn that this is being pushed by the United Nations. One of its Sustainable Development Goals is 'inclusive, quality education for all', which explicitly includes global citizenship as a target. Global citizenship, it says, consists of 'the social, political, environmental, and economic actions of globally minded individuals and communities on a worldwide scale.' It insists that 'promoting global citizenship in sustainable development will allow individuals to embrace their social responsibility to act for the benefit of all societies, not just their own.' The UN promises that by 2030, every child in every classroom around the world will 'acquire the knowledge and skills needed to promote sustainable development, including global citizenship.'[254]

But how does one go from being a boring old Brit to a 'global citizen'? According to Oxfam's *Global Citizenship in the Classroom*, it's quite easy. There is no requirement for historical grounding, civic literacy, critical distance, or nuance. All you have to do is 'be passionately committed to social justice, respects and values [sic] diversity, be aware of the wider world and take responsibility for your actions.'[255] You never know. One day you might even be like Greta Thunberg, who is widely featured across primary and secondary curricula, not just in the capacity of climate activist, but as a symbol of global citizenship and youth-led moral leadership.

Perhaps children's energies might be better directed towards ecological issues on their doorstep, such as the practice of some water companies to discharge sewage into rivers, or the tens of thousands of empty plastic bottles in Dorset rendering the sea inaccessible. They might also turn their attention towards the billions of Covid-era nonrecyclable polypropylene face masks, which can take 450 years to degrade, and which are still lying about in soil, rivers, and oceans.

It's not really about climate change; it's about a world-view based on social justice and identity politics. This is why Thunberg's 2025 pivot, from climate warrior to attempting to sail to Gaza, is entirely predictable. Her global role is not to promote scientific literacy or civic moderation, but to set an example of someone who has ideological conviction.

Children are being taught to see themselves not as members of a particular nation, but as members of humanity at large. This system is creating a generation of young people who think of themselves as global citizens first, long before they think of themselves as citizens of their countries. And remember, many are already deeply ashamed of their nations, so their attachment to them is already hanging by a thread. Global citizenship cuts that thread altogether.

7

Activist Teachers

In the lead-up to the 2024 US election, a schoolteacher addressed a Harris/Walz rally, declaring: 'I saw education for what it really was – the greatest instrument of Social Justice in this country.' As she delivered this revelation, cheers and whoops of delight erupted from her fellow attendees, many of whom were likely also in the business of education. No doubt their enthusiasm was heightened by the fact that Walz, the Democratic nominee for vice-president, had once been a high school geography teacher. In any case, their reaction to her proclamation reflects a broader shift in how the teaching profession sees itself, and her statement embodies the general belief among many teachers that their primary duty to society is a political one. Instead of using the classroom to transmit knowledge, a significant proportion of the teaching community believes they must dramatically remake society through the lens of Critical Social Justice.

This ideological shift in education has profound consequences. Teaching was once regarded as a noble profession dedicated to imparting knowledge, critical thinking, and civic responsibility. But it is now a highly politicised field, where teachers are shaped by the education faculties, the most ideologically captured of all departments. We have long since waved goodbye to stuffy old Mr. Chips with his tweed suit and well-thumbed copy of Virgil's *Aeneid*. Today we have Mx. Harper, who identifies as demigender and carries with her an equally well-thumbed copy of *Gender Queer: A Memoir*. Teaching colleges have produced the likes of Tim Walz, whose former students claimed that he didn't overload them with homework but challenged them in other ways, such as 'forcing them to wrestle with issues like the Cambodian genocide and how the French government treated its Muslim citizens.'[256] Later, as Minnesota governor, Walz forced himself to wrestle with biological reality and lost. His mandate of free menstruation products in boys' and girls' toilets earned him the sobriquet 'Tampon Tim'. A quick scroll of TikTok gives us a disturbing glimpse into the world of young female teachers with purple hair and nose rings, bragging about their intimate conversations with other people's children about their genitals or joyfully describing how they deliberately confuse little boys and girls by telling them that there is no such thing as little boys or girls.

Plato's Cave and the Bad Seeds

For much of Western history, education was grounded in the classical liberal model, designed to cultivate reason, virtue, and civic responsibility. In the 19th and early 20th centuries, classical education remained the foundation of elite schooling in the West, and it was seen as the foundation for a literate, informed, and virtuous citizenry. From the early 20th century onwards, a group of elite intellectuals, these 'key possessors of consequential knowledge', devoted themselves to a programme of disrupting the *status quo*. They decided that a society of literate, informed and virtuous citizens was not all that it was purported to be, and casting all tradition aside, supplanted the existing model with a new education theory.

The intellectual roots of this rebellion can be traced back to Switzerland, or more precisely, to the philosopher Jean-Jacques Rousseau (1712–1778), whose influence on education has been inestimable. In *Émile* (1762), Rousseau's most famous treatise on education and child-rearing, he argued that children should be raised with love and freedom, and that their education should be child-centred rather than knowledge-driven. He famously sought to 'liberate' children from formal learning, which he said was oppressive, proposing that they were perfect, created beings until civilisation and all its trappings came along and ruined them. He wrote,

'God made all things good; man meddles with them, and they become evil.' Among the things that Rousseau claimed were corruptors of men were books, so the only literature that our fictional hero, *Émile*, was permitted to read was Daniel Defoe's *Robinson Crusoe*. Presumably, Rousseau did not count his own works, of which there were several, as corruptors of men.

One of the fundamental difficulties with Rousseau (and there are many) is the vast chasm between what he preached and what he practised. For a man who made a living from theorising about children, he did not appear to like them or indeed know any. In the artist Eugène Delacroix's journal entry from 1824, he recounts a conversation with an elderly gentleman who had met Rousseau during a walk in the Tuileries Gardens. Encountering children playing with a ball, Rousseau expressed approval, saying, 'There, that is how I should like Émile to play.' However, when a ball accidentally hit his leg, Rousseau flew into a rage, chasing the child down with his cane and shattering the idyllic scene in seconds.

Rousseau's cruelty to his own children was, however, far more troubling than his cantankerousness. Despite his philosophical devotion to childhood, he forced his mistress, Thérèse Levasseur, to abandon all five of their infants to a Paris foundling hospital. None were named, and if any had survived childhood, they would have become vagabonds or beggars. 'How could I achieve the tranquillity of mind necessary for my work, my garret filled with domestic cares and the noise of children?' he asked. We might also ask how Rousseau achieved tranquillity of mind after these astonishing acts of cruelty. Easily, as it so happens. He justified his actions as a 'good and sensible arrangement', using Plato as his get-out clause. 'I thought I was performing the act of a citizen and a father and I looked on myself as a member of Plato's republic',[257] he later offered as a rather unconvincing excuse for his inhumanity.

Despite his significant shortcomings, Rousseau's ideas would not die with him but were resurrected a century later by Professor John Dewey (1859–1952), lauded among the modern-day teaching fraternity as the 'father of public education'. Not to be confused with the father of the decimal system, Melville Dewey, John Dewey's influence has been significant and long-lasting in the West. He explicitly rejected the idea that education should focus on knowledge acquisition and instead advocated for a 'learning-by-doing' approach, which is now known as child-centred learning, or 'Constructivism', which has proven to be an unmitigated disaster.

Dewey was a socialist in that he saw schools as a means to 'eliminate obvious social evils' and, in what will sound familiar to today's decolonisers, to weed out 'undesirable dead wood from the past'.[258] He completely dismissed the idea that education should transmit a culture's spiritual and intellectual values. Regarding problem-solving, children should work out their own solutions, with no help from the teacher who is merely a facilitator. His ideal syllabus would be devoid of 'facts, laws, information' and 'various bodies of external fact labelled geography, arithmetic, grammar, etc.'[259] This sentiment was echoed by a fellow educator, who exhorted teachers to 'overcome the fetichism [sic] of the alphabet, of the multiplication table, of grammars, of scales, and of bibliolatry',[260] which, if nothing else, is an interesting choice of phrasing.

From 1905 to 1930, Dewey taught at Columbia University's Teachers College, which was at that time the largest teacher training institution in the country. During his tenure, he was made Vice President of the *American Society for Cultural Relations with Russia*, which was a front for a Communist International propaganda organisation.[261] In 1928, Dewey travelled to the USSR with fellow academics on a 'fact-finding tour'. Given that their visit coincided with the early years of collectivisation and increasing political repression, it appears that Dewey and friends did not quite find *all* the facts. Indeed, he was so impressed by the experience that he wrote a memoir, admiring the Communists' use of propaganda to shape the population's thinking. Equally impressed was a fellow theorist at Columbia's Teachers College, George S. Counts, who made several extended visits to Russia during the 1920s and 1930s. While millions of peasants were being forcibly relocated and imprisoned in the name of building a new social order, Counts penned *Dare the School Build a New Social*

Order? (1932) in which he answered his own question in the affirmative.

During this period, legions of newly trained teachers were sent out into schools to test the new theories. Total anarchy ensued. No one did any work, children started calling each other names such as 'crazy stupid n***er' and even graffitied the walls with obscenities. This was entirely predictable because teachers essentially told children to 'do their own thing'. Yet, while Dewey conceded that there was a problem, he refused to admit culpability, and instead blamed extremists for having distorted his ideas. Later, William Coulson, a psychologist and former exponent of the philosopher's ideas, wrote that 'Dewey's experimentalism – the idea that the fund of accumulated knowledge should no longer control education – has turned out to exact a terrible price from American schools and their patrons.'[262]

Despite the demonstrable failures of Dewey's ideas, he continues to be revered within the educational establishment as a secular saint. As a professor of education at the University of Melbourne enthuses, 'reading Dewey on education often leads to marvelling at how his descriptions ring true in a twenty-first century world.'[263] His theories on 'learning by doing', student autonomy, and experiential learning are still held up as the gold standard of modern pedagogy. Daring to criticise Dewey within the educational community is akin to heresy because it challenges not merely his ideas but also the moral framework of modern education itself.

Bringing Children to Consciousness

As Communist sympathisers in the US were reprogramming the social order through the classroom, an actual Communist in Italy was developing the theoretical framework for a revolution through the classroom. Antonio Gramsci (1891–1937), leader of the outlawed Italian Communist Party and imprisoned by Mussolini in the 1920s, envisioned a cultural revolution waged through schools and other institutions. In his *Prison Notebooks*, Gramsci argued that the ruling class maintains dominance through economic power and control of cultural institutions, including schools. He took that to mean that if education was a tool of hegemony, then it was up to teachers to challenge dominant power structures and instil a revolutionary consciousness in their students. Gramsci, who ended up dying in prison, is still held up as a secular martyr by left-wing educationalists around the West.

This brings us to Brazilian Marxist Paulo Freire, who knew a thing or two about awakening people to consciousness. As previously discussed, the teaching community reveres him so much that it feels compelled to immortalise him in bronze. It is so keen on him that his *Pedagogy of the Oppressed* is the third most cited publication Chin the social sciences.[264] It seems that there can never be too much Paulo Freire.

Freire is the founding father of Critical Pedagogy, an educational theory and practice that views teaching and learning as inherently political acts aimed at empowering students to critically analyse and challenge systems of oppression, inequality, and social injustice. For an oeuvre purporting to lay out a brand-new theory of education, *Pedagogy of the Oppressed* is light on educational theorists but heavy on communist revolutionaries, with Marx, Hegel, Lenin, Mao Zedong, Castro and Che Guevara all quoted as positive exemplars.

No matter which way you look at it, *Pedagogy of the Oppressed* is an unapologetically revolutionary text. It is a call to arms, an invitation for teachers to be foot soldiers in the transformation of the classroom into a site of political awakening, while simultaneously promising that even those who have not yet realised how oppressed they are, will be liberated from oppression. Freire proposes that the acquisition of knowledge is corrupting, a tool of oppression because it impedes the students' ability to think about anything critically. Freire says that the acquisition of a critical consciousness is more important than knowledge, which is achieved through a process he invented called 'conscientização' or 'conscientisation'.

Like Dewey, Freire understood how important it was to capture the teaching colleges, so in 1968, he accepted a two-year lecturing position at the Harvard Graduate School of Education. In 1970, the newly formed World Council of Churches appointed Freire as educational consultant. However, 'decolonisation consultant' would have been a more fitting title. A few short years after he visited Mozambique, Angola, Guinea-Bissau, and Papua New Guinea, these nations threw off the yoke of colonial rule of Portugal and Australia, respectively. After returning to Brazil in the late 1970s, Freire became a professor at the Pontifical Catholic University of São Paulo, where he was to influence generations of educators.

But while Freire was bringing various peoples of the world to 'conscientização', a Canadian high school teacher named Henry Giroux picked up a copy of *Pedagogy of the Oppressed* and underwent an epiphany. 'It changed my life,' he wrote, 'because it gave me a language that enabled education to be understood as a political process.'[265] Before this revelation, Giroux had been struggling to have his radical ideas accepted in the school where he taught. It has even been suggested that Boston University's education faculty later denied him tenure because he was not only too radical but also too Communist.[266] Giroux's fixation with power, ideology, and social class suggests that he has been more inspired by Karl Marx's *Das Kapital* than by Edmund Burke's *Reflections on the Revolution in France*.

Revolutions, particularly the Marxist sort, appear to preoccupy Giroux. He informs teachers that they are vital political and cultural actors whose special mission is to empower students so that they question and then overturn the dominant ideologies (e.g., family, religion, tradition) using their political power. 'Young people', he says, 'have a lot of power':

> They can shut societies down. They can block streets, they can engage in direct action, they can educate their parents…They are a potent political force and I think what they need to do is to recognise themselves as a potent political force and they need to act. Because a discourse of anxiety should give way to a discourse of critique and a discourse of critique should give way to a discourse of possibility. And a discourse of possibility means that you can imagine a future very different from the present.[267]

Critical Pedagogy is pure politics. But it is not just any politics; it is a revolutionary politics with a distinctly Marxist flavour. It has always been revolutionary, from Jean-Jacques Rousseau's infamous and overrated statement that 'man is born free and everywhere he is in chains' to Henry Giroux's call for young people to shed their discourses, rise up and dismantle existing social structures. These men shared a deep discontent with the values and institutions of Western Civilisation, and a common ambition to replace it with a vision akin to a socialist utopia.

Social Justice Education

In the 1990s, the worst of both worlds collided. Critical Theory, which had already subsumed the humanities and social sciences, met Critical Pedagogy, which had overtaken education faculties, and they had a love child: Social Justice Education. Social Justice Education takes irrational theories about race and gender and combines them with the political activism of Critical Pedagogy. This ideology now dominates teaching colleges and education faculties across the West. It is not just one aspect of education – it *is* education. It is so ubiquitous that it is almost impossible to find a single education faculty that has not completely given itself to Social Justice. It is rare to find an academic in a teaching faculty not wholly preoccupied with race, gender, inequality, global challenges, colonialism or climate change.

In 2023, the British Educational Research Association (BERA) asked education researchers working in university departments, schools of education and education research centres to list up to five keywords/phrases describing their research focus. The responses revealed that 'Social Justice, Inequalities, and Diversity' were among the researchers' top three priorities, eclipsing the more tedious topics such as assessment and curriculum, STEM (Science, Technology, Engineering and Mathematics) and education policy.

Social Justice is not just a sideshow. It is the main event. It is the sole reason many people choose to dedicate their lives to education. Nearly 75 per cent of respondents said that their main motivation was 'Social Justice and Inequalities' and that 'education could and should contribute to a fairer, more equal and more peaceful society.'[268] This number is not confined to people specialising in actual Social Justice Education, which would make sense, but includes researchers of pedagogy, learning science, school improvement, teacher education and linguistics.

The symbiosis between education research and teacher training means that the UK's 260 or so teacher education providers are all suffering from the same condition. A perusal of units and courses on offer to trainee teachers is both predictable and disheartening on account of the sameness and narrowness of it all. Teachers themselves are being indoctrinated to indoctrinate. Take, for example, a unit entitled 'Education, Climate Change and Social Justice' that is mandated as part of a BSc in Education at the University of Bristol. Students are asked to consider if 'education [is] succeeding in preparing students to deal with the pressing challenges facing our planet and societies?' According to the unit director, the answer is a definitive 'no'. But by the time they complete their last assignment, he promises that they'll be able to solve 'key global challenges – the climate emergency, decolonialization, racism in education and the inequalities that have become apparent over 18 months of the Covid-19 pandemic.'[269] That's the least they can expect for £9,535 per year or £24,800 if they happen to be an international student.

But University College London has even more ambitious plans for its students. In 'Educating and Organising for Social Justice', they are let into the secret of how to 'use education effectively to transform society – to create a more just, equal, inclusive, democratic and sustainable society than the one we live in today.'[270] But, as envisaged by Freire, transformation goes beyond the classroom and demands activism in the community. At University College London, it takes putting on your Che Guevara T-shirt and going out into the community with a copy of Saul Alinsky's *Rules for Radicals* under your arm.

It takes teaming up with the militantly left-wing organisation Citizens UK and working on its 'Racial Equality in Education' campaign, which is based on the presupposition that schools are hotbeds of racism and oppression, a state of affairs that Citizens UK attributes to the overwhelming whiteness of teachers. 'In 2022, 60 per cent of schools in England had an all-white teaching staff,' it informs us, utterly horrified by these statistics. Worse still, '56 per cent of educators have not received any anti-racism Continuing Professional Development in the past two years.' Shocking! Finally, it claims that '67 percent of teachers, teaching assistants and school leaders admit to a lack of awareness about the effects of racism.'[271] A more accurate name for this particular campaign should be 'End Whiteness Amongst Teachers'.

This certainly seems to be the Scottish Council of Deans of Education's campaign through its 'Anti-Racist Framework' for Initial Teacher Education (ITE), which has been enthusiastically endorsed and implemented by ten universities, including the Universities of Glasgow and Edinburgh. In the framework, authored by Dr Khadija Mohammed, Associate Dean for Equality, Diversity, and Inclusion at the University of the West of Scotland, she insists that it is incumbent upon Scottish universities to produce teachers who are both 'race-cognisant and anti-racist'. Above all, Dr. Mohammed insists that they must be taught to 'disrupt the centrality of whiteness and enable different ways of seeing, thinking and doing', while being made to understand the full, and presumably negative 'impact of whiteness' in the classroom.[272] That this might be uncomfortable, even painful, for white teachers and students appears not to be a drawback but a feature of the process for Dr. Mohammed, who approvingly quotes interviews with trainee teachers reacting to this particular directive. 'I worry about saying the wrong thing and insulting someone without intending to,' says one. 'This session on race and racism has made me stop and think about what it is to be white,' admits another, seemingly internalising the guilt the session demands. The repercussions will soon be felt in the classroom, as teachers try to grapple with their own 'whiteness' while simultaneously trying to teach students how to read and write.

As one would expect from the country that gave birth to Critical Race Theory and intersectionality, there is also a great deal of grappling with 'whiteness' in American education colleges. Despite Robin DiAngelo's infamous pronouncement in *White Fragility* that she 'could get through a teacher-education program without ever discussing racism', race is not only one of the favourite topics of discussion but in many cases, it is the *only* topic of discussion. In the top-ranked colleges of education, 48 per cent of faculty staff were researching an aspect of Social Justice. And of those top-ranked colleges, 24 per cent of the staff listed race, diversity, or equity as their *primary* area of study. At the Berkeley School of Education in California, that number soars to 78 per cent.[273]

A perusal of the school's website certainly supports this proportion as well as its full dedication to the cause. One staff member happily reports that she 'applies critical, sociocultural, and translingual theories to examine the literacy and language practices of immigrant, transnational, and racialized bi/multilingual youth populations.' Another takes pride in exploring 'issues of equity and justice in higher education' while seeking to understand 'how Hispanic-Serving Institutions (HSIs) enact an organizational identity for serving Latine/x students and minoritized populations.' She tells us that as a 'critical scholar, she is race-conscious and equity-minded in her approach, seeking to empower historically marginalized populations and to create liberatory educational experiences in colleges and universities.'[274]

In April 2025, the department hosted Charlotte Tate, a self-described 'mixed ethnicity trans woman, a lesbian, and an intersectional feminist' and Professor of Psychology at San Francisco State University. Tate's speciality is the 'social identities of gender (trans* inclusive), sexual orientation (asexual inclusive), and ethnicity in the United States.'[275] The only minor problem with stating that one's specialities are gender and race is that they are everyone else's speciality too, which of course makes them infinitely less special. You would think that by now, everyone might be getting a little bored or at least be attempting to focus on something other than sexual orientation and skin colour. You would think that academics might be craving a break from the endless churn of identity politics, but their appetite remains insatiable.

Worryingly, or perhaps reassuringly, depending on which side of the ideological fence you sit, 70 per cent of American teachers are now processed through university education faculties, with only a quarter slipping through via alternative certification routes. The UK offers no real escape: most teachers pass through these same academic finishing schools, either entirely or via PGCE partnerships. Truly independent paths which might offer a different perspective are now little more than a quaint memory.

In Australia, a Bachelor of Education is essentially four long years of being re-educated by some of the most committed ideologues in the country. During your degree, you will spend the equivalent of one and a half of those years focusing on diversity, equity and inclusion, racism, gender and decolonisation, but only nine fleeting weeks on core skills like maths, phonics, and grammar combined. Developing actual teaching skills is an afterthought at the hands of your lecturers, who are not just dabbling in Social Justice and Critical Theory, they are submerged in it.[276]

At the University of Queensland, all first-year students, primary or secondary, are compelled to take 'A Sociological Orientation to Education' in which they must leave at the door their 'preconceived notions of schooling and education, including a consideration of appropriate learning and teaching practices for students with diverse linguistic, cultural, religious and socioeconomic backgrounds, with particular attention given to Indigenous students'. Prospective teachers at Monash University in Melbourne are promised that after completing the 'Theorising Social Justice' unit, they will have a strong grasp of the concept of 'cognitive justice, and the associated notions of epistemic and epistemological justice.' This will allow them 'to engage with and give value to, the diversity of thought and different ways of knowing that can be applied to the pursuit of social justice in local, national, and international contexts, in educational settings and beyond.' The words might be nonsensical, but the message is clear: teacher training in the West is no longer primarily about preparing individuals to teach. It is about preparing them to *change* the education system itself. The traditional teacher-as-expert has given way to the teacher-as-activist: not an instructor of subjects, but a political agent, a critical theorist, and a cultural interpreter.

But to truly comprehend the extent to which the politics of Social Justice has overtaken the institution of teaching, we need look no further than the 2024 Annual Conference of the UK's National Education Union. In his closing address, General Secretary Daniel Kebede did not hold back. He opened with 'What makes our union so great are the activists like you...', dispensing with the pretence that teachers are there to teach. From there, Kebede channelled his inner Karl Marx, criticising social media giants and private healthcare companies as 'privateers' and 'profiteers' in a world of 'corporate greed,' 'culture wars,' and 'class struggle'. He then claimed that 'Right-wing politicians' who 'scapegoat refugees for political gain need to realise is that every time they spill their bile about refugees, they are making life for many children in schools much harder' and are 'fanning the flames of racism.' He stated his support for Palestine and concluded with a final flourish that would not have been out of place in one of Lenin's addresses to the factory workers, soldiers, and peasants ahead of the October Revolution in 1917.

'Comrades,' he began. Well, almost. 'Conference,' he began. 'We will not stand idly by in the face of extremism':

> We will remain a union committed to the principles of equality and social justice. We will oppose racism, we will oppose antisemitism, we will oppose Islamophobia, we will champion the rights of women, we will stand up for LGBT+ and Disability rights. We will build alliances, we will work with others in the pursuit of a more inclusive, more just and more compassionate society.[277]

And with that, the conference closed. Not with a sober reflection on pedagogy or a call for improved classroom conditions, but with a speech that could have been ripped from the pages of a revolutionary manifesto. Roughly 30 per cent of the address touched on education; the remaining 70 per cent was unfiltered left-wing political rhetoric. In Kebede's vision, the teacher is no longer a professional, but a comrade in the great struggle for Social Justice.

The Price of 'Progress'

To paraphrase Thomas Sowell, something must always give way in any compromise. And in the case of the 'Progressive' education movement, literacy and numeracy are declining in the West faster than you can say diversity, equity and inclusion. Twenty years ago, a university lecturer, exasperated by his students' inability to form a cohesive sentence, took his grievances public. Writing to *The Independent*, he explained that he and his colleagues were not just teaching their subjects, but they were also forced to deliver crash courses in basic literacy, reading comprehension, and study skills. Even after what amounted to remedial intervention, many of the assignments remained, in his words, illegible.[278] It is a curious state of affairs that students taught in schools by university-trained teachers arrive at university only to discover, alongside their lecturers, that their foundational skills are, shall we say, a bit under par. In some circles, this might be called karma. In others, simply inevitability.

Coincidentally, it was just over twenty-five years ago that the OECD (Organisation for Economic Co-operation and Development) began testing fifteen-year-olds around the world in reading, mathematical, and scientific literacy through its Programme for International Student Assessment (PISA). Every three years, it releases a set of rankings and scores, in a ritual that has become oddly reminiscent of the Eurovision Song Contest, though with slightly less glitter and far grimmer results. Since the testing began in 2000, there has not been a single upward trend in the Anglosphere. Not once have we seen a renaissance of mathematical brilliance, a reading revolution, or a surge of scientific mastery among fifteen-year-olds in the UK, the US, or Australia. The promised flourishing of academic excellence has yet to materialise.

Nor have we witnessed a great flourishing among eleven-year-olds in England, who take the Standard Assessment Tests (SATs) at the end of primary school. Despite ten years of standardised testing, 'school improvement plans', and curriculum reforms, the average eleven-year-old today is performing no better in reading or maths than they were in 2014. In key areas, it's worse. In 2016, the Department for Education quietly lowered the pass mark and the bar for meeting the so-called 'expected standard'. It is now so low that your child can meet the maths standard without being able to add fractions or divide without a calculator. SATs do not diagnose illiteracy or innumeracy; they disguise it. Similarly, after decades of reform, inspection, and standardised testing, roughly the same percentage of students are still failing GCSE Maths and English as they were ten years ago. In 2024, only 59.9 per cent passed Maths and just 61.6 per cent passed English.[279] The government can shuffle grade boundaries or change how results are reported, but the outcome is the same: tens of thousands of young people are leaving school functionally underqualified in the very subjects that underpin every other academic or vocational path.

It is the same story in the US. Every year, the National Assessment of Educational Progress (NAEP) tests grades 4 (9-10-year-olds), 8 (13-14-year-olds), and 12 (17-18-year-olds) across a range of subjects including mathematics, science, writing, civics, US history and geography. If this is indeed the 'Nation's Report Card', then the Nation is in serious trouble. In 2024, 33 per cent of fourteen-year-olds did not even reach the NAEP's basic level.[280] What does this actually mean? It means that they can't locate and recall key facts or ideas, interpret simple relationships (like cause and effect), make straightforward conclusions based on what is explicitly stated, or understand basic text structures (e.g., chronology, comparison). It means that approximately 1.35 million American eighth graders, that is, students on the cusp of high school, simply do not understand what they are reading.

Meanwhile, over in the maths classes, 39 per cent of America's fourteen-year-olds are in a world of pain because they have not even mastered the most fundamental skills expected of nine-year-olds.[281] These teenagers cannot add ½ + ½ or form basic calculations without multiple-choice or pictures to help them, let alone apply them to real-world situations. PISA results in Australia since 2000 show a consistent decline across every sector, government, Catholic, and independent, and every socio-economic group. Moreover, its version of NAEP, which is called NAPLAN, reveals that one in three students are not meeting the basic standards of numeracy and literacy. The majority of Australia's Year 9 students use punctuation at a Year 3 level, which means that thirteen- and fourteen-year-olds are unable to convey complex ideas and are about as literate as eight-year-olds.[282]

It is no surprise that universities are reporting that there is a veritable abyss between the grades students achieve at school and the skills they actually possess when they turn up on campus. Just to be clear, we are talking about domestic students. International students are another kettle of fish entirely. Every year that a new cohort arrives, lecturers find themselves in the unenviable position of being torn between teaching course content and playing catch-up on the basics. Universities will often lay the blame on gaps in secondary education, over-reliance on technology, or a shift away from sustained writing practice before university. These are all valid reasons. But perhaps they might also look a bit closer to home for a clue. Perhaps they might turn their gaze onto their own education faculties, where their colleagues are doing a splendid job of teaching teachers how to wrestle with their white privilege but not so well when it comes to wrestling with the complexities of grammar or calculus. Universities are now dealing with a crisis for which they are partly responsible. None of this augurs well for suspension bridges, heart transplant patients or the citizenry at large.

We are at a point where literature professors are being given essays which read more like a text-message than they do academic papers, full of abbreviations – 'u' for 'you', 'bcos' for 'because', and completely devoid of paragraphs. They are finding that the bright students have just a passing acquaintance with spelling and are genuinely surprised when told that 'wiv' is not a suitable substitute for 'with'. They have never been taught how to structure an argument, and as one lecturer explained, 'I spent more time teaching basic grammar than discussing Dickens'. A linguistics lecturer at an older university, frustrated by students who continue to submit drafts riddled with the same issues, such as run-on sentences, no commas, vague pronouns, recounted:

> I'd spend 20 minutes annotating their work with suggestions – 'break this up', 'clarify this' – and the next version would be identical…It wasn't defiance; they just didn't know how to apply the advice. Writing's a skill, and they're arriving without it.

One suspects that if the feedback had read 'LMAO. Is this FR? I'm SMH. Pls c me l8r', the message might have landed more clearly. While this is a source of immense irritation for the lecturer who is not paid by the university to be a cryptanalyst, it is nothing short of mortifying for the student. Imagine dreaming of becoming a Professor of English Literature, yet you cannot reliably distinguish between 'their' and 'they're', or 'your' and 'you're'. Or imagine being a social science undergraduate who, along with your entire cohort, finds it 'a struggle', 'a chore', and 'pointless' to read academic literature, as one study recently found.[283] The following exchange between three of these students, who also happened to be trainee teachers, is as worrying as it is illustrative:

Jess: If I don't understand the words in the first paragraph, how am I going to understand the whole thing, let alone know what I'm supposed to take from it?

Emilia: I agree with Jess with that one. I feel like it's quite overwhelming when you don't really understand the words and then you've got to read a whole text on it.

Hannah: I'm the same. We had a reading last week for one of our modules and literally within the first, about halfway through the introduction… I'd run out of space to write down definitions of these huge words that I had no idea what they meant.

The interviews also revealed that students experienced a great deal of emotion in relation to their writing (e.g., anxiety, insecurity, shame) as well as a general lack of confidence in their academic writing abilities. Perhaps they might add 'anger' to their list of emotions, for they have clearly been shortchanged somewhere along the line. But their response is hardly surprising. If, as an aspiring linguist, you are stumped by the first paragraph of 'Modelling non-specific linguistic variation in cognitive disorders' in the Journal of Linguistics due to the 'huge words' contained therein, then yes, the struggle is real. And what's more troubling is that these students are not just struggling readers. They are trainee teachers.

Indeed, many students talk about reading as a 'struggle' or a 'battle' as they laboriously Google each individual word, just to be able to put a sentence together, and find that they lack the stamina to complete their readings before 'feeling saturated'.[284] This lack of stamina has less to do with intelligence and more to do with the fact that this generation has been raised on smartphones, and their attention is now so fragmented that even reading the first page of a novel feels like a marathon.[285] The National Literacy Trust has reported that only 35 per cent of children aged between eight to eighteen say that they enjoy reading, which is the lowest number since 2005.[286] Only 28 per cent said that they enjoy writing in their free time.[287] If they are not reading for fun, then it's hardly a mystery as to why reading dense academic prose is inducing anxiety attacks.

This battle extends beyond the written word to what is increasingly known as 'maths anxiety'. A 2016 review by the National Council on Teacher Quality (NCTQ) in the US found that only 13 per cent of 860 undergraduate elementary teacher-preparedness programmes covered critical maths topics such as problem-solving skills, geometry, data, and probability. Another NCTQ report in 2019 found that 25 per cent of teacher candidates failed the maths portion of a typical elementary licensing exam.[288] The report also addresses maths anxiety and the negative impact it has on students, teachers, and parents. Maths anxiety is defined in the review as 'a negative emotional response to mathematics tasks'. In the UK, a charity called National Numeracy was commissioned to test undergraduates through an aptly named online assessment tool called *Challenge*. Just 26 per cent of those assessed had the numerical skills considered sufficient for navigating daily life and the workplace. Presumably, the remaining 74 per cent must have floundered like a haul of haddock. Again, this does not reflect a lack of intelligence, but rather a failure of the education system to fulfil its basic purpose. Universities should not have to pick up the pieces left by the schools, but that is exactly what they are having to do. Queen Mary University of London has set up a 24-hour remedial service to help students read and write called 'Studiosity' so if you can no longer muster the strength to Google 'huge' words at 1am, there's someone on hand to help.

In the US, George Mason University offers a 'Math Boot Camp' for students such as computer science graduate Diego Fonseca, nineteen, of Ashburn, Virginia, who swallowed his pride and admitted that he 'really struggled when it came to higher-level algebra because [he] just didn't know anything'. This is a terrible admission to make to oneself at any stage in life, and it takes an immense amount of humility to admit to ignorance so openly. But as the Maths department head puts it bluntly, 'This is a huge issue. We're talking about college-level pre-calculus and calculus classes, and students cannot even add one-half and one-third.'[289] Through no fault of their own, students like Diego are arriving at university unprepared, not because they lack motivation, but because they have been failed by an education system that no longer prioritises literacy and numeracy.

Nowhere is this de-prioritisation more vividly illustrated than in Australia's National Curriculum, which is saturating children with identity politics, radical race theory, radical gender ideology and radical green ideology. If anyone needed a case study about how to effectively turn a syllabus into a political and ideological tool, then this is it. In fact, it would be surprising if the current review of the UK's National Curriculum, led by intersectional feminist Professor Becky Francis, were not looking to Australia for inspiration. When they devised this monstrosity of a curriculum back in 2011, its authors were so transparent about the ideology and politics they wanted, that they called them 'cross-curriculum priorities' and then embedded them into every subject from Foundation to Year 10. These are 'Aboriginal and Torres Strait Islander Histories and Cultures', 'Sustainability' and 'Asia and Australia's Engagement with Asia'.

One has to admire the creativeness and ingenuity of the curriculum's authors. No matter how unrelated the subject, one or all three of these priorities are dutifully shoehorned in, rather like Cinderella's ugly sisters trying to wedge their fat feet into the delicate glass slipper. You have four-year-olds in PE classes pondering the impact of systemic racism and discrimination on Aboriginal

Australians or devising raps about climate change in Art classes. In secondary school science, students are writing letters to newspaper editors about environmental issues affecting local ecosystems, and in French, they're organising 'protests or rallies to raise awareness of environmental, social or ethical issues such as le réchauffement de la planète, les droits des populations indigènes, le développement durable, les préjugés, la discrimination.' Given the Frenchman's penchant for protesting, this may be the one example that is not entirely far-fetched.

In general, however, the presence of these priorities is confusing for both teachers and students and detracts from the actual subject. At last count, the mathematics curriculum runs to 3,484 pages. In contrast, Singapore's primary mathematics curriculum is 49 pages long, with the various secondary school syllabuses coming in at well under 100 pages. Many Australian children cannot tell how much petrol is left in the tank from reading a fuel gauge or calculate the correct dose of medication. Meanwhile, Singaporean children who are participating in the junior division of the Singapore Mathematics Olympiad are able to work out the answers to questions like this:

> A painting job can be completed by Team A alone in 2.5 hours or by Team B alone in 75 minutes. On one occasion, after Team A had completed a fraction m/n of the job, Team B took over immediately. The whole painting job was completed in 1.5 hours. If *m and n* are positive integers with no common factors, find the value of $m+n$.

The answer, in case you are wondering, is 6.

In 2024, only 51 per cent of Australian students reached the National Proficient Standard in mathematics. Just 12 per cent performed at a high level, compared to 41 per cent in Singapore. Meanwhile, 26 per cent of Australian students are classified as low performers, more than three times the rate in Singapore, which is 8 per cent. The contrast is not just statistical; it is philosophical. Singapore's maths curriculum is shorter, sharper, and focused on mastery. It is actually about maths. Australia's, by contrast, is long-winded, bloated and incoherent. This is not a difficult problem to solve; just strip the curriculum of the ideological dross. But as yet, neither conservative nor Labor governments have had the political will, and as a result, children continue to suffer.

Turning children into indoctrinated, illiterate, and innumerate pupils, paralysed by climate anxiety, and all in the name of progress, is unforgivable. Small wonder, then, that parents are beginning to rethink their relationship with both kindergartens and schools, and are looking beyond the system altogether.

8

The State Wants Your Child

None of what has been discussed in this book so far can be understood in isolation. It all comes back to a larger reality, which is that what the state wants for children, and what parents want for children, are often diametrically opposed. Worse still, the state is doing a poor job of it, perhaps not surprisingly given that few things government touches are a roaring success. Yet failure alone would be one thing; failure combined with secrecy is quite another. Parents find themselves shut out of their child's formation, while the state exercises greater control combined with ever less transparency. This is an uneasy arrangement which sits at the heart of our current educational crisis, and it is here that the battle lines are being drawn.

And this is an arrangement that Clare Page discovered in 2023 when her fifteen-year-old daughter returned home from her school in southeast London disturbed by what she had learned in a Relationships and Sex Education (RSE) class. She had been told that society is 'heteronormative', and that this was a bad thing, and had been instructed to be 'sex positive' in her relationships. The lesson had been delivered by a third-party organisation, the School of Sexuality Education.[290] When Page requested the lesson plans and materials, the school refused. On further investigation, she discovered that one of the group's educators described themselves as a 'master fetish trainer' and that others delivering lessons 'had commercial interests in the sex industry'.[291] When she contacted the good folk at the School of Sexuality Education directly to see what they were teaching her child, they declined. Shockingly, instead of offering sympathy, the school's head teacher accused *her* of harassing the School of Sexuality Education, effectively slamming the door in her face.

The common saying that, 'when one door closes, another door opens' found quite the exception in Clare Page's journey to uncover the truth. After submitting Freedom of Information requests to access the lesson materials, she was blocked by the School of Sexuality Education which hid behind 'confidentiality' and 'copyright protections'. Undeterred, she then appealed to the Information Commissioner's Office (ICO), only to be told that the provider's copyright and commercial interests outweighed her right to know what her child was learning in school. Still not giving up, she pursued the matter to a first-tier tribunal, only for the tribunal to uphold the ICO's decision. In other words, three separate authorities sided not with the concerned parent, but with a private, ideologically driven organisation delivering highly questionable messages in schools. It's no wonder that parents are beginning to feel the entire system is not exactly on their side.

Although ministers only signalled in 2024 that parents should be able to see RSE materials, the July 2025 Statutory Guidance now gives parents a legal right to view all resources used with their child. And schools can no longer hide behind claims of commercial confidentiality or copyright. If parents still meet a closed door in practice, that only sharpens the underlying question: why are mothers and fathers being locked out of their own children's education? And the deeper question, on which society now seems divided, remains: to whom do children ultimately belong? Their parents, or the state?

The Great Abdication: Parents Step Back, the State Steps In

Many parents, either willingly or through circumstances, have waived their primary responsibility to care for their children, to ensure their wellbeing and pass on their culture. But having relinquished their duties to the state, some by choice, others through exhaustion or economic pressure, they have had quite a rude awakening. It turns out that the state's vision for their children is not quite the same as their own. Whereas most parents would prefer a literate, numerate, emotionally grounded, child who is prepared for a life of success, the state is hell-bent on producing ideologically re-engineered revolutionaries, programmed to fight against 'oppression', racism, sexism, bigotry, their own biology, and even the climate. If the education system were a business, parents would be asking for their money back.

Either that, or it would have gone into receivership long ago. Not just on account of failing to deliver the basics, but because of the way it treats its shareholders. Schools have adopted an attitude of 'we know best', behind which sit the government, unions and activist organisations. This is mainly because they genuinely believe that your children belong to them. At the conclusion of his speech at the 2025 Annual Conference, Daniel Kebede, General Secretary of the National Education Union, declared that 'It is what our parents demand and our children need!'[292]

Across the Atlantic, Kebede's colleague Randi Weingarten, President of the American Federation of Teachers, struck a similar tone. 'We are in a moment like never before,' she posted on X, 'and it's up to us to show up for our kids and communities, to defend democracy, and to envision a bold future where everyone can thrive.' The response from many American parents was swift and sharp: 'Our children, not your children.' When launching her new book online *Why Fascists Fear*

Teachers (2025), the fascists being those on the side of parents, Weingarten sported a T-Shirt emblazoned with *Protect Our Kids and Communities.*

While Kebede and Weingarten could not be more confident in their certitude, others appear to be rather hazy when it comes to the question of proprietorship. This confusion is laid bare in Joanna Williams' report, *Teachers or Parents: Who is responsible for raising the next generation?* which reveals that increasing numbers of children are being dropped off in nappies at the school gates, because they haven't the faintest idea about how to sit on a toilet. Teachers are reporting that a significant amount of the school day is spent cleaning up after bathroom related 'accidents', as well as helping children to dress and feed themselves. What is more, a third of children starting primary school are unable to hold a pencil or count to 10, while a quarter lack basic language skills. Teachers are understandably peeved, and justifiably so. They lose around 2.5 hours every day changing nappies, putting on shoes and buttoning up jackets. The term to describe this state of affairs is that they are not 'school ready'.[293] A more accurate term would be that they are not 'life ready', making their debut into society as helpless creatures at the mercy of strangers.

When asked why exactly it was that their five-year-olds were completely unprepared for life, 49 per cent of parents said that they didn't think it was really part of their job description. Meanwhile, the same proportion admitted to spending much more time on electronic devices than they did their progeny; scrolling through Instagram is much, much easier than running around after your toddler with a potty. As one teacher commented, 'Even when [parents] do know what the expectations are, they're fully aware their child's not there, but they may not have the resources, the knowledge, or the motivation to do anything about it anyway.'[294] This is a mess of the first order. The lines between parent and teacher have become so blurred that, as Williams points out in her report, the 'confusion all too readily morphs into blame, with each party accusing the other of not fulfilling their obligations. This, in turn, can prompt conflict. When children see their parents and teachers disagreeing, collective adult authority is undermined.'[295] Nobody wins in this sorry state of affairs.

But how did this collective abnegation of responsibility happen? Why have we let the state jostle into first position when it comes to child rearing? The answer lies with our old friends, Rousseau, Dewey, and Freire. Each man, in his own distinct way, contributed to the erosion of the family, which is the building block of society, by driving a wedge between parent and offspring, and leaving a gap into which the establishment has been quick to insert itself.

In *Émile, or On Education* (1762), Rousseau removes the little boy from his corrupting parents (the biggest corruptor of all being his mother!) and hands him over to a tutor. Rousseau planted the seed that children should be entrusted to the intellectual elite for their formation. Later, John Dewey would water that seed with his progressive vision that education was not about transmitting knowledge or faith from parent to child, but about preparing the child for political life. The home was not central but was incidental, perhaps even obstructive. The school, by contrast, became the surrogate parent, better aligned with the needs of the state and the future, than with the parochial loyalties of the family. By the time we arrive at Paulo Freire, the mission has become overtly revolutionary. In *Pedagogy of the Oppressed*, education is all about 'consciousness-raising'. The child is not to be nurtured but awakened, stirred into political struggle, questioning all forms of authority: religious, cultural, familial. Parents are no longer to be thought of as guides, but as potential agents of the oppressive system.

Fast forward to the twenty first century and we find the heirs of this movement claiming that parents never even had any rights over their children in the first place. According to some academics, parental rights are 'fiction', and that the only thing that should be afforded to them by law is a revocable 'child-rearing privilege'. The state, they say, has both the right and the duty to override parents in order to instil the 'substantive values' it deems essential.[296] In the UK, the Children Act 1989 deliberately replaced talk of 'parental rights' with the softer notion of 'parental responsibility'. The same move is reinforced by the UN, whose Convention on the Rights of the Child elevates the child's 'best interests' above parental authority, a principle that, in practice, places ultimate decision-making power in the hands of bureaucrats rather than mothers and fathers.[297]

An op ed in *The Washington Post* perfectly encapsulates the warped consensus among progressive education theorists with a piece entitled 'Parents claim they have the right to shape their kids' school curriculum. They don't.' The authors insist that the idea of parental rights is not a return to tradition, but a 'radical' innovation, that Critical Race Theory is a paranoid conspiracy, and that education must 'divide child from parent' for the child's own good. To add insult to injury, the article informs parents that if they are unhappy with the status quo, they can always opt out of the system and pay for private schooling.[298] So much for equity and inclusion. In this view, the state, not the family, is the rightful steward of the child. The task of shaping the child must therefore fall to teachers, to schools, to counsellors and to activist third parties. To anyone but the child's parents themselves.

What parents don't expect however, is the state turning their children against them. In climate change education, small children are urged to castigate their parents for eating too much meat, driving a petrol car, or, the worst sin of all, failing to separate plastics from cardboard. Researchers at an Australian university recruited seven-year-olds as part of 'Idle Off' project, which involved inveigling small children to nag their parents about turning their engines off whilst waiting for them at the school gates. During the day, children were put to work on a series of posters with captions such as 'Turn off your cars, you're going to die!!!' and 'Do you really want to make the environment worse?'[299] Even 'Comrade, report the enemy, even if he is your father!' would not have been completely out of place in this scenario.

But if climate change lessons turn children into parental scolds, sex education and gender ideology go further still: they cut parents out altogether. Parents are increasingly excluded from decision-making, dismissed as uninformed, and in some cases, legally prevented from knowing what their children are being told. To transform a child's worldview, you must first separate them from those who shaped their first one. This is why ideological education must bypass the home. When parents like Clare Page raise questions, they are, to use a pun, stonewalled, and not just figuratively. Stonewall, the influential LGBT charity, has actively encouraged schools to hide student name changes, pronouns, and 'gender identity' from parents. Some schools, following this advice, have even refused to disclose lesson content, citing student 'confidentiality' and 'privacy'.[300] In England, the 2023 *Asleep at the Wheel* report found that only 28 per cent of parents are reliably informed when their child expresses gender distress at school.[301] 'Parents have reported a mixture of evasiveness, secrecy and unfair treatment concerning enquiries they have made about RSE…Worryingly, some of this secrecy and discounting of parental wishes is clearly advocated by leading providers of RSE resources.'[302]

In February 2026, the Department for Education published draft revisions to its Keeping Children Safe in Education guidance. The proposals make clear that children as young as four may be 'socially transitioned' within school settings without clinical oversight and, in some cases, without their parents being informed — a position that would have been considered extraordinary only a few years ago.

In Australia, the same pattern is emerging. In some states, schools are legally permitted to socially transition a student without ever informing the family, provided the child is deemed a 'mature minor' by a principal or teacher. They do not have to undergo a psychological assessment, and there is no external oversight. Even the Australian Human Rights Commission and state education departments have issued guidance suggesting that student autonomy and privacy can outweigh parental rights. And the repercussions of this state-sanctioned secrecy are not insignificant, for it pits sons and daughters against their mothers and fathers, disturbing the precious unity of the family.

In one school, we hear that the 'wellbeing team' sent students confidential emails offering 'gender support' and explicitly reassuring them that 'If you choose to fill this out, your information will be private and we will not out you!'[303] Who are they promising to not 'out' the recipient of the clandestine correspondence to? It's clearly not the local constabulary. Here, the team is offering itself as an alternative to the child's family, with the chilling subtext 'your parents don't love you, but we do'. In another documented case, an autistic girl socially transitioned at school for months without her parents' knowledge. Her father, heartbroken, called it a 'complete betrayal of trust', made all the worse by the fact that 'this is a kid who only found out last year that Santa wasn't real.'[304] After all, what's the real difference between believing that a fat man in a red suit flies through the sky in a sleigh delivering presents, and believing that changing your name and declaring your pronouns to be 'he/him' will magically turn you into a boy?

In the United States, the situation is more legally fraught, but just as dire. A 2023 investigation by Parents Defending Education found that over 1,000 school districts, serving more than 10 million students, had adopted policies allowing, or even requiring, teachers to keep a child's gender transition secret from parents. Staff were told to use the child's chosen name and pronouns at school and then switch back to legal names and biological sex in emails or calls with the family. This is not passive neglect. Parental rights are being actively overridden. In a country known for its litigiousness, American parents are now filing lawsuits 'from coast to coast' to wrestle their rights back from the state. Yet, the gulf between parent and educator is not narrowing. One school superintendent dismissed parental concerns as nothing more than 'intolerance of LGBTQ people thinly veiled behind a camouflage of parental rights.'[305]

And this is the key point. Parents have put all their trust in the system, misguidedly believing that it cares as much for their children as they do. The sooner they realise the truth, the better. Families are being left battered and broken, caught in a tug of war with schools who are encouraging children, some as young as six or seven, to regard their families as the enemy and to lead double lives. The Cass Review describes how parents 'expressed concern about their child being socially transitioned without their involvement' and that they had felt compelled to 'affirm their child's assumed identity or risk being painted as transphobic and unsupportive.'[306] While indescribably painful for the parent, we must also consider the psychological toll on the child who is having to juggle two realities simultaneously.

While research on secret social transitioning is scarce (largely because it is framed positively in most academic discourse), child psychology does give us clear warnings about the harm of 'double life' situations. Child

Psychologist Clare Rowe comments that 'asking a child to conceal a core aspect of their daily identity from their parents creates what psychologists call role conflict – a form really of chronic stress where the demands of two environments are incompatible' and that 'over time, this can produce anxiety, hypervigilance, and identity confusion. Children in these situations can feel isolated and mistrustful and may struggle to integrate a coherent sense of self.' [307]

Finally, we need to consider who is to protect the child from danger, confusion, psychological burden, or identity instability, when the adults closest to them are cut out of the loop? Parents, barring cases of proven harm, should be the first port of call, not the last to know. Schools should be working with families, not against them. Because if we have reached a point where children are being trained to hide who they are from their own parents, then the system is broken and dangerous.

The Parental Rebellion: Opting Out

It is no wonder that parents are abandoning the system in droves. Once equated with 'end of world' cults and alternative lifestyles, the homeschooling movement has been growing rapidly in Britain, Australia, and the US. Covid is often cited as one of the main triggers, as parents were confronted with what their children were actually being exposed to, and realised that they could, in some cases, do a better job than teachers. In twelve years, homeschooling in the UK has tripled. In 2014, there were about 34,000 children being taught at home. Over the 2023/24 academic year, this number grew to 153,300 children, which is up from an estimated 126,100 the previous year.[308] In England, local authorities reported that 111,700 children were in elective home education (EHE), which is an increase from an estimated 92,000 in the previous autumn term.[309]

In Australia, over 45,000 students were registered for home education in 2024, almost double the figure in 2020. Still, in raw numbers, it's a drop in the ocean, with only 1.1 per cent of all Australian children and 1.5 per cent of children in the UK, and around 6 per cent of children in the US.

But where it becomes interesting is why parents are taking their children out of schools. In Australia, most were removed due to bullying, unmet special educational needs, or dissatisfaction with academic standards, though a notable minority cited a desire to shield their children from what they saw as politicised or activist teaching. In Queensland, surveys found that around 18 per cent of homeschooling families gave this reason.[310] Surveys in the US show the top two reasons for homeschooling are 'concern about environments at other schools' and 'dissatisfaction with academic instruction', which 'is a rejection of mainstream schools and, by extension, the professionals who run them.'[311] Still, in raw numbers, it's a drop in the ocean, with only 1 per cent of all Australian children and 1.4 per cent of children in the UK, and 6 per cent of children in the US.

But where it becomes interesting is why parents are taking their children out of schools. Surveys in the US show the top two reasons for homeschooling are 'concern about environments at other schools' and 'dissatisfaction with academic instruction', which 'is a rejection of mainstream schools and, by extension, the professionals who run them.'[312]

According to the DfE's national census for the Autumn Term 2024, the most common recorded reasons for British parents withdrawing children from school fall into five broad categories: Philosophical/Lifestyle/Religious (24.3 per cent), School Dissatisfaction (12.7 per cent), Health-Related (16.3 per cent), Administrative/Logistical (4.0 per cent), and a vast, opaque block of Unknown/No reason given/Other (43 per cent).[313] Insofar as the 'Philosophical' category is concerned, the DfE does not mean that parents are upset that too many teachers think of themselves primarily as Platonists rather than Aristotelians, or that there is too much Epicureanism and not enough Stoicism in the public education system. It is simply a polite way of referring to radical theories which, ironically, are devoid of philosophy.

What is more, these categories are hardly mutually exclusive, as illustrated with the testimony of one homeschooling parent who took her son out of school because he 'became completely overwhelmed by the school's LGBTQ agenda and sexualisation of children. He had nightmares and said that he wanted to die. He thought that he had to become a girl.'[314] As such, if we were to combine Philosophical, School Dissatisfaction and Health related, the official data alone suggests that over a third of cases (37 per cent) are clearly linked to values, beliefs, or dissatisfaction with what schools provide.

Yet this is almost certainly an undercount. The 'vague' category is a catch-all for missing data, parental refusals to explain, and reasons too politically awkward to record, such as objections to sex education, radical gender theory and climate activism. If even a quarter of that vague block concealed ideological motives, the share rises to nearly half. If half, the share rises to 58 per cent. If three-quarters, to almost 70 per cent. In other words, the official narrative dramatically underplays the extent to which parents are rejecting the cultural and ideological direction of the school system. The real figure is likely not just a significant minority, but possibly a majority of parents who are quietly but decisively rebelling against the system.

Independent surveys reinforce this picture. A 2022 report compiled by Education Otherwise based on a survey of 3,168 homeschooling parents, reveals that the most common reason was that home education provides a better education than school, at 40 per cent. 'General dissatisfaction' with school ranked second with 21 per cent, followed by the 'school curriculum not relevant or suitable' with 9 per cent, 'Health needs', including the child's mental health with 13 per cent, 'the school being unable to meet the child's special needs' with 10 per cent and 'bullying at school,' with 4 per cent. Two years later, the 2024 *Changing Cohorts* report painted a still sharper picture. It noted that growing numbers of parents were 'voting with their feet to remove their children from schools which they consider do not meet their children's needs,' with rising withdrawals linked not only to SEND (Special Education Needs and Disabilities) and bullying, but also to frustration with the quality and character of education itself.[315]

This is a damning indictment of a system that cannot even meet parents' most basic expectations. As one parent put it: 'There is no evidence that the National Curriculum constitutes an education, and millions of schooled children leave school without being able to read or add up. How can you possibly say that the UK has a "world class" education system?'[316] And yet many people do say this, including some politicians. And what's more, they say it with complete conviction. In a speech to the Centre for Social Justice in 2025, Education Secretary Bridget Phillipson declared: 'For the vast majority of parents in our country, what they want is a fantastic state education for their children. That's what we're delivering. That's what we're investing in.'[317] This statement will ring hollow to many of the parents who have withdrawn their children, not least because the official attitude towards home educators remains openly dismissive. One public official summed it up neatly: 'I don't really agree with home learning, some parents don't have any knowledge at all, what gives them the right to think they can home school their children, how do we know they are doing a good job?'[318] Given the current state of things, it would be nigh impossible to do a worse job.

Despite the absence of official UK performance data, international and historical studies consistently show that homeschooled children often outperform their traditionally schooled peers, particularly in literacy and general subject knowledge. A peer-reviewed *Journal of School Choice* overview found that of 14 quantitative studies on achievement, 78 per cent showed a clear academic advantage for homeschooled students. Research from the National Home Education Research Institute in the US similarly reports that home-educated children typically score 15 to 30 percentile points above average on standardised tests, regardless of parental income or education.[319]

Yet even as these results accumulate, the Starmer government is pushing ahead with a Bill that is not, it is fair to say, in the best interests of parents. Presented as a measure to improve child welfare and educational standards, the Children's Wellbeing and Schools Bill has been described by critics as an 'unprecedented intrusion into family life' that 'expands state power at the expense of families' and 'paves the way for a dangerous system of government surveillance, forced schooling, and punitive measures against parents.'[320] If parents felt beleaguered before this Bill, they will feel positively persecuted now. In many ways, it is the logical extension of a worldview dominant among progressive ideologues in government and education: that the state, not the family, should raise children, and that schools exist not primarily to teach literacy, numeracy, and knowledge, but to shape young minds into ideological activists.

In the US, Harvard Law professor Elizabeth Bartholet goes one step further, calling for a presumptive ban altogether. Her view is that homeschooling keeps children from the 'scrutiny of teachers and other professionals' and that it violates children's rights to a 'meaningful education' as well as protection from potential abuse. For Bartholet, abuse includes those parents who harbour 'conservative Christian convictions' and who will 'deliberately seek to withdraw their children from mainstream culture.' She portrays some of these parents as 'extreme religious ideologues' who question science and promote female subservience and even white supremacy. Bartholet reveals what truly troubles her: not poor outcomes or safeguarding failures, but parental authority itself. Her conclusion is stark: leaving children at home with their parents is, in her words, the most perilous arrangement of all. Channelling her inner Paulo Freire, she says 'I think it's always dangerous to put powerful people in charge of the powerless, and to give the powerful ones total authority.' [321] Spoken like a true apparatchik of the state.

Homeschooling is the clearest possible statement that a parent has lost complete faith in the state's educational offering, and not only that, are prepared to shoulder the full weight of responsibility themselves rather than submit their children to an environment they consider harmful. The reaction from the establishment is telling. There is no self-reflection, no pause to ask why so many families are leaving. Not once do we hear an admission that parents might be justified in trying to protect their five-year-olds from being told that they might have the wrong body parts. Instead, there is only a renewed, and perversely determined effort to control or even ban homeschooling altogether.

Parental Rebellion: Opting In

Where things get really interesting in this almighty tussle between parents and the establishment is when the public decides not to opt out but to stay and fight. Nowhere is this more gripping than in America, where parents have been turning up at school board meetings, running for parent-teacher associations, and building grassroots groups determined to wrest back control of what their children are taught.

At the centre of this insurgency are organisations such as Moms for America, which has over half a million members, and which focuses on grassroots mobilisation by training parents to challenge their local school boards and claim influence over dozens of elections. Another group, Moms for Liberty, founded in 2021 by three mothers in response to Covid school closures and mask mandates has broadened into a campaign against state indoctrination. Today it boasts more than 115,000 members and nearly 300 chapters across the country, and in 2022 it endorsed almost 500 school board candidates; more than half of them won. In Virginia, parents' outrage over Critical Race Theory helped sweep Republican Glenn Youngkin to victory in a state long considered safely Democrat.

The backlash against these movements has been vigorous, to say the least, because they have real political clout. The Southern Poverty Law Center piled on with its cheery *Year of Hate and Extremism* report (one can only imagine the Christmas party) slotting Moms for Liberty alongside the Ku Klux Klan and neo-Nazis. In Massachusetts, police training materials went further still, branding the group a 'hate organisation' in a course entitled *Freedom and Hate*.[322] In other words, ordinary mothers and fathers have been reclassified as literal enemies of the state. Within a generation, we have travelled from the notion that parents may not be the best educators, to the claim that they have no rights at all, to the astonishing reality that they are treated as dangerous subversives.

Britain's parents' movement is more polite, less brash, but stirring, nonetheless. Campaigns like Scrap the Schools Bill attracted more than 30,000 signatures, forcing ministers to retreat from proposals seen as authoritarian. In 2025, a broad coalition of home-educators, SEND advocates, faith leaders, and children's rights campaigners marched on Whitehall in the March for Children, flooding Parliament Square with banners declaring, 'No law can compel conscience'. Groups such as Safe Schools Alliance, Transgender Trend, Don't Divide Us, and Hands Off Our Children add intellectual firepower and grassroots reach.

But ultimately, all these battles over curricula, ideology, and parental rights are not isolated skirmishes. They are part of a larger war over the child. And if the state is prepared to fight this hard to keep every child within its grasp, then we must ask why. Why is it so determined that children be funnelled through the system? Why does the state want your children? Because it can't have any of its own. The only way it can survive is by taking the next generation. This is why it must recruit your children. Every state knows: whoever educates the children owns the future. A state monopoly produces citizens who are easier to govern, less likely to question, and more easily moulded to the prevailing ideology. If the system is broken, dangerous, and increasingly hostile to families, the question is no longer merely *what is wrong,* but *what must be done.* The next chapter turns from diagnosis to prescription: how parents, educators, and communities can begin to rebuild an education worthy of the children it claims to serve.

Conclusion

Here's a novel thought. The current education system is neither failing, nor is it broken. It's working exactly as its architects intended. What the system is interested in, and pursues with a monomaniacal obsession across the Anglosphere, is creating ideologically aligned, thoroughly malleable cogs in the machine. It is producing conformists and activists who are angry about the past, bitter about the present, and terrified of the future, and who will be ready and willing to help bring about a better, equitable, and socially just new world. Everything, then, is going perfectly according to plan.

Its genius, or its wickedness (depending on whether you are inside or outside the education system), lies in the fact that these cogs are not only unaware they are cogs, but unaware that there is a machine at all. The other genius is that they have been convinced that they are the rebels, bravely resisting the establishment, with all its heteronormativity, when in fact they are falling into lockstep with the establishment and unwittingly doing its bidding.

This is a system which has long abandoned any pretence of wanting to produce great men and women, or people who can think independently, who delight in the cut and thrust of debate, or who have enough humility to learn from our ancestors rather than pull down their statues. And of course, it is blindingly obvious that it prioritises ideology over teaching children how to read and write. We have known how to do this for centuries, and in many parts of the world, it is still known. It is hardly rocket science. But if we continue, say, to replace the maths curriculum with 'math ethnic studies', or teach addition through Aboriginal dance, there won't *be* any rocket science, because no one will be able to do the maths.

But we cannot say that we were not warned. In *The Closing of the American Mind,* Allan Bloom pre-empted 'identity politics' before it was even a thing. He thought that one of the most damaging beliefs of all for the university student was 'there is no truth, only opinion', which left the young rootless and incapable of critical thought. His call for a return to the canon brought criticism from his friends and colleagues, who called him a 'cranky conservative', 'elitist', 'sexist', 'Eurocentric', 'nostalgist', 'moral scold', and 'reactionary'. One critic even decreed that his was a book that 'decent people would have been ashamed to have written.'[323] Given that by the end of

1988, Bloom had sold 1 million copies, his was clearly a book that many decent people were not ashamed to read.

E.D Hirsch, who was a lifelong Democrat, also fell afoul of the establishment after exposing how progressive ideas deprived children of the cultural literacy they needed to function as free citizens. Accused of propagating 'cultural conservatism' and of being 'blind to multiculturalism', Hirsch's core-knowledge lists of names, dates, and concepts were dismissed as 'Eurocentric, patriarchal, and marginalising non-Western voices'. Teachers' unions and theorists were especially disturbed by his exhortation to memorise facts, which they referred to as 'drill and kill'. His critics were not early climate change activists worried about fossil fuels killing the environment, but proponents of the absurd notion that knowledge is an impediment to the children reaching their full creative potential.

Roger Scruton spent decades warning everyone that British schools and universities were sliding into ideological indoctrination, hollowing out the canon, and replacing scholarship with activism. He was vilified and cancelled repeatedly, yet his predictions about 'oikophobia', that is, hatred of one's own culture or civilisation, and the destruction of Western tradition now look prophetic. Are modern-day, decolonisation-infused history lessons anything other than instructions on how to be oikophobic? In her 1996 *All Must Have*

Prizes, Melanie Phillips, much like Bloom, cautioned that the rejection of objective truth and knowledge was wreaking devastation in schools, while children were left to 'explore their feelings' instead of being taught hard knowledge.[324] She too was mocked and marginalised as 'reactionary'. It turns out that the establishment does not take kindly to criticism.

We Have Been Here Before

Astute readers will know that this is hardly the first time in history that children have been hijacked by the state. They will also be aware that it has never ended particularly well. In Stalin's Soviet Union, children were to be shaped by the state's ideals into the 'New Soviet Child', while school lessons and propaganda glorified obedience to the Party above parental authority. Denouncing family members became framed as heroic, and loyalty to family was secondary to loyalty to the Party. In Maoist China, the Cultural Revolution turned schoolchildren into violent ideological enforcers, rewarded for turning on teachers and parents who showed 'counter-revolutionary' tendencies. Education was reduced to slogans, political theatre, and re-education camps. The damage reverberated for generations. In Germany, the Hitler Youth used children to bring about its goal of replacing family, church, and class-based social distinctions with a unified Volksgemeinschaft (people's community), totally subordinated to the state. And in Communist East Germany, schools and youth organisations promoted loyalty to the Socialist Unity Party (SED) and encouraged children to report 'anti-socialist' comments at home. Each attempt ended in mass suffering and collapse.

In 1920, Alexandra Kollontai, a leading Bolshevik and the Soviet Union's first Commissar for Welfare, declared that 'the responsibility for the child is passing from the family to the collective,' so that a 'new person' could be forged. For her, the traditional family was 'narrow and petty'.[325] A century earlier, Edmund Burke had already foreseen the danger. In *Reflections on the Revolution in France* (1790), he warned that revolutionaries would attempt to 'begin the world anew' by severing the chain between the generations. Society, Burke insisted, is a contract 'between those who are living, those who are dead, and those who are to be born.'[326] It is precisely this contract that today's regime is breaking, at great cost to the children entrusted to it. Even though today's commissars of education are more cautious in their vocabulary, using 'inclusion', 'equity', 'wellbeing', and 'global citizenship', the underlying ambition is much the same: to form children who reflect the values of the state, rather than those of their parents. The Soviets called it the 'new person'. We might call it the same thing.

The New Person

But what exactly does the contemporary Western version of the state-created 'new person' look like? In many cases utterly miserable, nihilistic, and sometimes suicidal. In an interview with a psychologist about why it was that some teens feel helpless or even suicidal, one such 'new person' replied, 'When we're struggling in school, we're told that going to school is a privilege, but when you're a teenager, it doesn't feel like that. You think about the big picture and the fact that in 100 years you'll be dead, and no one is going to remember you anyway, and it makes you feel like life is meaningless: So why even try?'[327] Why indeed. If you are taught that meaning can only be found through political activism, there is no point to anything if you are not out pulling down statues or vandalising paintings.

This is the fate of Gen Z, those born after 1997, whom Jonathan Haidt has rightly called the 'anxious generation'. He traces their plight to over-protection in the real world, and under-protection in the virtual one, suggesting that the appearance of the smartphone in 2012 coincided with rising rates of anxiety, depression, self-harm, and suicide.

The data bear this out. In the United States, emergency-department visits for self-harm among 10-14-year-old girls nearly tripled between 2010 and 2020, while among 15-19-year-olds they rose by more than 60 per cent. In the United Kingdom, hospital admissions for self-harm in girls have roughly doubled since 2010, while boys also showed increases, though from a lower base. In Australia, government health data report sharp rises in youth self-harm hospitalisations over the past decade – about 50 per cent for girls and 20 per cent for boys.[328]

But Haidt misses one crucial dimension. The advent of the smartphone arrived just as 'social justice' education was taking hold in schools, and in the last quarter century it has grown into a multi-headed hydra of anti-racism, decolonisation, sex education, and climate activism. Moreover, the content fed to children in the classroom is simply reinforced and magnified online via social media, so that they can't even escape it at home. Social media is simply the simulacrum of the classroom. The result is a perfect storm of indoctrination and despair.

Governments have responded to the dangers of social media by presenting themselves as guardians of childhood and by drafting laws to punish tech companies, mandating age checks, and even rolling out facial-recognition IDs in the name of 'safety'. Yet when we consider what children are being exposed to in schools, the hypocrisy is staggering. The real harm is not confined to screens but is inflicted daily in classrooms, sanctioned and facilitated by the state itself. If the British government were truly concerned about children's wellbeing, it would stop schools from hiring third-party providers such as Split Banana, which we discussed in Chapter Four, with its *Simple Guide to Great Sex-ed: How to Talk About Porn*, or the authors of classroom resources like *Masturbation – A Hands-on Guide*.[329]

After investigating the American public schooling system in *Race to the Bottom*, journalist Luke Rosiak concluded that sending your child to a public school is akin to 'child abuse'.[330] Critics will no doubt accuse Rosiak of moral panic and hysteria, but what else can we possibly call it? What else is it but abuse to burden children with adult sexual content at an age when they should be free to imagine, play, and grow without such intrusions? What else but cruelty to tell a child there is no such thing as truth, not even the truth of his own biological sex, so that he is left to drift forever in a sea of subjectivity? And what else but perverse to take the very institution meant to nurture children's growth, and twist it so that it stunts them instead?

But here's something to consider. What Rosiak describes in contemporary America, Aquinas had already diagnosed while writing the *Summa Theologica* in 13th-century Paris and Naples. To paraphrase Shelley, Aquinas would have looked upon the works of the critical theorists and despaired: despaired that children have become casualties in an unwinnable war against the natural order or the natural law. By this he meant that everyone is born with a knowledge of God and His law (eternal law) which can be accessed through reason. The fundamental principle of natural law is that good must be pursued and evil avoided, and that all people are naturally inclined to preserve life, nurture families, seek truth, live in community, and turn toward the divine. In simple terms, natural law is simply reason recognising that good is to be pursued. For Aquinas, this law was not a doctrine for Christians alone, but universal and accessible to all people through reason, whether they recognised its divine source or not.

On that basis, he concluded that human beings flourish only when they live in accordance with natural law: their created nature, rational and bodily, social and directed to God. Aquinas would have recognised that radical gender theory, intersectionality, Critical Race Theory, queer theory, fat studies, and the whole relativist postmodernist madness unleashed since the 1930s amounts to a wholesale rebellion against the natural order. And he would not have been surprised to learn that children taught this madness are turning against existence itself. They are anxious about the earth, anxious about themselves, and anxious about their countries. To raise children in this way is to disorder their lives, and disorder inevitably yields confusion and despair.

In *The Last Superstition*, philosopher Edward Feser draws the line clearly. The collapse of classical metaphysics, especially the abandonment of natural law and objective morality, has not led to enlightenment but to chaos. Feser identifies relativism as the 'last superstition', a dangerous belief that truth is subjective and morality a mere social construct. This worldview, he warns, has devastating consequences for children. They are no longer taught to seek what is good, true, and beautiful, but are instead indoctrinated with ideological fictions that distort their grasp of reality. When natural law is cast aside, childhood innocence is not preserved but politicised, pathologised, and ultimately destroyed.

Nil desperandum

Yet, for all the despair outlined in the pages of this book, there is genuine reason for hope. The architects of our new ideological education assumed that once indoctrinated, the youngest generation would carry their project forward without question. Far from passively absorbing every ideological label, they are beginning to resist. Aquinas would have been heartened by the fact that many of these children are rebelling against the rebellion. Having been offered only disorder and insanity, they are now seeking order and sanity. Having been raised on ideology, they are turning back to tradition, transcendence, and truth. One sign of this quiet revolt is that young people are making their way back to church.

In a recent survey, *The Quiet Revival*, commissioned by the Bible Society and conducted by YouGov, the number of eighteen to twenty-four-year-olds attending church in England and Wales has quadrupled, rising from just 4 per cent in 2018 to 16 per cent in 2024. Young men are particularly enthusiastic to take their place once again in pews. In 2018 only 4 per cent were going to church; by 2024 it was 21 per cent.[331]

The evidence also shows that those who believe in something beyond ideology are healthier in spirit as well as in mind. *The Quiet Revival* survey reports that young people returning to church describe themselves as less lonely, more hopeful, and more resilient than their peers. Even the World Health Organization, not exactly known for promoting spirituality, has now found that it matters. In its collaborative *Health Behaviour in School aged Children (HBSC)* study, which surveyed more than 42,000 children across eight countries, researchers reported that those with stronger spiritual health, especially a sense of meaning, purpose, and joy, consistently had better mental health and fewer symptoms of despair.[332] In short, even the WHO's own data now admits what common sense has long told us: children need a sense of purpose, not a constant barrage of nihilist propaganda.

While these are marginal shifts, they are shifts nonetheless, and signs of a generational backlash against the indoctrinators. They are waking up to what is being done to them. As Rosiak puts it, 'They take children who are joyous, carefree, and effortlessly living in a society that is more multicultural than any of these adults has ever known', he writes, 'and convince them that they are actually living in the midst of horrid oppression – an oppression that can, conveniently, be alleviated only by joining what is essentially a cult that the vast majority of adults would reject as ridiculous.'[333]

This is the cult, the Cult of DEI, that the young are beginning, at last, to reject. Research from King's College London shows that more than a third of British men aged sixteen to twenty-nine dismiss the term 'toxic masculinity' as unhelpful, a rejection rate nearly twice that of their female peers.[334]

The great social engineering project had already begun to falter in Australia in 2019. The ABC's 'Australia Talks' survey revealed that the public was split down the middle on the statement that there are more than two genders: 45 per cent agreed, but 38 per cent disagreed, while 15 per cent refused to endorse either side. This was hardly the universal youth consensus the architects of gender ideology had banked on.[335] When the survey was repeated in 2021, the question itself was gone. Perhaps they didn't want Australians talking about *this* particular issue.

What is to be done?

Let's start with higher education, where this book itself began. As of 2026, there are around 165 recognised universities in the UK. Virtually all are funded by the government, and virtually all are governed by sprawling Equality, Diversity and Inclusion (EDI) bureaucracies. Free speech on campus has become almost non-existent: invited speakers are routinely shouted down or physically driven out by students who also think that words are violence, aided and abetted by a bloated 'woke' bureaucracy. Progressive academics simply cannot see past Critical Theory, decolonisation, intersectionality and the politics of identity. Pity the poor undergraduate who longs for something more than an endless diet of race and gender.

There are, of course, pockets of resistance. A handful of academics still push back against the orthodoxy. But many eventually leave, exhausted and defeated by what political scientist Matthew Goodwin has described in *Bad Education* as 'deeply biased, openly political, highly activist and ideologically homogeneous institutions that have morphed into havens for liberal intolerance, crushing groupthink, and bureaucratic overreach.'[336] Goodwin, incidentally, was one of those who left after twenty years of teaching, much to his mother's chagrin. And if you imagine that Oxbridge remains a safe haven, you are mistaken. It is no coincidence that some of the most egregious examples documented in this book have come from the University of Cambridge itself.

That these censorious, stifling, identity-obsessed institutions have lost their way is incontrovertible. The public assassination of Charlie Kirk while he was holding a campus event at Utah Valley University, is perhaps the strongest argument of all for their catastrophic failure. If the universities were doing what they ought to be doing, that is, exposing students to new ideas, truly encouraging free speech and ultimately loosening the chains of ideological bondage, there would have been no need for Charlie Kirk to spend any time at all on university campuses. But he did. And in doing so, thousands of young Americans gathered to listen to him, converse with him, and debate him. He challenged them with concepts which they simply do not hear from their lecturers. And did not treat them as fragile snowflakes to be protected from 'dangerous' ideas.

Kirk was simply replicating outside what should be happening inside, and in this way, his presence on campuses was ultimately a very public shaming of academia and an exposé of its deficiencies. In addition, when recordings of these encounters spread on social media, they revealed to the world just how radicalised many students had become, especially on gender ideology, and in particular trans ideology. Kirk was hated not because of anything he had done, but because of what he had dared to say. And that fact alone should terrify anyone who still believes universities are places of free thought.

Can anything be salvaged from the wreckage? Some, such as Goodwin, seem to think that it can, proposing that universities are reformable, but not from the inside. The problem is so profound that he believes that we need to take an interventionist approach, which would look something like the Chicago Principles, the framework first adopted by the University of Chicago in 2015 and is widely regarded as the standard for protecting freedom of speech on campus. The principles are simple. The role of the university is to expose, rather than to shield students from ideas that they might find offensive or uncomfortable.[337] It is an attempt to put an end to the snowflakery, victimhood, deplatforming, and closed mindedness born of narrowness of teaching.

While more than 100 American universities have now adopted the Chicago Principles, it is almost impossible to know what the true student-to-snowflake ratio now is. The principles serve mainly as a reminder, and occasionally they give administrators a shield against censorship. But the evidence suggests little has changed in practice. The latest and fifth *College Free Speech Rankings*, compiled by the Foundation for Individual Rights and Expression (FIRE), do not suggest that academics are suddenly running weekly seminars on the glories of Western Civilisation. Even the University of Chicago itself ranked only 43rd out of 251 institutions, with an overall score of 55.2 out of 100, a 'slightly above average', which reads like the report card of a pupil who is failing badly, but whose teacher cannot quite bring herself to write the truth in red ink.

Goodwin believes that if such values were to be enforced in the UK, they would at the very least serve as a reminder to universities that their role is not to police thought, and that the best kind of diversity is intellectual diversity. And Goodwin does have experience in this field, as he was closely involved in the passage of the Higher Education (Freedom of Speech) Act in 2023, which compelled universities to publish codes of practice, nod gravely towards 'academic freedom', and promise not to use NDAs against students. It was progress of a sort, at least an acknowledgement that free thought on campus was under threat.

But since then, the Starmer Labour government has made its own modifications. Most notably, it has removed the right of students to sue universities for censorship, which then lets student unions, often the most zealous censors of all, entirely off the hook.[338] And, most significantly, the Act does not require universities to dismantle their DEI bureaucracies which are, in many cases, holding the institutions ideologically hostage. As long as those bureaucracies remain entrenched, there is little hope of change.

In the middle of 2025, America's elite universities were hit with something they never expected. Washington turned off the money tap. The Trump administration began freezing billions of dollars in federal research grants in response to what it described as 'institutional antisemitism' and entrenched ideological bias on campus. This was not about trimming a few research assistants or scholarships but involved staggering sums.

At Harvard, more than £1.63 billion ($2.2 billion) in active federal research grants was suddenly frozen, halting everything from medical research to space science, until a federal judge in September 2025 ruled the freeze unlawful and ordered the funds restored.

Columbia University saw £296 million ($400 million) frozen in March, followed by another £185 million ($250 million) in April, before it eventually reached a £163 million ($221 million) settlement with the government to restore access under new oversight.[339] Other institutions such as Brown, Penn, Cornell, Princeton, Northwestern, Johns Hopkins, and UCLA faced similar freezes or threats; in UCLA's case, roughly £430 million ($584 million) in grants was frozen before a federal court ordered the money released later that month.

Naturally, most university presidents, 94 per cent to be precise, are convinced that the Trump Administration is waging war on higher education, yet when asked what the most accurate criticism of their sector might be, only 19 per cent pointed to faculty political bias and the lack of a free speech culture, while a mere 9 per cent blamed unfair admissions practices.[340] The overwhelming majority preferred to deny that anything fundamental was wrong at all, which rather proves the Administration's point. And for all their boasting about vast endowments and independence, it turns out that they are not so independent after all.

But many Americans see it differently. Whatever one thinks of Trump, the freeze has exposed a reality: supposedly sovereign institutions have long been propped up by federal support, and Washington can hold them to account if it chooses. Gallup shows public confidence in higher education has risen for the first time in a decade.

In 2015, 57 per cent of Americans expressed confidence in the sector. By 2024, that figure had collapsed to 36 per cent, the lowest ever recorded. Yet in June 2025 it rose to 42 per cent.[341] Coincidental? I wonder.

Ultimately, it appears that 'what is to be done?' cannot be left to the universities themselves. The solution, therefore, lies outside the system. And in this respect, America is leading the way. There, individuals with dedication, energy, and awareness of how precarious things have become, are establishing new universities. Their aim is simple; to restore the university to its true purpose and ensure that they are not beholden to the state.

While hardly new (it is now in its 182nd year), Hillsdale College in Michigan has for the last 42 years refused every cent of government funding. It is an independent, private, conservative Christian liberal arts college. You would struggle to come up with a more left-progressive triggering set of adjectives and nouns if you tried. In addition to offering undergraduate degrees in Business and Economics, Sciences, Social Sciences, and Humanities, the general public can sign up to free, online courses such as 'The Great American Story: A Land of Hope', 'Theology 101: The Western Theological Tradition', 'Great Books of Western Civilisation' and 'Mathematics and Logic: From Euclid to the Modern World'. Titles like these are enough to send progressive activists into full-scale meltdown.

Over in Texas, some remarkable individuals, among them Niall Ferguson, Heather Heying, Bret Weinstein, and Jonathan Haidt, backed the founding of the University of Austin in 2021, with the first students arriving in 2024. 'We are here not just to build a great new college in Austin,' they declared, 'but also to reinvent American higher education for the 21st century as profoundly as Chicago and Stanford did when they were founded more than a century ago, and to grow as rapidly as they did, to become competitors with and influencers of the established northeastern Ivy League institutions.' Their mission is nothing less than to reaffirm 'the fearless pursuit of truth as the core purpose of a university, and the indispensable roles of academic freedom and meritocracy in that mission.'[342] This mission will be made all the more possible following the donation of $100 million by businessman Jeff Yass in November 2025, which guarantees free tuition in perpetuity.

And then there is Ralston College in Savannah, which launched its flagship Master of Arts in the Humanities in 2022. The programme begins in Greece, where students immerse themselves in the study of ancient and modern Greek, before returning to Savannah to grapple with the great works of Western Civilisation. In its first year, Ralston received 3,000 expressions of interest and over 1,000 applicants for only 24 spaces. As its president Stephen Blackwood wrote, 'And how could it not be so? The problem with our culture, and the problem with higher education in particular, is not one of demand. It is a problem of supply; it is a failure to offer what is highest and best, to preserve and pass on what the late Roger Scruton once called, "the things we have loved." The young and indeed the not-so-young, still seek to live lives of purpose, dignity, and self-understanding.'[343]

And the young appear to agree. 'I felt I had missed out on being educated,' commented a Columbia maths graduate. A computer science graduate from MIT admitted that, even after completing her degree, she felt 'some really important part of my soul was missing.' A Princeton alumnus, trained in both classics and psychology, said he had grown 'sick of the destructive' ways the humanities so often treated the classics and that Ralston, at last, offered the antidote.[344] Even further outside the system is the online Peterson Academy, launched in 2024, which proves that the old model of a brick-and-mortar campus can be bypassed altogether. Marketed as offering 'higher education at 1% of the price', it allows anyone, anywhere, to sign up for lectures from world-class academics in history, politics, social science, philosophy, and mathematics. Its existence raises an uncomfortable question: do we really need universities in their current form at all?

Things are not so easy in Britain. The University of Buckingham, founded in the 1970s with the open support of Margaret Thatcher, is the sole, lonely institution which challenges the monopoly. Its radical principle was that universities should be independent of government. Buckingham remains the only British university where a student can still receive an education relatively untouched by the DEI commissars. It even offers a course on 'woke' ideology, taught by Eric Kaufmann, a small but telling act of defiance. Yet even Buckingham is not immune to the reach of the progressive bureaucracy. In 2025, its Vice-Chancellor, James Tooley, was reinstated after having been forced out in what he himself described as a politically motivated plot by his left-wing colleagues.

It is much harder to start a university in the UK than it is in the US. In order to call yourself a 'university', you must secure a Royal Charter or the blessing of the Privy Council, but even if you get to this stage, you are still locked out of the student loan system. In England, a three-year BA is around £27,750, excluding living expenses, but most students do not pay this up front, so the state-backed universities win by default. The government funds the system, and the system reproduces the government's ideology. The situation in Australia is very similar, where starting a university plunges you into a world of red tape and government hoops. Campion College in Sydney, founded in 2006, offers a small but serious liberal arts education rooted in Western Civilisation, while Alphacrucis University College, a Pentecostal university, offers Arts, Education and Ministry, Business and Counselling courses. However difficult, it is still possible to teach, to think, and to pursue truth, provided you can break free from the grip of state funding.

Schools

The only way to fully guarantee children both intellectual formation and freedom from indoctrination is either to do it yourself (homeschooling, co-op, parallel networks) or to build institutions intentionally designed to resist the tide. But what can be done about the schools themselves? Can the public education system be saved, or is it simply a case of starting new institutions? Rosiak is convinced there is no hope for America's public schools. Policymakers may mandate reform, but implementation is left to entrenched insiders such as superintendents, union leaders, and administrators who can ignore, delay, or quietly subvert those reforms. Their record, he points out, is one of manipulating data and keeping parents at bay, so that victories on paper rarely translate into change in classrooms. The rot, Rosiak argues, is simply too deep.

But it does seem that both reform and regeneration are possible in America. At the political level, education has become such a powerful issue that it is reshaping school boards, legislation, and even national elections. Parents are particularly energised, busily forming themselves into highly effective grassroots movements. Across the country, Moms for Liberty and similar groups have won seats on local school boards, removed books such as *Gender Queer*, *All Boys Aren't Blue* and *This Book is Gay* from libraries, and managed to block activist curricula. In Virginia, Glenn Youngkin's 2021 gubernatorial victory, powered by parents angry about CRT and gender ideology in schools, forced state-level reforms. In Florida, Ron DeSantis's 'Stop WOKE Act' and overhaul of civics education has already changed curricula. In February 2026, DeSantis announced that 21,000 teachers had taken a new on-line civics course for teachers where they are taught the full sweep of Western Civilisation. Meanwhile parental rights laws now give families more control over what is taught.

In addition, there is a strong school choice movement, led largely by 'school choice evangelist' Corey DeAngelis. In his 2024 *The Parent Revolution: Rescuing Your Kids from the Radicals Ruining Our Schools*, DeAngelis promotes systems where public funds (or a portion) can follow students to charter schools, private schools, or homeschooling. He argues that Covid school closures, ideological curricula (CRT, gender theory, *1619 Project*), and union obstructionism woke parents up to what was happening in classrooms, and that in the US, school choice is no longer radical but is becoming mainstream, and it's winning.

Down in Texas and Arizona, school choice legislation has expanded dramatically, making it possible for parents to send their children to charter or private schools with state-backed vouchers. Vouchers are essentially public grant money which gives families the genuine freedom to decide where their children are educated, and to take them out of the ideologically captured public system.

Vouchers don't just give parents freedom to choose, they open up an immense range of choices. Parents can send their children to one of seventy-five Chesterton schools, whose curriculum is everything that today's state system is not. Children are immersed in Homer, Dante and Shakespeare. Where government schools strip away the arts, Chesterton insists every child must paint, sing, and perform. There is no climate change anxiety, no gender confusion and no racial tensions.

Parents can also choose to educate their children in micro-schools or hybrid home schools, and to large privately funded networks such as Cristo Rey which was founded in Chicago in 1996 by Jesuits specifically to serve low-income families, many of whom are Hispanic. This variety is possible because of a unique combination of decentralised governance, a strong tradition of philanthropy, religious institutions that are able and willing to found and fund schools, and a legal framework which recognises the rights of parents to take their children out of the public system. They are fortunate indeed.

In the UK and Australia, the state remains the dominant force in schooling. Government sets the curriculum, controls examinations, regulates teacher accreditation, and funds the vast majority of education provision. Around a third of Australian children attend non-government schools, but these schools are still required to follow government-mandated curricula, teacher-training rules and assessment regimes. Independent schools exist, but they are not genuinely independent of the state's control.

In Britain, Katharine Birbilsingh's state-funded Michaela School in Wembley, London, is a rare beacon of excellence, but unless you live in the local catchment area you cannot hope to secure a place. Beyond Michaela, a handful of grassroots organisations such as UsForThem, the Safe Schools Alliance, and Don't Divide Us, are beginning to push back against ideological excesses in British schools.[345] Yet these are isolated campaigns, lacking the scale and political leverage of their American counterparts.

Elite schools too are not necessarily free from indoctrination. Readers may recall the dismissal of Will Knowland, an English master at Eton from 2010 to 2020 accused of 'gross misconduct' after uploading a lecture entitled *The Patriarchy Paradox* which questioned feminist orthodoxy and suggested that male traits such as courage, strength, and chivalry might benefit women as much as men. Grammar schools, meanwhile, remain strong in core subjects but are still bound by state mandates on 'anti-racism', Relationships and Sex Education, and of course, climate change education.

In Australia, too, there are occasional green shoots, such as the newly founded St John Henry Newman College in Queensland, or small schools operating under homeschooling legislation, but these remain fragile exceptions in a system otherwise dominated by state control. All in all, parents have little real choice. Unless they can afford to opt out entirely, they must accept what the state offers.

Yet there is one place where parents always have a choice: in the home. To reclaim education, they must first reclaim their role as parents. It is mothers and fathers who bring children into the world, who give them their moral and spiritual formation, not the state. They must start to recognise the ideological dangers that the system is posing to their offspring and become far less trusting. It is time for parents to stop outsourcing authority and for the family, that building block of society, to reclaim the child. This means rejecting the Rousseau-inspired deception that only experts can raise children which has permeated Western culture, and which has to some extent, given parents licence to abnegate responsibility.

And if parents are to once again reclaim their authority over their own children, we must also remind ourselves again about what a child actually is, for we appear to have forgotten that too. The government schooling system treats children as adults in miniature. They might have little arms and legs, but apparently their heads are perfectly capable of processing adult themes about sex and race, as they are conditioned for lives of politicking and activism. And the younger the better. Wearing a nappy does not protect children from radical gender theory. Sociologist Frank Furedi has long been warning us about the fact that modern culture simultaneously infantilises and prematurely adultifies the young. Adults project their own anxieties onto children, expecting them to shoulder emotional burdens they cannot carry.

And then there is the question of children needing to be protected from adult themes; a concept which is absent from government education, and whose absence explains the phenomenon of wholly inappropriate classroom activities, often imported by third-party groups.

What the system is doing to children today is stripping away childhood innocence, which is something every serious moral tradition for millennia has recognised as sacred and in need of protection. We once understood instinctively that children must be shielded from adult burdens until they are ready to face them. Yet in our new culture of 'safetyism,' we have arrived at the absurd situation in which children are deemed too young to walk to school alone, but not too young to be encouraged to question their 'assigned sex', to declare their pronouns, to shoulder guilt for centuries of racial oppression, and to bear responsibility for saving the planet.

This is a deep tragedy. The struggle for young minds is ultimately a struggle for the soul of our civilisation. Throughout these pages we have traced how the radical theories about gender and race, as well as identity politics and decolonisation, are replacing knowledge. Unformed, malleable minds are being closed, not opened, drilled to echo slogans without comprehension. But most egregious of all is that these minds are being closed to the most basic realities, which is that there are two sexes, that mathematics has right and wrong answers, and that history is more than a catalogue of grievances. How can a society function properly if we can no longer agree on these realities? And we have seen how children are taught to regard their countries and Western Civilisation, not just with disinterested contempt, but with visceral hatred. Again, how can a civilisation continue if most people have neither the will nor the inclination to defend it? Furthermore, we have examined how children are no longer being taught to see themselves as autonomous sovereign individuals responsible for their own lives but are locked into roles of guilt or grievance.

Where we go from here will decide whether the Western mind survives. If children continue to be subjected to mass conditioning while being denied the chance to flourish in truth, beauty, reason, and reality, then Western Civilisation itself will not endure. The closing of the Western mind is not merely an educational crisis but a civilisational one. We are teetering on the edge, but it is not too late. Our survival will depend on the rising generation now rebelling against the system, whose minds remain open enough to chart a course out of the ideological doldrums into which we have drifted.

Endnotes

1   Throughout this book, "public education" refers to government-run schools. In Australia and the United States these are typically called public schools; in the United Kingdom they are usually referred to as state schools. In the UK, the term "public school" traditionally refers to elite fee-paying institutions such as Eton or Harrow. To avoid confusion, unless otherwise specified, "public education" here means the government-run system of schooling.

2   Daniel Trilling, 'Why is the UK government suddenly targeting "critical race theory"?', *The Guardian*, 23 October 2020, https://www.theguardian.com/commentisfree/2020/oct/23/uk-critical-race-theory-trump-conservatives-structural-inequality.

3   Lottie Moore, *Asleep at the Wheel: An Examination of Gender and Safeguarding in Schools*, Policy Exchange, 2023, 11.

4   Zachary Goldberg, 'Yes, Critical Race Theory is Being Taught in Schools', *City Journal*, 20 October 2022, https://www.city-journal.org/article/yes-critical-race-theory-is-being-taught-in-schools.

5   Chelsea Ritschel, 'Teen launches scathing takedown of dead father in damning funeral speech to shocked mourners', *The Independent*, 17 November 2022, https://www.independent.co.uk/life-style/funeral-speech-father-tiktok-racist-b2226711.html.

6   State Government of Victoria, *Rainbow Toolkit for Public Libraries*, 2024 (no longer available online).

7   Moms4Liberty, 'Just what you want your child to hear from their teacher, "F*** your mom."', X, 12 September 2023, https://x.com/Moms4Liberty/status/1701353453082071242.

8   US House Committee on the Judiciary, 'DOJ labeled dozens of parents as terrorist threats', 20 May 2022, https://judiciary.house.gov/media/press-releases/us-house-judiciary-republicans-doj-labeled-dozens-of-parents-as-terrorist.

9   Jack Schneider and Jennifer Berkshire, 'Parents claim they have the right to shape their kids' school curriculum. They don't,' *The Washington Post*, 21 October 2021, https://www.washingtonpost.com/outlook/parents-rights-protests-kids/2021/10/21/5cf4920a-31d4-11ec-9241-aad8e48f01ff_story.html.

10   Katy Watson, 'How Brazil's culture wars are being waged in classrooms', *BBC,* 7 May 2019, https://www.bbc.com/news/world-latin-america-48039435.

11   Hazel Shearing, 'Cambridge sculpture makes a stand on culture wars', *BBC*, 26 November 2021, https://www.bbc.com/news/education-59406106.

12   Brian Dillon, '"An Event, Perhaps" by Peter Salmon review – a timely biography of Jacques Derrida', *The Guardian*, 27 November 2020, https://www.theguardian.com/books/2020/nov/27/an-event-perhaps-by-peter-salmon-review-a-timely-biography-of-jacques-derrida.

13   CS Lewis, *Surprised by Joy* (London: Fontana, 1959), 167.

14   Allan Bloom, 'Our Listless Universities', *National Review*, 10 December 1982, 1544.

15   University of Cambridge, https://cpgj.wordpress.com/about/, (accessed 12 October 2025).

16   Ibid.

17   University of Cambridge, https://www.classics.cam.ac.uk/events/bridging-binaries-lgbtq-tour-14 (accessed 28 September 2025).

18   Yale University, https://www.coursetable.com/catalog?course-modal=202501-24201 (accessed 23 March 2025).

19   Harvard University, https://www.english.fas.harvard.edu (accessed 23 March 2025).

20   Kaetlyn Liddy, 'The art of studying Taylor Swift: College campuses embrace themed courses', *NBC News,* 28 December 2023, https://www.nbcnews.com/pop-culture/taylor-swift-college-courses-review-rcna128236.

21   Yamini Narayanan, 'An Ecofeminist Politics of Chicken Ovulation: A Socio-Capitalist Model of Ability as Farmed Animal Impairment', *Hypatia*, 39 (2024), 568–588.

22   H. Howitt, 'How we fuck: assembling intimacy-as-method to research trans sex practices', *Gender, Place & Culture*, 31 (2024), 523–542.

23   Will McKeithen, 'Queer ecologies of home: heteronormativity, speciesism, and the strange intimacies of crazy cat ladies', *Gender, Place & Culture*, 24 (2017), 122–134.

24   Susan McHugh, 'Bitch, Bitch, Bitch: Personal Criticism, Feminist Theory, and Dog-writing', *Hypatia*, 27 (2012), 616–635.

25   Max J. Andrucki and Dana J. Kaplan, 'Trans objects: materializing queer time in US transmasculine homes', *Gender, Place & Culture*, 25 (2018), 781–798.

26   Thomas Wimark, 'Homemaking and perpetual liminality among queer refugees', *Social & Cultural Geography*, 22 (2019), 647–665.

27   Jacob Henry, 'The unspeakable whiteness of volunteer tourism', *Annals of Tourism Research*, 76 (2019), 326–327.

28   Rachel Lewis, 'Feline Entanglements: Feminist Interspecies Care and Solidarity in a Post-Pandemic World', *Hypatia*, 39 (2024), 795–811.

29   Matthew Lesh, 'Australia's Decaying University', in *Reclaiming Education*, ed. by Catherine Runcie and David Brooks (Sydney: Edwin H. Lowe, 2018), 77.

30   Mathew Goodwin, *Is Academic Freedom Under Threat?* Legatum Institute, 2022.

31   Michael Langbert, 'Homogeneous: The Political Affiliations of Elite Liberal Arts College Faculty', National Association of Scholars, 2018, https://www.nas.org/academic-questions/31/2/homogenous_the_political_affiliations_of_elite_liberal_arts_college_faculty

32   Noah Carl, *Lackademia: Why Do Academics Lean Left?*, Adam Smith Institute, 2017.

33   Goodwin, *Is Academic Freedom Under Threat?*, 2.

34   Centre for the Study of Partisanship and Ideology (CSPI), 'Academic Freedom in Crisis', https://www.cspicenter.com/p/academic-freedom-in-crisis-punishment (accessed 10 December 2025)

35   Hugh Campbell, 'The Truth About Noah Carl', *The Spectator*, 4 May 2019, https://www.spectator.co.uk/article/the-truth-about-noah-carl/.

36   Eric Kaufmann, *Academic Freedom in Crisis*, Centre for the Study of Partisanship and Ideology, Report No. 2, 1 March 2021, 19.

37   Speech First, *No Graduation without Indoctrination: The DEI Course Mandate*, April 2024.

38   Hannah Forsyth, 'How a fake free speech crisis could imperil academic freedom', *The Conversation*, 6 August 2020, https://theconversation.com/how-a-fake-free-speech-crisis-could-imperil-academic-freedom-144272.

39   *The Times Higher Education Academic Freedom Survey*, 2024, https://www.timeshighereducation.com/depth/times-higher-education-academic-freedom-survey-2024 (accessed 5 July 2025).

40   Chavan Kissoon and Terence Karran, 'Academic Freedom in the Digital University', *University and College Union (UCU)*, 2024.

41   Research Team, 'Academic Freedom in Our Universities: The Best and the Worst', *Civitas Institute for the Study of Civil Society*, December 2023.

42   Brianna McKee, *Free Speech on Campus Audit 2023*, Institute of Public Affairs, 2023.

43   Steve Stevens and Greg Lukianoff, 'The Unholy Alliance; How college administrators and students unite to silence speakers'. *Substack,* 12 February 2025.

44   Christopher Rufo, 'Critical Race Briefing Book', *Substack,* 15 February 2023.

45   Douglas Murray, *The Madness of Crowds: Gender, Race and Identity* (London: Bloomsbury, 2019), 58.

46   Doug Stokes, *Against Decolonisation: Campus Culture Wars and the Decline of the West* (Cambridge: Polity Press, 2023), 31.

47   University of Cambridge, https://www.undergraduate.study.
      cam.ac.uk/fees-and-finance/tuition-fees (accessed 11 March
      2025).

48   Pieter Garicano, 'Dean of the Faculty of Law launches #Ra-
      ceMeToo', *Cherwell*, 31 July 2021, https://www.cherwell.
      org/2021/07/31/dean-of-the-faculty-of-law-launches-race-
      metoo/

49   Columbia University, https://www.english.columbia.edu (ac-
      cessed 8 March 2025).

50   Ayça Çubukçu, 'At Columbia and beyond, disobedience for
      Palestine becomes a duty', *The New Arab*, 6 May 2024, https://
      www.newarab.com/opinion/student-intifada-disobeying-pales-
      tine-becomes-duty.

51   David Ludden, 'I Was One of 19 NYU Faculty Members Ar-
      rested For Protecting Student Protesters. Here's What I Think',
      The Wire, 1 May 2024, https://thewire.in/politics/david-lud-
      den-nyu-palestine-protest-arrest.

52   Faculty and Staff of Oxford University, 'On the Oxford Action
      for Palestine Solidarity Encampment', 6 May 2024, https://
      oxfordgazastaffsolidarity.wordpress.com/

53   Brendan O'Neill, *After the Pogrom: October, Israel and* the
      Crisis of Civilisation (London: Spiked, 2024), 79.

54   John Brady, 'Academics at Britain's top universities are ac-
      cused of legitimising Hamas attacks…', *Daily Mail Online*,
      11 October 2023, https://www.dailymail.co.uk/news/ar-
      ticle-12615859/

55   Claudine Gay, 'Resignation Letter', *The New York Times*, 19
      June 2024, https://www.nytimes.com/2024/01/02/us/clau-
      dine-gay-resignation-letter-harvard.html.

56   Lydia Evans, 'Ibram X. Kendi responds to layoffs, allegations
      in Q&A', *The Daily Free Press*, 2 October 2023 (accessed 2
      February 2025).

57   *The Coddling of the American Mind*, documentary, 2023,
      https://www.imdb.com/title/tt15130080/.

58   FIRE, 'Student Acceptance of Violence in Response to Speech
      Hits Record High', https://www.thefire.org/news/student-ac-
      ceptance-violence-response-speech-hits-record-high (accessed
      25 September 2025).

59   David Montgomery, 'What Americans really think about political violence', *YouGov*, 13 September 2025, https://today. yougov.com/politics/articles/52960-charlie-kirk-americans-political-violence-poll.

60   Lionel Shriver, 'The Trouble with a "decolonised" Curriculum', *The Spectator*, 3 October 2020, https://www.spectator.co.uk/article/the-trouble-with-a-decolonised-curriculum/.

61   Bella d'Abrera, 'Universities always said we were racist. Now look at their dilemma', *The Australian*, 15 June 2020, https://www.theaustralian.com.au/commentary/universities-always-said-we-were-racists-now-look-at-their-dilemma/news-story/111ba35e0377e437f7c9c8171ef5f4b3.

62   Nick Reimer, 'After Christchurch, universities have a re-sponsibility: abandon Ramsay', *Sydney Morning Herald*, 19 March 2019, https://www.smh.com.au/national/after-christ-church-universities-have-a-responsibility-abandon-ramsay-20190318-p5154r.html

63   Stokes, *Against Decolonisation*, 18.

64   A. Quayson and A. Mukherjee, eds., *Decolonizing the English Literary Curriculum* (Cambridge: Cambridge University Press, 2023), 43.

65   Ross L. Jones, James Waghorne and Marcia Langton, eds., *Dhoombak Goobgoowana: A History of Indigenous Australia and the University of Melbourne, Volume 1: Truth*, https://www.unimelb.edu.au/dhoombak-goobgoowana.

66   SOAS, University of London, *Decolonising Philosophy: A Toolkit*, 4, https://www.soas.ac.uk/decolonising-philosophy-curriculum-toolkit.

67   Stokes, *Against Decolonisation*, 31.

68   The Ashmolean Museum, Oxford, https://www.ashmolean.org/colonialism (accessed 17 April 2025).

69   University of Birmingham, https://www.birmingham.ac.uk/news/2023/decolonising-a-business-school-going-beyond-the-curriculum (accessed 6 May 2025).

70   University College London, '8 Reasons the Cur-riculum is White', 23 March 2015, https://novaramedia.com/2015/03/23/8-reasons-the-curriculum-is-white/.

71   University of Cambridge, https://www.english.cam.ac.uk/
      admissions/undergraduate/student-views.htm (accessed 6 May
      2025).

72   Giorgia Lambert, 'Students can't read long books anymore,
      says Oxford professor', *The Times*, 7 October 2024, https://
      www.thetimes.com/uk/education/article/students-cant-read-
      long-books-any-more-oxford-professor-says-tn7tcczmm.

73   Will Humphries, 'Of Mice and Men taken off Welsh GCSE
      list for being "psychologically damaging"', *The Times*, 23 De-
      cember 2024, https://www.thetimes.com/uk/education/article/
      of-mice-and-men-removed-gcse-curriculum-wales-7wnvzdhr7.

74   Rachel Roberts, 'Decline and fall? Students' perspectives on
      A-level English at 16', *BERA Blog*, 16 May 2024, https://www.
      bera.ac.uk/blog/decline-and-fall-students-perspectives-on-a-
      level-english-at-16.

75   Cambridge OCR A Level English Literature, Teacher Guide,
      'Different Interpretations, English Literature. Girl, Woman,
      Other by Bernadine Evaristo.'

76   Lana Starkey, *Illusion of Choice. New Rules Mandate Woke Texts
      in Victorian Schools*, Institute of Public Affairs, February 2024.

77   Ibid.

78   Washington Office of Superintendent of Public Instruction,
      Tribal Sovereignty Curriculum, https://ospi.k12.wa.us.

79   Joseph M. Hanneman, 'California ethnic studies pushes
      in-school pagan prayers to Aztec gods', *The Catholic World
      Report*, 7 September 2021, https://www.catholicworldreport.
      com/2021/09/07/california-ethnic-studies-pushes-in-school-
      pagan-prayers-to-aztec-gods/.

80   Australian National Curriculum, Version 9.2, HASS F–6, Year
      2 'Skills: Interpreting, analysing and evaluating.'

81   Watarraka Foundation, 'The Tradition of Aboriginal Music',
      https://www.watarrkafoundation.org.au/blog/the-tradition-of-
      aboriginal-music

82   Australian National Curriculum, Version 9.2, Teacher Back-
      ground Information, Science, Year 1 'Science understanding
      – Biological sciences.'

83   Australian National Curriculum, Teacher Information, Science
      Year 2, 'Science as a human endeavour – Use and influence of
      science.'

84   Bella d'Abrera, *Who's Teaching the Teachers? An Audit of Teaching Degrees at Australian Universities*, Institute of Public Affairs, September 2023.

85   Ibid.

86   Rodger Beehler, 'Grading the "cultural literacy' project", *Studies in Philosophy and Education*, 10 (1991), 315–335.

87   Robert Pondiscio, 'At long last, E.D. Hirsch, Jr. gets his due: New research shows big benefits from Core Knowledge.' Thomas Fordham Institute, 13 April 2023, https://fordhaminstitute.org/national/commentary/long-last-ed-hirsch-jr-gets-his-due-new-research-shows-big-benefits-core.

88   Martin Robinson, 'Sixty children as young as FOUR are sent home from school every day for racism, says study', *Daily Mail*, 2 September 2024, https://www.dailymail.co.uk/news/article-13804593/Sixty-children-young-FOUR-sent-home-school-racism.html.

89   National Education Union, *Framework for Developing an Anti-Racist Approach*, 2024, 5.

90   Frederick Attenborough, 'Give white children more money in Monopoly to teach racism and privilege, councils tell parents', Free Speech Union, 30 October 2024, https://freespeechunion.org/give-white-children-more-money-in-monopoly-to-teach-racism-and-privilege-councils-tell-parents/?v=7885444af42e.

91   Rhi Storer, 'All teachers should have anti-racism training, says NAHT', *Schools Week*, 11 April 2025, https://schoolsweek.co.uk/all-teachers-should-have-anti-racism-training-says-naht/.

92   Anti-Racism Education, 'Primary Resources, Key Stage 1, Lesson One: Talking about race and racism', https://www.antiracism.education/primary.

93   Ibid.

94   Don't Divide Us, *Who are the Experts*, 2023, 25.

95   Graeme Paton, 'Children reprimanded for racist behaviour', *The Telegraph*, 14 September 2011, https://www.telegraph.co.uk/education/educationnews/8760676/Children-as-young-as-four-reprimanded-for-racist-behaviour.html .

96   Megan Howe, 'Children as young as four among 15,000 sent home from school for "racist" behaviour', Evening Standard, 26 August 2025, https://www.standard.co.uk/news/uk/children-sent-home-school-racist-behaviour-b1244461.html.

97   Robinson, 'Sixty children as young as FOUR are sent home from school every day for racism, says study'.

98   The Manifesto Club, https://manifestoclub.info/the-myth-of-racist-kids/ (accessed 5 February 2025).

99   Department for Education, 'GCSE Results, 2022', https://explore-education-statistics.service.gov.uk/find-statistics/key-stage-4-performance-revised.

100   Ibid.

101   Howe, 'Children as young as four among 15,000 sent home from school for "racist" behaviour'.

102   Education Committee, *Forgotten: White Working-Class Pupils Let Down by Decades of Neglect*, 2021, https://committees.parliament.uk/publications/6218/documents/68719/default/.

103   Tony Sewell et al., *Commission on Race and Ethnic Disparities: The Report*, March 2021.

104   Eric Kaufmann, *The Political Culture of Young Britain*, Policy Exchange, 2022.

105   Bella d'Abrera, *De-Educating Australia. How the National Curriculum is Failing Australian Children*, Institute of Public Affairs, February 2023.

106   RacismNoWay, 'Anti-racism education for Australian schools. Teaching resources', https://racismnoway.com.au/teaching-resources/anti-racism-activities/lesson-ideas/racist-behaviour/.

107   RacismNoWay, 'K–12 Understanding Prejudice: "The Sneetches"', https://racismnoway.com.au/teaching-resources/anti-prejudice-activities/kindergarten/sneetches/.

108   Ibid.

109   Jason Reynolds and Ibram X. Kendi, *Stamped: Racism, Antiracism, and You* (New York: Little Brown Books for Young Readers, 2024).

110   Woke Kindergarten, https://www.wokekindergarten.org/ (accessed 15 April 2025).

111   *The Ben Shapiro Show*, episode 2139, The Daily Wire, 15 February 2025.

112   Summit Ministries and McLaughlin & Associates, Poll: More Than Two-Thirds of American Voters Say Critical Race Theory is Further Dividing Young People, 18 January 2023.

113 Harry Wallop, 'My son thinks I'm racist — he might be right', The Daily Telegraph, 15 April 2016, https://www.telegraph.co.uk/family/parenting/when-your-child-calls-you-a-racist/.

114 Jonathan Osler, 'Explaining to my eight-year-old that yes, she too is racist', EmbraceRace, https://www.embracerace.org/resources/explaining-to-my-eight-year-old-that-yes-she-too-is-racist.

115 Andrew Grant Thomas, 'Your 5-year-old is already racially biased', EmbraceRace, https://www.embracerace.org/resources/your-5-year-old-is-already-racially-biased-heres-what-you-can-do-about-it.

116 Phyllis A. Katz, 'The Development of Racial Attitudes in Children', in *Towards the Elimination of Racism*, ed. Phyllis A. Katz (New York: Pergamon Press, 1976), 55.

117 Frances E. Aboud, Children and Prejudice (Oxford: Basil Blackwell, 1988), 45.

118 David R. Hirschfeld, Race in the Making: Cognition, Culture, and the Child's Construction of Human Kinds (Cambridge, MA: MIT Press, 1996), 43.

119 Thomas Sowell, *Is Reality Optional?* (Stanford: Hoover Institution Press, 1993), 4.

120 Goldwater Institute, 'Teacher Blows the Whistle on Critical Race Theory in California School', 31 January 2022, https://www.goldwaterinstitute.org/teacher-blows-the-whistle-on-critical-race-theory-in-california-schools/.

121 Matthew Goodwin, 'Stop Dragging Our Kids into the Culture War', Substack, 14 June 2023.

122 Bari Weiss, 'The miseducation of America's elites', City Journal, 9 March 2021, https://www.city-journal.org/article/the-miseducation-of-americas-elites.

123 Douglas Murray, *The War on the West* (London: HarperCollins, 2022), 54.

124 Kaufmann, *The Political Culture of Young Britain.*

125 Weiss, 'The miseducation of America's elites'.

126 Luke Rosiak, *Race to the Bottom. Uncovering the Secret Forces Destroying American Public Education* (Washington, DC: Regnery, 2021), 64.

127   Tim Sigsworth, 'Toddler kicked out of nursery for being transphobic', The Telegraph, 31 March 2025, https://www.telegraph.co.uk/news/2025/03/31/toddler-kicked-out-of-nursery-for-being-transphobic/ (accessed 7 October 2025).

128   Rebecca Whittaker, 'Toddler accused of being transphobic or homophobic was suspended from nursery', The Independent, 31 March 2025, https://www.independent.co.uk/news/uk/home-news/toddler-suspended-nursery-transphobic-b2724495.html.

129   Department for Education, 'Suspensions and permanent exclusions in England, Academic Year 2023/2024', https://explore-education-statistics.service.gov.uk/find-statistics/suspensions-and-permanent-exclusions-in-england/2023-24.

130   Brooke Pessin-Whedbee, *Who Are You?: The Kid's Guide to Gender Identity* (London: Jessica Kingsley Publishers, 2017).

131   The Christian Institute, 'BBC "100 genders removed"', YouTube video, https://www.youtube.com/watch?v=wqryurd_WfA (accessed 7 October 2025).

132   Michel Foucault, The History of Sexuality, Volume I: An Introduction (New York: Pantheon, 1978); Jacques Derrida, Of Grammatology (Baltimore: Johns Hopkins University Press, 1976); Annamarie Jagose, Queer Theory: An Introduction (New York: New York University Press, 1996).

133   Judith Butler, *Gender Trouble: Feminism and the Subversion of Identity* (New York: Routledge, 1990).

134   Helen Pluckrose and James Lindsay, *Cynical Theories: How Activist Scholarship Made Everything About Race, Gender, and Identity — and Why This Harms Everybody* (North Carolina: Pitchstone Publishing, 2020), 99.

135   Ibid., 94.

136   Ibid., 89.

137   Balázs Boross, 'Queering babies: (Auto)ethnographic reflections from a gay parent through surrogacy', *Journal for the Psychoanalysis of Culture and Society*, 4 December 2024.

138   Harper Keenan and Lil Miss Hot Mess, 'Drag Pedagogy: The playful practice of queer imagination in early childhood', *Curriculum Inquiry*, 50 (2021), 1–21.

139   John Colapinto, 'The True Story of John/Joan', *Rolling Stone*, 1997, https://www.rollingstone.com/culture/culture-features/david-reimer-john-money-john-joan-1235282697/.

140   Lauren Smith, 'Dr John Money and the sinister origins of gender ideology', *Spiked*, 5 February 2023, https://www.spiked-online.com/2023/02/05/dr-john-money-and-the-sinister-origins-of-gender-ideology/.

141   Pluckrose and Lindsay, *Cynical Theories*, 154.

142   Raewyn Connell, 'Masculinities', https://www.raewynconnell.net/p/masculinities_20.html (accessed 7 October 2025).

143   Sex Matters, 'Helen Joyce on sex, gender identity and human rights', 20 December 2024, https://sex-matters.org/posts/healthcare/helen-joyce-on-sex-gender-identity-and-human-rights/.

144   State Government of Victoria, 'Respectful Relationships', https://www.vic.gov.au/respectful-relationships (accessed 2 May 2025).

145   Department for Education, *Statutory Guidance: Relationships and Sex Education* (RSE) (Secondary).

146   In the 2023–24 financial year, the charity received approximately £618,757 in government grants, an increase from £572,868 the previous year. These funds come from a mix of UK government departments, devolved administrations like the Scottish and Welsh governments.

147   Mermaids, https://mermaidsuk.org.uk/professionals/ (accessed 5 May 2025).

148   Miriam Cates, 'What is being taught in Relationships and Sex Education in our schools?', *New Social Covenant Unit*, 2023, 76.

149   Ibid., 62.

150   'Tender Education and Arts', https://charityawards.co.uk/tender-education-and-arts/ (accessed 7 October 2025).

151   Misogyny Resource, 'Pyramid of Sexual Violence', https://tender.org.uk/ (accessed 30 September 2025).

152   Ibid.

153   Our Watch, *Men in Focus Practice Guide: Addressing Masculinities and Working with Men in the Prevention of Men's Violence Against Women* (Melbourne: Our Watch, 2022).

154   IPSOS, Emerging tensions? How younger generations are dividing on masculinity and gender equality, February 2024.

155   Ibid., 58.

156   Matthew Smith, 'Should pupils be taught about gender identity in schools?', *YouGov*, 17 May 2024, https://yougov.co.uk/politics/articles/49445-should-pupils-be-taught-about-gender-identity-in-schools.

157   Pew Research Centre, *Race and LGBTQ Issues in K–12 Schools*, 22 February 2024.

158   Daniel Buck and Jay Richards, 'Gender Ideology as State Education Policy', *The Heritage Foundation*, 18 December 2024, https://www.heritage.org/education/report/gender-ideology-state-education-policy.

159   Bella d'Abrera, *Radicalism in Early Childhood Education*, Institute of Public Affairs, May 2024.

160   State Government of Victoria, 'Respectful Relationships'.

161   Transgender Trend, https://www.transgendertrend.com/ (accessed 7 October 2025).

162   Judith Butler, *Undoing Gender* (New York: Routledge, 2004), 155.

163   NAHT, 'Comments on government's promised review of sex education', *The School Leaders' Union*, 8 March 2023, https://www.naht.org.uk/News/Latest-comments/Press-room/ArtMID/558/ArticleID/1983/NAHT-comments-on-governments-promised-review-of-sex-education.

164   Mati Keynes, 'For the first time, the curriculum in Australian classrooms has a focus on truth-telling', *Pursuit*, 28 May 2024, https://pursuit.unimelb.edu.au/articles/for-the-first-time-the-curriculum-in-australian-classrooms-has-a-focus-on-truth-telling.

165   John Elledge, 'The history of the British Empire is not being taught', *The New Statesman*, 12 June 2020, https://www.newstatesman.com/politics/uk-politics/2020/06/history-british-empire-not-taught-schools-curriculum.

166   Zachary Marsh and Iain Mansfield, *Lessons from the Past: The State of History in English Secondary Schools*, Policy Exchange, 2025.

167   Graeme Paton, 'Horatio Nelson "was French football captain",
       say children', The Telegraph, 20 October 2010, https://www.
       telegraph.co.uk/education/educationnews/8075874/Horatio-
       Nelson-was-French-football-captain-say-children.html.

168   TES, 'The History of India – 11. The Bengal Famine 1943',
       https://www.tes.com/teaching-resource/the-history-of-india-
       11-the-bengal-famine-1943-12799295 (accessed 7 October
       2025).

169   Katherine Burn and Richard Harris, *Historical Association
       Survey of History in Secondary Schools in England in 2021*,
       Historical Association.

170   Liverpool International Slavery Museum, *Teachers' Pack*,
       National Museums Liverpool, 2020.

171   The Black Curriculum, *Black British History in the National
       Curriculum Report*, 2020, 1.

172   Runnymede Trust, *The Runnymede School Report. Race, Educa-
       tion and Inequality in Contemporary Britain*, 2015, 5.

173   Donna Ferguson, 'Students need to know the harrowing truth':
       teachers on black history in the curriculum', *The Guardian*, 3
       October 2020, https://www.theguardian.com/education/2020/
       oct/03/teachers-on-black-history-in-the-curriculum.

174   David Abulafia, 'The strange attempt to find Muslim Vikings'
       The Spectator UK, 4 June 2025, https://www.spectator.co.uk/
       article/the-strange-attempt-to-find-muslim-vikings/.

175   Ed Griffiths, 'Vikings were "not all white and some were Mus-
       lim", pupils told in effort to ditch "Eurocentric Ideas"', GB
       News, 6 June 2025, https://www.gbnews.com/news/vikings-
       non-white-muslim-eurocentric-ideas.

176   The Brilliant Club, *Friends or Foes, Vikings in Medieval Eng-
       land*, Key Stage 2 Programme.

177   Burn and Harris, *Historical Association Survey of History in
       Secondary Schools in England in 2021*, p.1.

178   GCSE OCR, 'A Migration to Britain c1000 to c2010', https://
       www.bbc.co.uk/bitesize/topics/z9hx2p3 (accessed 7 October
       2025).

179   The Black Curriculum, *Black British History in the National
       Curriculum Report*, 2020.

180 A History Teacher, 'What can a school history of West Africa tell us about English education?', *History Reclaimed*, https://historyreclaimed.co.uk/what-can-a-school-history-of-west-africa-tell-us-about-english-education/.

181 The Secret Teacher, '"Do you hate Britain?" I asked my pupils. Thirty raised their hands', The Times, 20 April 2024, https://www.thetimes.com/world/asia/article/do-you-hate-britain-i-asked-my-pupils-thirty-raised-their-hands-35gxx2t6n.

182 Zachary Marsh and Iain Mansfield, *Lessons from the Past. The State of History in Secondary Schools*, Policy Exchange, 17 May 2025, 41.

183 Carl Bennet, 'Winston Churchill's role in World War Two not known by a third of Britons in staggering statistic', *GB News*, 22 February 2023, https://www.gbnews.com/news/winston-churchills-role-in-world-war-two-not-known-by-a-third-of-britons-in-staggering-statistic/446332.

184 Joel Rogers de Waal, '"What's D-Day?", says half of British respondents', *YouGov UK*, 5 June 2019.

185 OCR, *Striking the Balance: A Review of 11–16 Curriculum and Assessment in England*, 2024, 4.

186 Robert Tombs, 'Towards a revised School History Curriculum', *History Reclaimed*, 2024, https://historyreclaimed.co.uk/towards-a-revised-school-history-curriculum/.

187 Rosiak, *Race to the Bottom*, 145.

188 Knight Foundation, 'Howard University: Nikole Hannah-Jones', https://knightfoundation.org/employee/nikole-hannah-jones/ (accessed 25 September 2025).

189 Economic History Association, 'Slavery in the United States', EH.Net Encyclopedia, https://eh.net/encyclopedia/slavery-in-the-united-states/ (accessed 25 September 2025).

190 Matthew Desmond, 'In Order to Understand the Brutality of American Capitalism, You Have to Start on the Plantation', *The New York Times Magazine*, 14 August 2019, https://www.nytimes.com/interactive/2019/08/14/magazine/slavery-capitalism.html.

191 Tom Mackaman, Interview with Peter Wood, *World Socialist Web Site*, 28 November 2019, https://www.wsws.org/en/articles/2019/11/28/wood-n28.html.

192 Tom Mackaman, Interview with James McPherson, *World Socialist Web Site*, 14 November 2019, https://www.wsws.org/en/articles/2019/11/14/mcph-n14.html.

193 Ibid.

194 Rosiak, *Race to the Bottom,* 146

195 Timothy Sandefur, 'The 1619 Project: An Autopsy', *Cato Institute*, 27 October 2020, https://www.cato.org/commentary/1619-project-autopsy.

196 Pulitzer Center, *K–12 Curriculum Guide for the 1619 Project (Penguin Classroom),* 3.

197 Ibid., 12

198 Nigel Biggar, *Colonialism. A Moral Reckoning*, (London: Harper Collins, 2023), 147.

199 Sarah Ison, 'There's no shame in gap: Blainey', *The Australian,* 20 October 2023, https://www.theaustralian.com.au/nation/politics/geoffrey-blainey-says-indigenous-australians-far-far-better-off-since-1788/news-story/e326a2e93ce20b034a9e-924239dadb48.

200 d'Abrera, *Radicalism in Early Childhood Education*

201 Teaching Brave, '*Reconciliation, National Sorry Day and NAIDOC Week in Early Childhood*', https://teachingbrave.com/reconciliation-national-sorry-day-and-naidoc-week/ (accessed 7 October 2025).

202 '"There's just nothing they've done wrong": families outraged by preschool curriculum on Australia's colonisation', *Nine News*, 22 August 2023, https://www.9news.com.au/national/new-south-wales-preseschool-kids-sorry-cards-first-nations-people-parent-outrage/2c1a1926-6a33-4247-aef5-a96304ba8c00.

203 d'Abrera, *De-Educating Australia. How the National Curriculum is Failing Australian Children.*

204 Ibid.

205 Murray, *The War on the West,* 16.

206 Lorena Allam, 'Dark Emu's Infinite Potential: "Our kids have grown up in a fog about the history of the land"', *The Guardian*, 24 May 2019, https://www.theguardian.com/books/2019/may/24/dark-emus-infinite-potential-our-kids-have-grown-up-in-a-fog-about-the-history-of-the-land.

207   John Roskam, 'There Will be Consequences', *Spectator Australia,* 8 June 2024, https://www.spectator.com.au/2024/06/there-will-be-consequences.

208   Ibid.

209   Daniel Wild, 'Almost half of young Australians are too ashamed for fight for their nation', Institute of Public Affairs, 18 September 2024, https://ipa.org.au/publications-ipa/media-releases/almost-half-of-young-australians-are-too-ashamed-to-fight-for-their-nation.

210   Eliana Silver, '"Disgrace!" Gen Z says UK is "racist" and would not fight for UK as army chief issues warning', GB News, 10 February 2025, https://www.gbnews.com/news/genz-uk-racist-fight-britain-farage-disgrace.

211   The Secret Teacher, 'Do you hate Britain, I asked my pupils.'

212   Dylan Difford, 'What Does Gen Z Think About Britain?' *YouGov*, 21 February 2025, https://yougov.co.uk/society/articles/51658-what-does-gen-z-think-about-britain

213   Jack Blackburn, 'Less than half of young people know what happened on D-Day', *The Times*, 21 May 2024, https://www.thetimes.com/uk/history/article/fewer-than-half-of-young-people-know-what-happened-on-d-day-zc6xc2zxp.

214   George Chesterton, 'Why our young people are scared to wear the poppy', *The Telegraph,* 10 November 2024, https://www.telegraph.co.uk/news/2024/11/10/why-young-people-are-scared-to-wear-the-poppy/.

215   Michael Hand and Jo Pearce, 'Patriotism in British Schools: Principles, Practices and Press Hysteria', *Educational Philosophy and Theory*, 44 (2012), 621–636.

216   Ibid.

217   Michael Taylor, 'National Identity', in Katherine Birbalsingh (ed.), *The Power of Culture*, 84.

218   Education Reform Act 1988, Section 8(3).

219   Ofsted, *Deep and Meaningful? The Religious Education Subject Report*, 17 April 2024, https://www.gov.uk/government/publications/subject-report-series-religious-education/deep-and-meaningful-the-religious-education-subject-report.

220   Richard S. Lindzen, 'Resisting Climate Hysteria: A Case Against Precipitous Climate Action', Science & Public Policy Institute, 2009.

221   John Clauser, *Quantum Korea 2023 Keynote Address*, https://
       co2coalition.org/media/quantum-korea-2023-keynote-ad-
       dress-dr-john-clauser/ (accessed 20 October 2025).
222   World Wildlife Fund, https://www.wwf.org.uk/get-involved/
       schools/resources/climate-change-resources (accessed 25 Sep-
       tember 2025).
223   World Wildlife Fund, 'Our Frozen World', Climate Resources,
       https://www.wwf.org.uk/sites/default/files/2020-01/Our_
       Planet_ourfrozenworlds_0.pdf.
224   Claire Rowe, 'Climate Anxiety in Pre-Adolescent Children:
       A Neuroscientific and Psychological Perspective', Institute of
       Public Affairs, May 2025, 9.
225   World Wildlife Fund, 'Our Frozen World'.
226   Rowe, 'Climate Anxiety in Pre-Adolescent Children', 3.
227   Jeffrey Kluger, 'Climate Anxiety Is Taking Its Toll on Young
       People', *Time Magazine*, 29 April 2025, https://time.
       com/7280989/climate-anxiety-mental-health-young-people/.
228   Rowe, 'Climate Anxiety in Pre-Adolescent Children', p. ii.
229   Royal College of Psychiatrists, https://www.rcpsych.ac.uk/
       mental-health/parents-and-young-people/eco-distress-for-
       young-people (accessed 17 July 2025).
230   Ibid.
231   Ibid.
232   Helena Horton, 'BBC removes Bitesize page on climate
       change 'benefits' after backlash', *The Guardian,* 2 July 2021,
       https://www.theguardian.com/media/2021/jul/02/bbc-re-
       moves-bitesize-page-climate-change-benefits-backlash.
233   Rita Soaores Pinto and Sally Grove-White, 'From Climate
       Anxiety to Resilient Active Citizenship: when primary schools,
       parents and environmental groups work together to catalyse
       change' *Forum*, 62 (2020), 252.
234   Stella Fleetwood et al., *Climate Literacy Amongst School Leav-
       ers: Research Report*, Department for Education, Government
       Social Research, October 2024.
235   Royal Meteorological Society, https://www.rmets.org/news/
       department-education-climate-literacy-survey-2024 (accessed
       28 September 2025).

236 Caroline Hickman et al., 'Climate Anxiety in Children and Young People and Their Beliefs About Government Responses to Climate Change: A Global Survey', The Lancet Planetary Health, 5(12), e863–e873.

237 Aaron Kulakiewicz, Rob Long and Nerys Roberts, 'Inclusion of Sustainability and Climate Change in the National Curriculum', House of Commons Library, Debate Pack No. 166, 25 October 2021

238 WWF, *Introduction to Climate Change: Teacher Activity Guide for Ages 7–11*, 11, https://www.wwf.org.uk/sites/default/files/2021-11/WWF_ClimateChangeResourcePack.pdf.

239 Teach the Future, https://www.teachthefuture.uk/ (accessed 28 September 2025).

240 Birbalsingh, *The Power of Culture*, 147.

241 B. Verlie and A. Flynn, 'School strike for climate: A reckoning for education', *Australian Journal of Environmental Education*, 38 (2022), 1–12.

242 Michael Shellenberger, 'Why Climate Alarmism Hurts Us All', *Forbes*, 4 December 2019, https://www.forbes.com/sites/michaelshellenberger/2019/12/04/why-climate-alarmism-hurts-us-all/.

243 Birbalsingh, *The Power of Culture*, 150.

244 Abby Tabor, 'Human Activity in China and India Dominates the Greening of Earth, NASA Study Shows', NASA, 11 February 2019, https://www.nasa.gov/centers-and-facilities/ames/human-activity-in-china-and-india-dominates-the-greening-of-earth-nasa-study-shows/.

245 Celine Wadhera, '"An Absolute Disgrace": BBC Bitesize Condemned for Listing "Positive" Impacts of Climate Crisis', The Independent, 1 July 2021, https://www.independent.co.uk/climate-change/news/bbc-bitesize-climate-change-reactions-b1876100.html.

246 Horton, 'BBC removes Bitesize page on climate change "benefits" after backlash'.

247 WWF, *Introduction to Climate Change, Climate Resource Pack*, 8-9.

248 Ibid.

249   Michael Shellenberger, *Apocalypse Never: Why Environmental Alarmism Hurts Us All* (New York: HarperCollins, 2020), 140.

250   Joanna Williams, *Teachers or Parents: Who Is Responsible for the Next Generation?* Civitas, 2024, 10.

251   Met Office, 'Exploring Climate Impacts', https://weather.metoffice.gov.uk/learn-about/met-office-for-schools/themes-for-7-11/resources-7-11/exploring-climate-impacts (accessed 29 September 2025).

252   Let's Go Zero 2030, *Climate Activity Pack*, Ashenden, 2025, https://letsgozero.org/.

253   Department for Education, *Sustainability and Climate Change: A Strategy for the Education and Children's Services Systems*, 20 December 2023, https://www.gov.uk/government/publications/sustainability-and-climate-change-strategy/sustainability-and-climate-change-a-strategy-for-the-education-and-childrens-services-systems.

254   United Nations, 'Global Citizenship', https://www.un.org/en/academic-impact/global-citizenship#:~:text=The%20concept%20of%20global%20citizenship… (accessed 29 September 2025).

255   Oxfam, Global Citizenship in the Classroom: A Guide for Teachers, https://www.oxfam.org.uk/education/who-we-are/global-citizenship-guides/.

256   Katherine Kim, 'Tim Walz Was My Teacher Twenty Years Ago. Here's What I Learnt', Politico, August 2024, https://www.politico.com/news/magazine/2024/08/08/tim-walz-was-my-teacher-what-i-learned-00173212.

257   Paul Johnson, Intellectuals (London: HarperCollins, 1988), 21–23.

258   Thomas Sowell, Social Justice Fallacies (New York: Basic Books, 2023), 93.

259   John Dewey, The School and Society (Chicago: University of Chicago Press, 1902), 92.

260   C. Bradley Thompson, 'Progressive Education and Our Killing Schools', Substack, 31 May 2022.

261   Central Intelligence Agency, Soviet Sponsored Societies of Friendship and Cultural Relations (October 1957), Freedom of Information Electronic Reading Room, https://www.cia.gov/readingroom/.

262 Melanie Phillips, *All Must Have Prizes* (London: Little, Brown and Company, 1996), 216.

263 John Quay, 'Conference on the Legacy of John Dewey on Contemporary Pedagogy' (paper presented at the Australian Association for Research in Education Conference, February 2022).

264 David Corey, 'Paulo Freire's Oppressive Pedagogy', *National Affairs*, no. 62 (Winter 2023), https://www.nationalaffairs.com/publications/detail/paulo-freires-oppressive-pedagogy.

265 João França, Interview with Henry Giroux, CCCPLAB (YouTube video), 2 July 2019, https://www.youtube.com/watch?v=LCMXKt5vRQk&t=44.

266 James Lindsay, *The Marxification of Education* (New Discourses, 2022), 24.

267 França, *Interview with Henry Giroux*

268 Rebecca Morris et al., *Education: The State of Discipline* (London: BRERA, May 2023), 44.

269 University of Bristol, https://www.bristol.ac.uk/unit-programme-catalogue/UnitDetails

270 University College London, https://www.ucl.ac.uk/module-catalogue/modules/educating-and-organising-for-social-justice-EDPS0012.

271 Citizens UK, *Citizens Manifesto General, Election 2024l*, 28.

272 Khadija Mohammed, *The National Anti-Racism Training for Initial Teacher Education (ITE)*, Scottish Council of Deans, 2023, 5.

273 Frederick M. Hess and Lindsey M. Burke, 'Does Race Get Short Shrift in Education Research and Teacher Training?', The Heritage Foundation, 5 April 2021.

274 Lindsey M. Burke, *It's Time for States to Break Up with Education College,* The Heritage Foundation, 16 September 2022.

275 University of California, Berkeley, 'Charlotte Tate: Gender Is for the Birds', https://events.berkeley.edu/ipsr/event/295642-charlotte-tate-gender-is-for-the-birds.

276 Bella d'Abrera, *Who's Teaching the Teachers. An Audit of Teaching Degrees Offered at Australian Universities*, Institute of Public Affairs, October 2023.

277   National Education Union, General Secretary address to Annual Conference, 6 April 2024.

278   'Lecturers have seen standards plummet', Letter to *The Independent*, 26 September 2005.

279   National Education Union, General Secretary Address to Annual Conference, 6 April 2024.

280   National Assessment Governing Board, 'Ten takeaways from the Newly Released 2024 NAEP Results'

281   NAEP Report Card, *Mathematics, Grade 8*.

282   Australian Education Research Organisation, Writing Development: What Does a Decade of NAPLAN Data Reveal?, October 2022, 4.

283   W. Mason and M. Warmington, 'Academic Reading as a Grudging Act: How Do Higher Education Students Experience Academic Reading and What Can Educators Do About It?', Higher Education, 88 (2024), 839–856.

284   Ibid.

285   This brings us to the growing body of research on technology and attention. Jonathan Haidt's *Anxious Generation* argues that the rise of the smartphone has led to a "great rewiring" of childhood — one that has caused social deprivation, sleep disruption, fragmented attention, and even addiction. The implications for education and mental health are beyond the purview of this chapter. But we can already conclude from university classrooms is clear: there is a widening gap between the basic demands of academic reading and writing, and students' capacity to meet them.

286   Christina Clark et al., Children and Young People's Reading in 2024, National Literacy Trust, 2024, 6.

287   Ibid.5.

288   Lauren Provencher, 'SREB Report Relates Importance of Maths Education', 27 February 2020.

289   Collin Binkley, 'College Students Are Still Struggling with Basic Math. Professors Blame the Pandemic', *The Hechinger Report*, 31 August 2023.

290 The School of Sexuality Education's mantra is that 'There are a variety of sexual preferences and practices – we're all a little different. Being sex positive is about accepting and learning about that diversity in order to approach sex with a nuanced awareness of everybody's multi-faceted, fluid sexual identity. This includes being nonjudgemental and accepting sexual practices that are considered to deviate from the norm.'

291 'Mother Loses Campaign to Have RSE Material Released', Care, 14 June 2023, https://care.org.uk/news/2023/06/mother-overruled-by-courts-to-obtain-sex-education-materials-taught-in-daughters-class.

292 National Education Union, Annual Conference 2025 Highlights, https://neu.org.uk/about/about-us/annual-conference/annual-conference-2025-highlights.

293 Kindred2, *2024 School Readiness Survey*, https://kindredsquared.org.uk/school-readiness-survey.

294 Ibid.

295 Williams, *Teachers or Parents: Who Is Responsible for the Next Generation?*

296 James G. Dwyer, 'Parents' Religion and Children's Welfare: Debunking the Doctrine of Parents' Rights', California Law Review, 82, no. 6 (1994).

297 United Nations, Convention on the Rights of the Child, Article 3.

298 Schneider and Berkshire, 'Parents claim they have the right to shape their kids' school curriculum. They don't.'

299 Ibid.

300 Hilary Cass, *Independent Review of Gender Identity Services for Children and Young People: Final Report* (London: Department of Health and Social Care, 2024), 233. https://www.gov.uk/government/publications/independent-review-of-gender-identity-services-for-children-and-young-people.

301 Moore, *Asleep at the Wheel*, 38.

302 New Social Covenant, 'What Is Being Taught in Relationships and Sex Education', 6.

303 Binary Australia, https://www.binary.org.au/.

304 Carly Douglas, '"Devastated" Victorian Parents Left in the Dark as Schools Allow Their Kids to Socially Transition', Herald Sun, 21 June 2024.

305   Sarah Marshall Perry, 'Parents Are Fed Up with Public Schools Secretly Transitioning Children', The Heritage Foundation, 18 March 2023, https://www.heritage.org/gender/commentary/parents-are-fed-public-schools-secretly-transitioning-children.

306   Cass, *Independent Review of Gender Identity Services for Childre and Young People,*160.

307   Clare Rowe, personal communication to the author, 13 August 2025.

308   Anna Fazackerley, '"I Felt Absolutely Lost": The Crisis Behind the Rising Number of Children Being Homeschooled', *The Guardian*, 21 September 2024.

309   Department for Education, Elective Home Education Statistics, https://explore-education-statistics.service.gov.uk/find-statistics/elective-home-education/2024-25-autumn-term.

310   Rose Innes and Hayden Johnson, 'Why Parents Are Pulling Children Out of School', *Courier Mail*, 21 August 2024.

311   Rachel Alexander Cambre, 'Homeschooling, Homesteading, and the Renewal of American Citizenship', The Heritage Foundation, 4 March 2025.

312   Rachel Alexander Cambre, 'Homeschooling, Homesteading, and the Renewal of American Citizenship', The Heritage Foundation, 4 March 2025.

313   Department for Education, Elective Home Education Statistics.

314   W. Charles-Warner, 'England: Why Parents Choose Home Education', *Education Otherwise*, August 2022, 19.

315   Ibid.

316   Ibid., 9.

317   Department for Education, 'Education Secretary Speech on New Era of School Standards', https://www.gov.uk/government/speeches/education-secretary-speech-on-new-era-of-school-standards.

318   Charles-Warner, 'England: Why Parents Choose Home Education', 9.

319   National Home Education Research Institute, *Research Facts*, https://nheri.org/research-facts-on-homeschooling/.

320   *The Home Ed Daily*, https://www.thehomeeddaily.co.uk/article/2025/02/17/whats-wrong-children-s-wellbeing-and-schools-bill-overview-key-issues.

321   Elizabeth Bartholet, 'What Rights Do Children Have in Homeschooling?', Harvard Magazine, 13 September 2023.

322   Mairead Elordi, 'Moms for Liberty Called a "Hate Group" in Massachusetts Police Trainings', *Daily Wire*, 1 August 2025, https://www.dailywire.com/news/exclusive-moms-for-liberty-called-a-hate-group-in-massachusetts-police-trainings.

323   David Rieff, "Bloom in Full," *Los Angeles Times Book Review*, 21 June 1987.

324   Phillips, *All Must Have Prizes,* 42

325   Alexandra Kollontai, 'Communism and the Family' (1920), https://www.marxists.org/archive/kollonta/1920/communism-family.htm.

326   Edmund Burke, *Reflections on the Revolution in France* (London: Penguin, 1986 [1790]), 194.

327   John G. Cottone, 'Gen Z Takes on Mental Health: I Wanted to Know What Gen Z Teens Thought About Mental Health. So I Asked One', *Psychology Today*, https://www.psychology-today.com/us/blog/the-cube/202405/gen-z-takes-on-mental-health.

328   Jonathan Haidt, *The Anxious Generation* (New York: Penguin Press, 2024), 30–44.

329   Cates, 'What Is Being Taught in Relationships and Sex Education in Our Schools?', 52.

330   Rosiak, *Race to the Bottom*, 257.

331   Bible Society and YouGov, *The Quiet Revival: Religion among 18–24-Year-Olds in England and Wales* (London: Bible Society, 2024).

332   Valerie Michaelson et al., 'Establishing Spirituality as an Intermediary Determinant of Health among 42,843 Children from Eight Countries', Preventive Medicine 179 (2024).

333   Rosiak, *Race to the Bottom,* 259

334   Ipsos and King's College London, 'Young Men and "Toxic Masculinity"', *Ipsos MORI Social Research Institute*, June 2023.

335   Catherine Hanrahan, 'Are There More Than Two Genders? Australia Talks Survey Reveals Split Opinions', ABC News, 20 November 2020, https://www.abc.net.au/news/2019-11-20/gender-diversity-splits-australians-in-australia-talks-survey/11714302.

336   Matthew Goodwin, *Bad Education: Why the Education System Is Failing a Generation and How to Fix It* (London: Biteback, 2023), 196.

337   University of Chicago, *Report of the Committee on Freedom of Expression* (Chicago: University of Chicago, 2015).

338   Richard Adams, 'Ministers to Revise University Freedom of Speech Legislation', *The Guardian*, 16 January 2025.

339   'Columbia University and the Trump Administration Reach Settlement', NPR, 25 July 2025, https://www.npr.org/2025/07/25/nx-s1-5479240/columbia-trump-administration-settlement-details.

340   Jeffrey Sonnenfeld and Steven Tian, 'College Presidents Are Right to Defy Trump's War on Higher Education', *Time*, 4 February 2025, https://time.com/7212572/college-presidents-defy-trumps-war-on-higher-education.

341   Association of American Universities, 'Americans' Confidence in Higher Education Increases', 18 July 2025, https://www.aau.edu/newsroom/leading-research-universities-report/americans-confidence-higher-education-increases.

342   University of Austin, Strategic Vision and Plans, https://uatx.webflow.io/news/strategic-vision-and-plans-for-the-future.

343   Stephen Blackwood, 'Ralston's Year in Review', *Newsletter*, 2022.

344   Mark Bauerlein, 'At Ralston College, the Humanities Are Alive — and So Are the Students', *Mind the Campus*, 8 April 2025, https://www.mindingthecampus.org/2025/04/08/at-ralston-college-the-humanities-are-alive-and-so-are-the-students/.

345   https://dontdivideus.com, https://safeschoolsallianceuk.net, https://usforthem.co.uk/.

Index

www.ingramcontent.com/pod-product-compliance
Lightning Source LLC
Chambersburg PA
CBHW032137050726
47590CB00008B/3131